Rare
Tongues

Lorna Gibb was born and grew up in Bellshill, North Lanarkshire. She has a PhD in Linguistics from Edinburgh as well as a BA and MA from the University of London. She's currently an Associate Professor at the University of Stirling but has worked at universities in London, Hertfordshire, Essex, Qatar, Monaco and France. Before going to university, Lorna worked as a professional dancer in Italy and the UK. She also worked in the City of London as an IT programme manager and consultant for several years, and as a journalist. *Rare Tongues* is her sixth book.

Rare Tongues

The Secret Stories of Hidden Languages

Lorna Gibb

Atlantic Books
London

Published in hardback in Great Britain in 2025 by Atlantic Books,
an imprint of Atlantic Books Ltd.

10 9 8 7 6 5 4 3 2 1

A CIP catalogue record for this book is available from the British Library.

Hardback ISBN: 978 1 83895 177 1
E-book ISBN: 978 1 83895 179 5

Printed in Great Britain by CPI Group (UK) Ltd, Croydon CR0 4YY

Atlantic Books
An imprint of Atlantic Books Ltd
Ormond House
26–27 Boswell Street
London
WC1N 3JZ

www.atlantic-books.co.uk

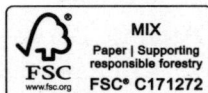

MIX
Paper | Supporting
responsible forestry
FSC
www.fsc.org
FSC® C171272

For my mum, Jessie, and for Alan, of course

Contents

Introduction

THERE ARE LANGUAGES like German and Cantonese that will be familiar to you, even if you don't know anyone who speaks them. But I would bet that you've never heard of Hmong, the whistling language of the Himalayas. Or Guarani, the majority language of Paraguay, which is too often disregarded, despite being more widely spoken than Spanish in the country. *Rare Tongues* is a journey through some of the more esoteric languages of our planet and what they can tell us about ourselves and our more familiar languages. Some languages I have studied and travelled to explore. Others have been chosen because of the crucial knowledge that they carry, knowledge that is in danger of being lost forever. Some of them have fascinating features that may make you question what we regard as a language at all. Others have turbulent histories and carry painful memories for those who dared to speak them amid political upheaval. And a few of them are under threat, their continued existence in question, because of creeping linguistic homogeneity, moving like a silencing killer across our landscapes, rendering words unspoken and forgotten.

Every language is unique and has something important to tell us about the world we live in. Each one of them can enlighten us about the manifold roles that they play in defining society, in enriching it, in enabling diverse communities to share knowledge and histories. This is what is at risk: when a language is no longer understood, an essential and inimitable way of seeing the world, of interacting with it, disappears too – and there is an undeniable link between the erosion of diverse cultures and climate change. Awareness is growing, but slowly. We are currently in the United Nations decade of indigenous languages (2022–2032), and activists and academics are highlighting what we still have and what we are in danger of forgetting. This book is my contribution to that chorus of voices: a personal call to reflect.

Since childhood, I've been fascinated by languages. In the seventies and eighties, when I was growing up on a sprawling council estate in Bellshill, North Lanarkshire, Scotland, you didn't hear many people who sounded like me in the media. However, I discovered, even before I went to secondary school, that I could have two different types of language just by copying people on the television. I didn't use what my family proudly called 'Lorna's posh voice' very often, but I switched it on when I had to read something aloud at school or act in a play, or at the ballet school where I was the only kid from a council estate and it made me fit in better. And it wasn't just the variations of my native tongue. Before I was born, my mum was the manager of a record shop, and so I was raised on all kinds of music, but especially the operas of Puccini. I'd follow the Italian words in English on those dual-language scripts you used to get inside opera album boxed sets, while my friend, whose dad ran the local Chinese restaurant, taught me Cantonese phrases in the playground, which I proudly repeated at home in the evening.

When I moved to London to study for my first degree in English Language and Literature, I learned that what I had always thought of as upper-class accents and my own, very different, way of articulating at home were more than just a way of speaking: they were a way of being. The soft, persistent rain that I called 'smirr' did not exist in London, and a phrase I might use with friends at home, teasing, 'you silly cunt' or saying 'cunts everywhere' to describe a busy street, represented something far stronger and more forbidden in the south.

I knew words that did not exist in Standard English and used them as part of my everyday vocabulary without even considering that people in my new home city might not understand them. In a second year phonetics class, we spoke of sociolinguistics and how class and accent were linked, a fashionable theory at the time. Our phonetics lecturer asked me if I would stand up and say a sentence to a packed lecture hall, so that everyone could hear a Scottish working-class accent. I was embarrassed, already finding it difficult to fit in with most of my peer group, who were from far wealthier backgrounds than me and didn't have to juggle learning with jobs to finance their studies. But I stood up anyway, and aggression, which came more naturally to me than tears when

I felt cornered, made me say, 'This is a really ridiculous thing to ask me to do' in the strongest accent I could muster. The lecturer, who was well-known, didn't even have the awareness to blush, just thanked me and told me to sit down again.

Afterwards, though, I did come close to tears when I overheard two wealthy fellow students mimicking my accent and calling me the 'Scottish charity case' when I walked past the common room.

Yet, conversely, the fact that I had studied five years of Latin at my very rough comprehensive (because it was still regarded as a good thing to do in those days in Scotland) meant my first job as a cash-strapped student paid more for a day than I had earned in a month in my Saturday shop jobs at home. My English literature tutor asked me to help him translate some Medieval Latin texts for a book he was writing. It was a pleasure; I would have done it for half the cash, and he always arrived with wonderful cheese from Neal's Yard and a glass of good wine for our sessions. He brought in texts that we then worked on together, acquired a British Library reader's pass for me (it was still located in the British Museum then), and watched with amusement while I fell in love with Medieval Latin bestiaries and their beguilingly beautiful gilded illustrations. It was the best job I ever had as a student; in fact, it was the best job I had for a good few years afterwards too.

All this happenstance and accident of birth consolidated into a curiosity about how humans communicate with each other. What makes languages different from each other? How are language and landscape and language politics related? Which aspects of language develop because of where we live and how we live? And why do some languages die? What does it mean when they do?

It wasn't until I began my postgraduate studies in linguistics, or, more precisely, in phonetics and phonology, and began to look at the sounds of languages across the world that I realized just how diverse and fascinating, and filled with local knowledge and history and culture, these systems of sounds could be. Moreover, it wasn't just a particular accent that people assumed was indicative of your birthplace, your class, and even sometimes, ridiculously, your intelligence. Rather, there were entire languages haunted by a huge collection of assumptions that people could and did make when they encountered them.

These assumptions could work for you or against you, in terms of where you were placed in society, who you were judged to be, and what opportunities were open to you. So, despite being the most widely spoken language in Paraguay, Guarani speakers there are presumed to be poor and uneducated, unlike Spanish speakers. But in the United States, first-language Spanish speakers may be ridiculed and discriminated against, even when they are perfectly fluent in English. And when Singhalese became the official language of Sri Lanka in 1948, Tamils could no longer work in the government or in the civil service, even though there had been Tamil speakers in Sri Lanka since the second century BCE. Colonization in its myriad forms often attempts to eradicate and forbid the use of the language of the colonized in the name of assimilation and education.

Wars have been waged over the right to speak a language and wars may also have the eradication of a language as an aim. But they can also be used to establish a common peace and wipe out nationalism. This is what happened in 2017 when the four languages of former Yugoslavia, that is Bosnian, Croatian, Montenegrin, and Serbian, were declared to be four different versions of a single language. In an attempt to suppress strong national identities that had led to years of war, thirty linguists from across all four countries testified to the statement, which was greeted with dismay and disbelief by nationalists but welcomed by most speakers in each of the countries, whose only question was what a single language might most fairly be called.

And it is not only the power of language, but also its variety that makes it fascinating. There is articulation – the way our lips and tongues and teeth and the shape of the inside of our mouths can fashion sounds that seem impossible to one person yet are part of everyday communication to another. There are the words that these sounds make and how we use them. There are the spoken and unspoken meanings behind them, the way these are perceived. There are concepts hidden in a sentence or a whole perspective on a philosophy of a way of living encoded in a single word.

Agglutinative languages see what English speakers think of as suffixes and prefixes as building blocks to create a single word with a different purpose, so that 'in the flower', which has three distinct words in English, becomes the single word 'kukassa' in Finnish, with the ending 'ssa' showing that the word is what's called *inessive* and refers to something being inside the named noun. And there are the structures that dictate the order in which words should appear, sometimes with a verb at the end, such as 'Je t'aime' in French, or sandwiched between subject and object, as in 'I love you'.

Many Asian and African languages are tonal – that is, the meaning of a word is conveyed by pitch rather than by a series of sounds. The word 'ma' in Mandarin can mean 'mother', 'horse', or 'to scold', depending on whether your tone is level, high then low then high again or falling. The distinction is clear to a Mandarin speaker, yet the three words will often be indistinguishable to a speaker of an Indo-European language, such as Italian, German, English, or Hindi. Yet when, in accordance with his parents' regional tradition, I was invited to choose an English name for my Chinese godson, I avoided any with the phonemes /r/ and /l/, opting for my late dad's name, John, because I knew that neither of his parents, despite their excellent command of English, had ever mastered those particular sounds.

And landscape, the geography of where we live, can shape our communication too. Languages that are whistled rather than spoken exist in mountainous regions around the world. Historically, one language grew from Native American signing languages in the Great Plains of the eighteenth-century United States to meet the need for different linguistic communities to speak to each other; it went on to become one of the most important languages used for trade and inter-community exchange in the world.

And while our environment can shape language, those same words often carry information about the land and all that live in it. The loss of a language, therefore, can mean the disappearance of unique ecological knowledge. By revitalizing and promoting a multitude of tongues, linguistic activists are preventing rich and important knowledge about our world from being lost forever.

Languages can be the gateway to secret groups, societies, and clans and become the basis of criminal masterminding, allowing their speakers to discuss schemes and plots without fear of discovery. The language of the Hmong people in the Himalayas may be used to find a mate, and afterwards may grow and be adapted into something shared only by the couple who used it in their courtship, akin to the languages shared by twins as children, known and understood only by the two people who have created it.

When I began writing this book I was working and living just outside London. But then the pandemic happened, bringing new realizations of what is most important and new ways of working that, in my case, meant being able to be closer to family. So I returned to my linguistic beginnings, to Central Scotland. My accent grows stronger, day by day. I relearn words that I had stopped using because English friends and colleagues could not understand them. 'Dreich' (grey, wet, miserable weather), 'greetin' (crying/weeping), 'chappin' the door instead of knocking, 'bletherin' (either idly gossiping or saying something nonsensical or untrue), 'hingin aboot' (waiting), and 'scunnered' (sickened) are, once again, words I hear and use every day. It feels as if I am coming home to my own tongue as well as to my kin: it brings awareness and sorrow for those who may never experience that, because their mother tongue is no longer spoken or in decline, and happiness that my own Scots language, my mother's tongue, is now on the rise, with young, brilliant, creative people sharing it as a badge of pride, and a new understanding of nuance and expression. I find myself grinning when I come across a phrase I haven't heard for years: 'Ma heid's birlin' (My head's spinning), 'Away n bile yer heid' (Get lost), 'Gie's a lenny that' (May I borrow that?). And at first, I was also slightly amazed that I understood them immediately, without any hesitation at all, as if they were somehow imprinted onto who I am linguistically. This persistence isn't true of languages I've worked hard to learn. Despite living in Finland for almost two years, and once having a reasonable fluency in the language, I can barely manage a sentence in Finnish any more and can no longer understand even the simplest WhatsApp message from old friends without recourse to an online dictionary. With age, there is also a realization and sense of regret that I will never, ever achieve anywhere near the level of fluency in the other languages I know as that which I possess in my native tongues.

The intricate dynamics of language evolution, conflict, and extinction can serve as a microcosm for the broader sociopolitical landscapes in which they exist, illuminating how unusual, threatened, and extinct languages are not merely footnotes in linguistic catalogues but vibrant markers of cultural identity and historical evolution.

In my own journey, I've come to see that these rare tongues are intricately composed musical notes in the symphony of our human experience. These are not mere words and syntax but the keepers of unique worldviews, the battlegrounds of ethnic clashes, and the cries of societies struggling to preserve their heritage. Each one carries deeply personal stories; each one is a living testament to human resilience, adaptability, and the enduring quest for identity in a rapidly changing world.

This book is a tour of this glorious kaleidoscope. The chaotic, seemingly arbitrary differences, the incredible similarities and commonalities. Above all, it is about what we can learn from a closer look at the communication systems that are so fundamental to our human nature, and why their diversity matters.

1

---◁▷---

Latin and How Languages Develop

'History does not merely touch on language but
takes place in it.'

—Theodor Adorno, *Minima Moralia:
Reflections on a Damaged Life* (2005)

'Historia magistra vitae est' (History is the teacher of life)

—Cicero, *De Oratore* II-36

I N AN ORNATE Roman Catholic church in central
London, tucked anachronistically just behind Selfridges,
I find myself transported back simultaneously to medieval times and to my own childhood. I am not Catholic,
but the Latin mass is a thing that evokes mystery and awe
and for me, having grown up in a violently sectarian part of
Scotland, hints at a childhood curiosity about those kids who
went to the other school across the road. It's a complicated
thing. I studied Latin at my rough comprehensive secondary
school for five years and took a course in Medieval Latin as
part of my undergraduate degree. The Catholic priest from

11

the church at the edge of our estate gave me a Latin prayer book, and some neighbours gossiped for days about whether my parents were going to have a convert to deal with. To my mother and father's credit, they just shrugged and said it was up to me.

As the service progresses those gentle wafting smells of incense bring back to me those heady scents that emanated intriguingly through a chink in the door of the local Roman Catholic church as I passed by.[1] Yet the only time I attended an RC service in my home town, again with the friendly priest, I was disappointed to my core, in a way that perhaps only adolescents can be, because the service itself was in English and the candles were little bulbs that came on when you inserted a coin.

Latin was an oddity on our curriculum. One of our Latin teachers was the dread of school bullies, and in fact had taught my mother's generation too, although she had never been taught by him; she'd had to leave school at fourteen to bring in the money our family needed just to get by. Even still, she knew his formidable reputation. But because Mr Laird was hated by bullies, he was adored by me. Unlike many classes, his was a place of respite from torment. His ability to give the belt was legendary, although I never actually saw him belt anyone, but stories circulated of students with broken fingers and slash marks on their hands that took weeks to heal. I was grateful for the mythology, and happy too for the peace it afforded me. The first-year Classical Background class he taught only hinted at language, but there was promise that the unfolding understanding of Latin and ancient Greek would allow us to enter a world of metamorphoses and magical imaginings. In second year, language lessons began: tables of verbs and nouns in cases that I can still recite in my fifties; the strange classifications of words according to what they did in a sentence – nominative (the subject), vocative (direct address), accusative (the object), genitive (belonging to), dative (to or for), ablative (by, with, or from). It was years before I knew that these terms were also a window to learning other languages, and when I started on Finnish I recalled my Latin teachers and gave them more thanks than I ever had as a student. In second year, my teacher was one of our youngest. She was easy to like, and the bullies had mostly been weeded out at the end of first year, so a new world of possibilities opened to us. There were competitions in spoken Latin that involved a day off other classes and a minibus ride to a posh school in Glasgow (invariably the hosts were private schools). I won two years running, reading prose, Vergil and Pliny:

Quam quam animus meminisse horret, incipiam.
(Although my mind shudders at the thought, I will continue.)

But in the third year, I lost my place to a pupil at the hosting private school whose parents proudly boasted about the excellent tutor they had employed to lead her to success. Our practice classes were at odd lunchtimes, hours kindly donated by the teachers, both Mr Laird and Miss Tweedie, that I wish I had appreciated more at the time. But my teenage soul raged against what I thought of as inequity.

I didn't know then that the chance to do Latin at all at a comprehensive school was far from usual. There was talk at parents' day as to whether it was a useful subject. 'Papish,' some said, 'should only be for Catholics', 'But you need it to be a doctor,' others would retort, only for a third parent to chime in, 'Like anyone from here is going to get into medicine.'

Less than a decade after I left school it was removed from the curriculum, discarded as outmoded and non-vocational. By then I had begun a PhD in Linguistics, had the best-paying student job I ever found using Latin, and had published a couple of short stories heavily influenced by classical myth. I wasn't alone, far from it, in finding value in the skills learned from a language labelled as dead and dying, but I was to be the last generation of working-class kids to have the opportunity at all.

Even now, just as a tourist, exploring Pompeii and Herculaneum with my husband, I find a little gleam of pleasure when a familiar Latin word is legible on a faded fresco. I loved telling him about Pliny the Elder and Pliny the Younger, and how the latter's account is how we know so much about the eruption of Vesuvius. For me, there was a thirty-five-year gap between translating Pliny's words and seeing the two towns being carved and dug out of the ashes and the mud, but the continuity of history preserved and the thread of this ancient language running through my own life only seemed to highlight the relevance of history, and the languages of history, to all of us, no matter where we come from or who we are.

In those decades between the classroom and my imaginings of a lost world captured in a language described as dead, and my visit to a society still being discovered day by day, I had experienced first-hand what linguistic discrimination was. I changed from trying to disguise my own origins with an accent that was more respected to being proud of who I was and where I came from. My working-class dialect and vocabulary and the way I saw them interpreted by people I thought of as better, richer, more educated was the first time I had seen language as part of a societal marking; but it was only the beginning of a continuous experience. Only recently do things seem to be changing, only now is linguistic diversity celebrated, only now are many of the words that are intrinsic to my mother's tongue, and to my own, seen as part of a language, Scots, rather than mere oddities of dialect and class.

But during that intervening time, I also encountered people whose languages and culture were threatened with a devastation more complete than even that of a volcanic eruption, for whom there would be no trace, no thread of understanding or being understood, passed down through millennia. I have spoken to others whose language is a way of keeping secrets and to those who want to make their words known and spoken by the masses as a way of preserving a culture, its stories, its history. But for me, because it is the beginning of my own story, my own endless fascination with languages, this book begins with Latin, its rise, decline, and legacy, and the story of why, although it might be the instance most familiar to many of us, it's not the only language to have followed that trajectory.

Latin is the rarest of languages now, yet once it carried prestige and honour wherever it was spoken. Even this, the most powerful of historic languages, had a lifespan, its evolution and decline, over centuries, a perfect example of the way that language changes and is not always predictable in how it does so. It is a testament to how even the greatest of monolingual spreads can diminish and vanish, become no more than archaic mementos. The Latin mass, in particular churches or held only at occasional times, and the scientific nomenclature given to objects and creatures are the living memories of a language that once dominated the world.

A very brief introduction to Latin grammar

Latin grammar is known for its systematic and precise structure, and many traces of it remain in languages familiar to us today, including English. Looking in some detail at the grammar and how it's structured will be helpful when we look at the evolution and description of some of the other rare tongues later in this book.

One of the fundamental aspects of Latin grammar is its system of cases. Nouns, pronouns, and adjectives are declined into various cases, indicating their grammatical function within a sentence.

Latin nouns are inflected, meaning they change their endings to indicate grammatical case, number, and gender. Nouns belong to different declensions, and mastering these declensions is crucial for accurate translation and sentence construction. There are five main noun declensions in Latin, each with its own set of endings and patterns.

Latin is a fusional language. That means that when you add a morpheme (a segment) to a base word, it tells you more than one thing about the word. One of the properties it indicates is case. Latin employs six main cases, each serving a specific grammatical function within a sentence. Nouns, pronouns, and adjectives change their endings to indicate the case to which they belong. Because the notion of cases will feature in several of the languages we'll look at, let's look at the cases of Latin and what they mean a word is actually doing in a sentence.

In Latin, the nominative case is used for the subject of a sentence or a predicate nominative (a noun or pronoun that follows a linking verb and renames or describes the subject):

Puella ambulat. (The girl walks.)

A genitive suffix indicates possession or relationship, often translated as 'of' or 'belonging to':

Liber magistri. (The book of the teacher.)

The indirect object, or the person or thing to or for whom something is done, is denoted by the dative:

Donum amico dedi. (I gave the gift to my friend.)

And the accusative marks the direct object of a verb:

Puellam vidit. (He saw the girl.)

The ablative is slightly more complex because it can have different functions, including indicating the means or instrument by which something is done, or its location and separation:

Cum amico ambulo. (I walk with my friend.)

Finally, the vocative is used to address or call someone or something:

Salve, amice! (Hello, friend!)

Recognizing the case of a noun is essential for understanding its role in a sentence and determining the appropriate form and agreement of other words within the sentence. Adjectives in Latin agree with the nouns they describe in case, number, and gender. For example, the adjective 'magnus' (big) would become 'magna' when describing a feminine noun in the nominative singular (e.g., 'magna domus' – big house). Prepositions in Latin usually require nouns to be in either the accusative or the ablative case. For example, 'in' can take the accusative when it means 'into' (e.g., 'in domum' – into the house) or the ablative when it means 'in' (e.g., 'in domo' – in the house).

Just as in English, Latin verbs undergo conjugation to express tense, mood, voice, and person. There are four main conjugation patterns that verbs can follow. For instance, the verb 'amo' (I love) belongs to the first conjugation. In the present indicative tense, it changes as follows: 'amo' (I love), 'amas' (you love), 'amat' (he/she/it loves), 'amamus' (we love), 'amatis' (you all love), 'amant' (they love). Latin verbs also have different moods, including the indicative (stating facts), subjunctive (expressing doubt, possibility, or necessity), and imperative (giving commands). Each mood has its own set of endings and conveys different nuances of meaning and attitude. For example, the present subjunctive of 'amo' is 'amem' (I may love), 'ames' (you may love), and so on.

Latin verbs express various tenses to indicate the time at which an action occurs. The main tenses in Latin include the present (corresponding to, for example, I love), imperfect (I was loving or used to love), future (I will love), perfect (I loved), pluperfect (I had loved), and future perfect (I will have loved).

Unlike English and many other languages, Latin employs a relatively flexible word order due to its inflected nature.

While the typical word order is subject-verb-object (SVO), Latin allows for variations to emphasize certain elements or achieve stylistic effects. Instead of relying heavily on word order, Latin uses noun cases to establish relationships between words within a sentence. This brief overview of Latin will help us understand some of the links to contemporary languages in the following chapters, as well as to illustrate the legacy of Latin.

A short history

Archaeology indicates that people lived around the area we now call Rome as early as 1000 BCE. And by the eighth century BCE a small settlement had mushroomed in the area around what we still know as the Roman Forum. The way of life of the very first people who lived there remains shrouded in mystery, but they did use a form of the Latin language and were already literate, after less than two hundred years had passed, because an inscription on the Forum Romanum dates from the sixth century BCE.

Latin was only one of the languages used within the continental mass we now call Italy. Oscan and Umbrian were native to the area too, the former in much of southern Italy, the latter in Umbria, and early inscriptions show that all three languages had many similarities, although they were different enough that it's unlikely a speaker of one could understand and communicate with a speaker of the others. All these languages had only a small number of speakers and with other languages in the region formed a group we now label as Italic languages. Italic languages, however, are another subset of the Indo-European languages we mentioned earlier, a group that also includes languages as different as Gaelic, Bengali, and Latvian, and whose diversity gives us a plethora of information about early migration and trade. The Etruscans were yet another neighbour of this small Roman settlement. The two groups were politically, economically, and socially intertwined, and, although their two languages were unrelated, their alphabets were not, with the Romans adopting a modified version of the Etruscans' alphabet to write their own language. This is the same alphabet we use for many languages, including English, today. From the fifth century BCE, the Roman settlers were farmers and fighters. And it was by combining these two skills that Latin slowly began to spread throughout Italy and, eventually, much further afield.

As the soldiers conquered and occupied neighbouring territory, they brought their language and customs to an ever-widening area. Soldiers were rewarded at the end of their service with parcels of land in the new colonies, where they could farm and raise families. They settled like this, not only across Italy, but even as far as North Africa, modern-day Tunisia. Yet, despite this, the Romans were not yet the most important culture of the time: that was a distinction held by the Greeks. Like the Romans, the Greeks were intrepid fighters, but they were also sophisticated, creating works of literature and art. When the Romans finally conquered southern Italy and Sicily, which had hitherto been Greek, they encountered a highly developed culture and a new language. Retaining Latin, they adopted Greek as a second language, with most prominent Romans knowing it fluently, and began to build a literature of their own.

By 300 BCE, Latin was the official language of the empire. The first literature was unsophisticated, usually rough translations of Greek genres and forms. Initially, although it was used for law, politics, and religion, it coexisted alongside Greek dialects, but when Latin was made a compulsory language, the use of which could bring reward and recognition, it quickly surpassed other tongues. The Romans continued to conquer and occupy, taking their language with them, and the peak of Latin's linguistic development was achieved in 100 BCE with the literature of Cicero, Vergil, and Ovid. Latin's success, its growth and usage, was a manufactured thing, part of a skilful Roman strategy to maintain unity and control over their conquered nations, and Romans made their language a mark of prestige as well as a sign of their dominance, promoting stories where knowledge of the language brought great reward.

There was the tale of Vindicius, a young slave whose knowledge of Latin enabled him to discover a rebellious plot and whose reward was freedom and Roman citizenship, told by Livy in the first year of the Roman Republic. According to the story, the House of Tarquin were angry and defiant at the loss of royal privilege they had enjoyed under the monarchy. Many of their friends and allies were similarly disaffected; no longer able to go to the king for favours, they felt that the laws of the republic had reduced them to a position no better than slaves. The former king, Tarquin the Proud, petitioned to have his property returned to him. Afraid that refusal would be seen as a declaration of war, most of the senate acquiesced, allowing the exiled royal and his entourage to delay their departure from the city while the means to transport their belongings was arranged. In fact, the whole petition was a cover for a plan to regain the crown.

As the former king and his loyal supporters dined together, they were overheard by Vindicius, a young slave of the household that was hosting them. Unusually for a slave, Vindicius was fluent in Latin and was able to not only understand the overheard conversation but also read documents in the Latin language. Realizing that the word of a slave was likely to be doubted, he found papers to substantiate his eavesdropping and took them to the consuls, who immediately arrested the perpetrators.

When the issue of the restoration of property was raised again, it was decided that it should be given to the slave, as well as his freedom and Roman citizenship. His knowledge of the language had saved the republic as well as brought him personal wealth and position. It's unlikely that Livy's story – although regarded for centuries as history – is true.[2] But it served as perfect propaganda for how knowledge of the Latin tongue could lead to success and prosperity and make emancipation an aspiration, not just a dream. It's a tale that we'll see repeated again and again over centuries: the prioritization, the apparently unstoppable domination, of the dominant tongue.

The growth of literature fixed the classical language so that, for the first time, officialdom and literature mirrored each other in a formal and prescribed form. But a popular, more colloquial language continued to develop too, and a divergent form, Vulgar Latin, gradually emerged. This was not a separate language, but rather a different form. Vulgar, the word, comes from 'vulgaris', meaning common, but it's often noted, correctly, that the written evidence and traces we have of Vulgar Latin are not from slaves, servants, or those at the lowest levels of Roman society – because, for the most part, these groups would have been unable to leave any – but rather from the middle and merchant classes, who had learned how to write. As in English, even in Roman times the word 'vulgar' had derogatory connotations and could refer to a lack of education or someone from a 'lower class', but the language was far more widespread than that suggests.

As noted, Classical Latin was already established with a body of written work. But there are literary remnants of colloquial Latin too: the works of Roman playwright Plautus, even though they date from the very earliest period of what is usually regarded as Vulgar Latin, show examples of this in their dialogue.

Titus Maccius Plautus was a Roman playwright of the third century BCE, best known for his comedic works. His work offers a glimpse into the Latin of the people and shows us its humorous scope, while its use helped to develop the characters of slaves or lowlife figures, such as Ballio, a pimp, in his play *Pseudolus*.

Plautus' knack for employing wordplay and witty remarks, combined with the novelty of this technique, which created comedic effects in his plays, gave him popular celebrity. By using colloquial forms and vocabulary, he captured the everyday language and humour of the general populace, as well as gifting posterity with grammatical clues as to the development of the language.

At Herculaneum, ancient graffiti also attests to the pervasiveness of Vulgar Latin. At Herculaneum Bar, we learn that 'Two friends were here. While they were, they had bad service in every way from a guy named Epaphroditus. They threw him out and spent 105 and half sestertii most agreeably on whores.' Then we can smile a little at the words next to a drawing of a phallus, which read 'Handle with care'.[3]

By the second century, Vulgar Latin was in the ascendant – even civil and religious documents were being transcribed into Vulgar Latin so that they might be shared with a wider readership. The nineteenth-century linguist Wilhelm Meyer-Lübke argued convincingly that Vulgar Latin, the everyday spoken language, was in fact the prototype for the numerous European languages that would later evolve, with the static written Classical Latin being a far more artificial, prescribed form that was lauded, but not actually used.

A more modern parallel to Meyer-Lübke's insight might be the position the so-called 'Queen's English' held across Great Britain for much of the twentieth century. Even in my 1980s university seminar group, taught by some of the world's best-regarded linguists, it was referred to as the 'correct form' —despite being a form of English rarely heard outside a very small, and dwindling, group of British speakers.

Let's look at the ways in which the two Latin forms differ, in the light of Meyer-Lübke's claim. The distinction between Vulgar Latin and Classical Latin encompasses differences in grammar, vocabulary, pronunciation, and syntax. Vulgar Latin displayed a simplification of the verb system compared to Classical Latin. Verb conjugations became more regularized, with fewer distinct endings. Irregular verb forms were often simplified or replaced with more regular patterns. The synthetic future tense, for example, was gradually replaced by periphrastic constructions with the verb 'habere' (to have) and the infinitive. One of the most significant grammatical changes in Vulgar Latin was the erosion of the case system found in Classical Latin, which we looked at earlier. We saw that Classical Latin had a robust case system with six cases (nominative, accusative, genitive, dative, ablative, and vocative); however, Vulgar Latin experienced a reduction in case distinctions. Nouns began to rely more on prepositions to express relationships and the functions of cases. Vulgar Latin increasingly employed prepositions to convey the meanings that Classical Latin expressed through case endings. Prepositions provided more explicit indicators of relationships between nouns and their modifiers. This shift led to the development of prepositional phrases, just as we have in English today, as an alternative to the more inflected phrases of Classical Latin.

Word order became more fixed, with subject-verb-object (SVO) becoming the predominant word order, whereas Classical Latin allowed for more flexibility in word placement due to the inflectional endings indicating grammatical roles. This change meant Vulgar Latin now had similar word order patterns to those found in modern Romance languages.

Vulgar Latin exhibited changes in the pronoun system, including the loss of some distinct forms and the emergence of new ones. For example, the third-person pronoun 'ille' developed into Romance-language equivalents such as 'el' (Spanish) and 'il' (Italian), while the second-person pronoun 'tu', now familiar to us from modern-day French, replaced the Classical Latin 'vos' as the singular pronoun for 'you'.

Vulgar Latin also incorporated a considerable number of loanwords from neighbouring languages and dialects. This influx of new vocabulary enriched the lexicon and contributed to the formation of the Romance languages. Loanwords from Germanic tribes, such as the Visigoths and Lombards, and Celtic and Arabic languages influenced the development of Vulgar Latin vocabulary. This continuum of linguistic changes that occurred over time in the evolution of Vulgar Latin eventually led to the emergence of the distinct Romance languages, each with its own grammar, vocabulary, and phonological features.

Rome's growth and expansion, and most importantly, the central control that had brought some consistency to the language used across its vast territory, came to an end in 476 CE. But its disintegration had begun much earlier. Under Constantine's rule, Christianity had become the dominant religion, and the new faith consequently spread across the empire. The notion of the emperor as divine ruler, among a panoply of other worshipped gods, was in direct contradiction to the Christian idea of a single supreme Lord God. Constantine also split the empire into two – western and eastern – establishing the capital in the latter of these, which he named Constantinople after himself. Many scholars believe that this original split was made to create a new city, detached from the corruption that Constantine saw as all-pervasive in Rome. The Byzantine Empire, as the eastern side, used Greek as its primary language. The Latin-speaking Roman Catholic territory of the western empire owed huge amounts of debt to the east and suffered a series of weather incidents that led to decreased food production and higher prices, popular revolts, and the inability to halt invasions by Germanic barbarian tribes. It was the success of a ruler of one of these tribes, Odoacer of the Sciri tribe, that brought the defeat of the last Roman emperor. In a haunting memory of one of the founders of the empire, Romulus, it was the death and deposition of a namesake that brought the western part of the empire to the end of its long existence. Meanwhile, in the eastern Mediterranean, Greek continued to retain its hold as the lingua franca, and the gradual dwindling of

Latin's linguistic hegemony across the western region began. With a dearth of common infrastructure between occupied territories, Latin changed into distinct Latinate languages, such as French, Spanish, Italian, Catalan, and Portuguese.

Latin did not die. It evolved. It continued to be the language of the Roman Catholic Church, providing continuity and stability during this period of political and social upheaval. Latin was still used for liturgical texts, theological works, legal documents, scientific writings, and philosophical treatises. During the Middle Ages, Latin developed regional variations and absorbed elements from the vernacular languages spoken in different parts of Europe. This resulted in the emergence of distinct local forms of Medieval Latin. For example, in areas heavily influenced by the Germanic languages, such as Germany and England, Latin incorporated grammatical and lexical features from Old High German and Old English. These traces remain in many modern languages today.

Even in English, where Germanic roots dominate, we still find many Latin forms, often in words we think of as more learned or formal – for example, 'Ego' meaning 'I' in egotistical, 'Mater' and 'Pater' meaning 'Mother' and 'Father' in words like maternal and paternal, 'pulcher' meaning 'beautiful' in the English 'pulchritudinous'. The Church retained it as the language of worship, and thus, as the Church gained power and influence, so did the language once more.

Latin would once again regain its power, stretching its reach to countries that even the Romans had not introduced it to. While the populations of Europe spoke their own distinct language derivatives, priests and intellectuals continued to use Latin, and from the eighth to the fourteenth century Latin enjoyed a whole new heyday. This form of the language, Medieval Latin, the Latin of the Middle Ages, or Ecclesiastical Latin, was used in Europe from the sixth to the fifteenth century. Charlemagne, also known as Charles the Great, king of the Franks from 768 and the emperor of the Carolingian Empire from 800 until his death in 814, played a significant role in the promotion and preservation of the Latin language.

Latin had already undergone significant changes from its classical and vulgar forms and had evolved into what is now called Late Latin, which was influenced by Germanic and Romance languages. However, it remained the language of the Church, administration, and scholarship throughout Western Europe. Charlemagne recognized that Latin could be a unifying force within his empire, which spanned much of modern-day Western Europe. He saw the preservation and promotion of Latin as a way to maintain continuity with the Roman Empire and to establish a cultural and intellectual legacy for his reign.

To achieve these goals, Charlemagne implemented several language-related initiatives. He sought to establish a standardized form of Latin that could be used for administration, education, and religious purposes. He supported the work of scholars such as Alcuin of York and encouraged the creation of standardized grammars, dictionaries, and textbooks.

These efforts aimed to stabilize and regulate the use of Latin across different regions of his empire. Charlemagne's reign witnessed a period of cultural and intellectual revival known as the Carolingian Renaissance. He established a court school at his palace in Aachen, attracting scholars from across Europe. The school emphasized the study of Latin literature, grammar, rhetoric, and theology. Charlemagne himself was known to be a patron of learning, and he actively participated in scholarly discussions and debates.

One of Charlemagne's most lasting contributions to Latin was the establishment of the Carolingian minuscule script, a clear and legible handwriting style that replaced the earlier uncial and half-uncial scripts. This new script facilitated the copying and dissemination of Latin manuscripts and became the basis for the development of Medieval Latin scripts. Then, in 787, Charlemagne issued the Capitulary on Education, a decree that aimed to improve the education system within his empire. The decree emphasized the importance of Latin as the language of instruction in schools and monasteries. It required the establishment of schools in every diocese and monastic community, where Latin grammar, rhetoric, and other subjects would be taught. Recognizing and promoting the value of Classical Latin literature, Charlemagne sought to preserve ancient works that were at risk of being lost. He ordered the copying and preservation of manuscripts containing important classical texts. Monastic scriptoria played a crucial role in this endeavour, as monks diligently transcribed and preserved

Latin manuscripts, including works by Roman authors like Cicero, Vergil, and Ovid.

Charlemagne's efforts to promote and preserve Latin had a profound and lasting impact on European culture and education. The educational reforms he initiated laid the foundation for the medieval educational system, with Latin remaining the primary language of learning for centuries to come. His support for scholarship and the preservation of Latin texts contributed to the transmission of classical knowledge to subsequent generations. Moreover, the Carolingian minuscule script became the basis for the development of various European scripts, including the script used for writing the Latin language.

Charlemagne's reign marked a crucial period in the history of the Latin language. His championing and promotion of the language had vital roles in the continued significance and influence of Latin in medieval Europe, ensuring that Latin was once again esteemed as a language of intellectual and cultural exchange. Medieval Latin was the language of scholarship and intellectual discourse throughout Europe. Monks, scholars, and theologians used Latin to write and translate works in various fields, including theology, philosophy, law, medicine, and science. Prominent figures like St Thomas Aquinas, Roger Bacon, and Hildegard of Bingen composed their influential works in Medieval Latin.

But with the emergence of the Renaissance, just as the Middle Ages ended, the use of Medieval Latin began to decline again. A revival of interest in the classical world and the growing importance of vernacular languages led to the transition from Medieval Latin to Renaissance Latin. This latter sought to revive the purity and elegance of Classical Latin as part of a wider movement towards the restoration of classical influence and literature.

The Renaissance period, spanning roughly from the fourteenth to the seventeenth century, marked a significant shift in intellectual, cultural, and artistic pursuits throughout Europe. This revival of interest in the classical world was coupled with a desire to emulate the achievements of ancient Rome and Greece. It was a time of intellectual and cultural rebirth, characterized by a renewed interest in the literature, philosophy, and art of ancient Greece and Rome. The rediscovery and renewed popularity of classical texts, such as those of Cicero, Vergil, and Ovid, sparked a movement to revive and imitate the language and style of Classical Latin. Humanist scholars, inspired by the ideals of the ancient world, played a crucial role in promoting the use of Renaissance Latin. Renaissance Latin aimed to emulate the purity, elegance, and stylistic norms of Classical Latin. Scholars and writers sought to revive the language of classical authors, often referred to nostalgically as the 'Golden Age' of Latin literature. The emulation extended to the vocabulary, grammar, and rhetorical devices used in classical texts, with the new form including many of the linguistic features and grammatical structures of Classical Latin. However, it also developed its own distinct characteristics. It incorporated neologisms and loanwords from contemporary vernacular languages to express new concepts. In an odd return to its history, the general syntax of Classical Latin returned, with the use of cases, declensions, and conjugations. However, the use of complex sentence structures and rhetorical devices became more refined. Eloquence and clarity of expression were emphasized and admired. Writers often employed rhetorical devices, such as metaphor, alliteration, and antithesis, to enhance the persuasive and aesthetic qualities of their texts, with the use of rhetorical figures and devices aiming to recreate the rhetorical tradition of ancient Rome.

Renaissance Latin was primarily used in scholarly and intellectual circles and increasingly came to serve as the language of diplomacy, scientific discourse, legal texts, philosophical treatises, and theological works. Renaissance scholars composed works in Latin to reach a wider European audience and to establish continuity with the intellectual traditions of the past. Latin became the lingua franca of learned communities throughout Europe, allowing scholars from different regions to communicate and share knowledge. But while Renaissance Latin remained a dominant language in academic and intellectual spheres, the growing influence of vernacular languages cannot be overlooked. The rise of national languages, such as Italian, French, and English, led to the development of a bilingual culture. Scholars and writers often wrote in both Latin and their native languages, selecting the appropriate language for the intended audience and subject matter.

The use of Renaissance Latin gradually declined with the advent of the printing press and the dissemination of vernacular literature. The increasing availability of books written in local languages led to a shift away from Latin as the primary language of communication and scholarship. It did, however, leave a legacy, and the influence of Renaissance Latin on the development of modern European languages, as well as the formation of scientific terminology, is apparent in our world today.

And there's a literary facet to our heritage from Renaissance Latin too. Many of the best-known British writers of the time borrowed from the classics, even if it wasn't always direct. Several of the stories in Boccaccio's *Decameron*, which in turn would be an inspiration for both Chaucer and Shakespeare, were borrowed from Ovid's *Metamorphoses* – although the plagiarism doesn't begin with Chaucer because Ovid himself was not a creator, but rather a collector and translator of myths and legends, which he cleverly collated under the theme of transformation, thus creating the early Latin inspiration for many of those we regard as the canonical writers of the Renaissance.

When Chaucer wrote his beautiful *Troilus and Criseyde*, he announced that he was translating the story from the Latin works of Lollius. But Lollius did not exist, was part of the fiction itself, a nod to the prestige that could be had by showing a link to ancient, less well-known Latin texts, and Chaucer took the story from Boccaccio's *Il Filostrato* (c. 1335) and Benoît's *Le Roman de Troie* (c.1155–60). The influence of *Il Filostrato* is especially obvious, with stanzas matching almost word for word and the whole scene structure clearly taken from Boccaccio's story.[4] Shakespeare, too, borrowed heavily from Bocaccio with *Othello*, *The Two Gentlemen of Verona*, and *As You Like It* having few divergences in their narratives from the *Decameron*. The prestige and importance of Latin, its association with scholarliness and culture, made it important for writers who wished to be treated seriously to show their links with its past; but to retain an aura of originality, they obscured the true Latin roots and created new, more exciting, unknown ones to impress and attract their readers.

The Renaissance was the last glorious rise of Latin. Thereafter, it was confined to certain spheres – medicine, the Church, science – where it resides today, its traces running through our lives, rarely acknowledged or even fully understood but nevertheless familiar.

Manchu: the language of a lost empire

The longevity of Latin and its spectacular past are mirrored in another language, much less well-known in the west, which also once held a great empire together. Although they belong to different language families and emerged in very distinct cultural and geographical contexts, the Manchu language has a similar trajectory to Latin, mirroring its history of prestige and power and eventual decline.

Also known as Manchu-Tungusic, Manchu belongs to the Tungusic language group, one of a family of languages spoken in Eastern Siberia and Manchuria by Tungusic peoples. Historically, it was the official language of the Qing dynasty in China and was spoken by the Manchu people, who ruled over China from the mid-seventeenth century until the early twentieth century.

Originally a semi-nomadic people, the Manchus lived in Manchuria, an area encompassing present-day north-eastern China, parts of Russia's Far East, and the Korean Peninsula, around the Amur. It's a place of fast-flowing rivers and mountains whose summits are hidden in clouds throughout much of the year, a region that reflects the original hunting-and-gathering way of life of its people. The early history of Manchu is closely intertwined with the rise of the Jurchen people, who established the Jin dynasty in the twelfth century. The Jurchen language, also belonging to the Tungusic language family, was spoken by these early ancestors of the Manchus. The Manchu language gradually evolved from Jurchen as the Jurchen people assimilated with other Tungusic-speaking tribes in the region. The emergence of the Manchu language as a distinct entity can be attributed to the consolidation of power by the Aisin Gioro clan, who eventually established the Qing dynasty.

When the Manchus conquered China and established the Qing dynasty in 1644, they adopted many aspects of Chinese culture and governance. However, they also maintained their distinct Manchu identity, including their language, making Manchu the official language of the imperial court alongside Chinese. During the Qing dynasty, the Manchu language played a crucial role in government administration, with all important documents and official communications being conducted in Manchu. The ruling class, including the emperor and the nobility, were required to be fluent in Manchu, while Chinese was mainly used by the common people. The language of a small group of hunters grew to become one of diplomacy, culture, and control.

Manchu was written using what was known as 'Manchu script' or 'Manchu alphabet'. It was derived from Mongolian script and bears some resemblance to it. Initially, Manchu script was primarily used for writing administrative documents, historical records, and literature related to the ruling class, but ultimately it came to be the principal language for the translation of Chinese classics and the compilation of official historical texts.

Like Classical Latin, Manchu underwent processes of standardization. We've seen how Latin evolved through its different varieties and how the standard form of the language was used for formal communication, literature, and government affairs throughout the Roman Empire. Similarly, Manchu went through a standardization process during the Qing dynasty when, under the patronage of the emperors, it was codified and developed into a literary language with its own grammatical rules and norms.

Manchu has a complex system of vowels and consonants, with a total of fifteen vowels and twenty-one consonants.

It too is an agglutinative language so, like Latin, affixes are added to the end of words to indicate tense, aspect, mood, number, possession, and other grammatical functions. This agglutinative nature allows for the creation of complex words with multiple affixes.

It has six grammatical cases – it does not include the Latin vocative case, but has nominative, accusative, genitive, dative, ablative, and locative. The cases are indicated by adding suffixes to the noun. One distinctive feature of the Manchu language is its use of classifiers, which are used to indicate the number and type of objects being referred to. For example, instead of saying 'three horses', a Manchu speaker would say 'horse three heads'.

The language thrived, adapting and absorbing influences from the diverse cultures that coexisted within the empire's borders. Manchu absorbed loanwords from Mongolian, Tibetan, and Chinese and became the lingua franca of disparate cultures and peoples for almost three centuries.

But, as the nineteenth century unfolded, Manchu faced its first tribulations. The ruling elite, in a bid to solidify their position and reconcile with their Chinese subjects, gradually adopted the language and aspects of the culture of the people they ruled. This led to a decline in the use of the tongue among the ruling class and the general population. As China modernized in the late nineteenth century, the use of Mandarin Chinese became more widespread, and the Manchu language began to lose its prominence.

The social and political changes that accompanied the fall of the Qing dynasty in 1912 and the establishment of the Republic of China further marginalized the Manchu language. Mandarin was promoted as the national language, and policies were implemented to unify the diverse linguistic landscape of the country under a single language. These efforts resulted in the reduced use and recognition of minority languages, including Manchu. What had once been a prominent and influential tongue in China now found itself in a precarious state, facing the challenge of a quickly dwindling number of speakers, who often suffered from persecution and discrimination.

Today, it's officially classified as an endangered language. The remaining Manchu speakers are almost exclusively elderly individuals who have inherited the language from earlier generations, and they are concentrated in China's north-eastern regions, particularly in Heilongjiang, Jilin, and Liaoning provinces, although the language is also spoken by some Manchu communities in other parts of China and in the diaspora. The exact number of Manchu speakers is difficult to determine, as there are no comprehensive surveys or official statistics available. Though many Manchus adopted Chinese names and assimilated into society to escape the persecution that followed the 1911 revolution, there are estimated to be ten million ethnic Manchus around the world. The number of fluent speakers is reckoned to be less than twenty.[5]

But Manchu language instruction and preservation efforts have gained some momentum in recent years. The Chinese government, as well as various academic institutions and cultural organizations, have recognized the importance of preserving the Manchu language as an integral part of China's cultural heritage. Manchu language classes have been introduced in universities and research institutions across China. These programmes aim to train new generations of Manchu language specialists and promote the use of the language in academic and cultural contexts. Additionally, there are initiatives to develop language-learning materials, dictionaries, and textbooks to support the study and revitalization of the language.

Beyond China, there are also efforts to maintain and promote the Manchu language. In the Manchu diaspora communities, particularly in countries like Russia, South Korea, and Japan, there are individuals and organizations working to revive the language and its cultural significance. But revitalizing any language is a complex task. The intergenerational transmission of the Manchu language has been irreparably disrupted, and the language faces challenges in being adopted and used in contemporary settings. Chinese government support tends to centre on the language as a historical artefact, rather than as a language to be reintroduced to modern society. The dominance of Mandarin Chinese and the influence of global languages like English further complicate efforts.

The digital age has opened up new possibilities for the preservation and promotion of the language. Online platforms, websites, and social media communities have emerged as spaces where Manchu enthusiasts and speakers can connect, share resources, and engage in language-related discussions. The internet offers a means of reaching a wider audience and fostering a global community interested in the preservation of endangered languages. Manchu Sky, an online forum with more than five thousand members, is uniting Manchurians across great geographical distances. Members can share sound clips, language-learning initiatives, and even Manchu songs.

With help from a Cantonese friend, Xiao Lee, I briefly join the forum. Many posts are in Cantonese, as well as Mandarin, and there are subgroups where people post in Russian and Korean. Xiao engages with a thread about the language on my behalf. It's just a glimpse at the threads that bind the people who congregate here, and it feels like a fragile thing. One woman posts that she is learning the language; two others, who won't say where they are geographically, say it's impossible to find classes in their region. There are several posts about ancestry and pride in the history of the Manchu people, but far fewer with details of new projects attempting to rekindle it. It seems to me that the Manchu language is at a critical juncture in its history. As with so many languages at risk, there are clearly passionate, dedicated individuals and organizations actively working to preserve and revitalize it. An AI project in northern China is attempting to develop technology to speak and understand the language to help redress the dwindling number of speakers before it is too late. An article in the *Beijing Review* recounts the story of a young Manchu woman, Dekjin, who works in Beijing.[6]

Saddened that so few of her Manchu friends and acquaint-ances could speak the language, she set up a training centre. While hunting for teachers, she found a pocket of fluent speakers in north-east China, the Xibe ethnic group. Most of these speakers cannot write the language, so her plan is to combine their spoken proficiency with Manchu texts as part of a project. Once again, there is hope and determination.

2

---◇---

Khoisan – The Languages
with Many Sounds

'In my native village, in Johannesburg
There is a song that we always sing when a young girl gets married
It's called The Click Song by the English
Because they can't say ngqothwane
Igqira lendlela nguqo ngqothwane
Igqira lendlela kuthwa nguqo ngqothwane'

—Miriam Makeba, 'The Click Song'

LANGUAGES WOULD ONCE again rescue me from student penury when I was midway through a postgraduate course at the School of Oriental and African Studies. I had only scant knowledge of the country, Namibia, and its many languages and had been instead working on the phonology of Kikuyu, a language spoken in Kenya and one that the PhD I intended to move on to would feature.

But a job opportunity arose in the shape of a role on a dictionary project, run from the University of Windhoek. The language of the dictionary in progress was Nama, also known as Khoikhoi, one of a large group of languages called the Khoisan languages. When my supervisor asked if I was interested, I immediately said yes. The dictionary project offered me an opportunity to study a fascinating language whose consonants included many of the 'click' sounds I had been learning in preparation for my practical phonetics examination.

I discovered almost immediately that the word 'Nama' used to refer to the language was believed by many speakers to exclude them; Nama is an ethnic group in Namibia that does speak Khoikhoi, but the language is also indigenous in other parts of continental Africa in other ethnic groups. Sometimes it's also spelled Khoekhoe, but one activist pointed out to me that this was the Afrikaans spelling of his language. Out of respect for this, I'm using Khoikhoi throughout.

Khoikhoi

The late singer and civil rights activist Miriam Makeba brought knowledge of the click sounds, common to many African languages, to a global audience with her single 'The Click Song' in 1963. Like all students of phonetics and phonology, I had learned to pronounce and recognize the different click sounds as a part of studying the International Phonetic Alphabet, which states the symbols to be used for every known sound in the world's languages. What this scant knowledge had not prepared me for was the sheer number of different sounds that the addition of these clicks could result in. Nama, the language I was about to start researching, had twenty clicks! These clicks can have one of four places of articulation: dental, alveolar, lateral, or palatal, and use symbols to denote them, like this:

/!/ – alveolar click produced with the tip of the tongue against the roof of the mouth (like a cork pulled from a bottle).

/ǁ/ – lateral alveolar click produced by the side of the tongue against the back of the side teeth, like to a horse to speed up.

/ǂ/ – palatal click made with a flat tongue. This has a softer popping sound than the alveolar click.

/ǀ/ – dental click

Their phonemic designation can be seen in the following Khoikhoi examples:[1]

!am: to light
ǁam: clap
ǂam: exclusive
ǀam: demolish
!au: scream
ǁau: thick
ǂau: slow
ǀau: reprimand

Each of the clicks can be nasal, aspirated, voiceless aspirated, or glottalized, or 'tenuis' (which means that it doesn't contain any of the other features), thus giving us twenty distinct sounds.

Consider that English has forty-six phonemes, sounds that are used to differentiate one word from another. The number of phonemes is not the same as the number of letters in the alphabet, but instead is the number of distinctive sounds. Thus, we have 'pet' and 'bet', two different words that mean very different things, where the two phonemes /p/ and /b/ correspond to letters of the alphabet; but we also have 'ship' and 'chip' with the phoneme sounds /ʃ/, the sound you make to say 'hush', and /tʃ/, 'tch', which don't correspond to letters at all (see the appendix for more on phonology).

One of the other languages in the same group as Khoikhoi is called !Xóõ and is believed to have the biggest number of phonemes of any language in the world, a staggering 112 different sounds that can be used to contrast the meaning of words. The name of the language itself includes the symbol for an alveolar click, the very first symbol /!/, which sounds a bit like a cork being pulled from a bottle, while the /X/ that follows it is the sound you hear at the end of the word 'loch' when it is pronounced by a Scottish person. Unlike most languages that include them, clicks have important phonological functions in the languages within this group. Academic research suggests that, although rare now, these click noises used to be a worldwide feature of all human speech.[2] One posited reason for this is human anatomy. Studies suggest that click-language speakers have smaller alveolar ridges. Anyone with a larger alveolar ridge has more difficulty producing the sound, with the production requiring more effort.[3]

A history of Khoikhoi

The Khoisan languages are believed to be among the oldest language families in southern Africa, with roots dating back thousands of years. Originally a single homogenous group, over centuries they evolved into three distinct categories, nowadays known as Northern, Central, and Southern.

The Khoisan people, including the Khoikhoi and San groups, have inhabited the region for tens of thousands of years, and their languages were once widely spoken across southern Africa, including present-day Namibia, Botswana, Angola, South Africa, and parts of Zimbabwe. But colonization and numerous attempts to destroy indigenous culture and language have meant that this is no longer the case.

The San and the Damara ethnic groups are the first known peoples of present-day Namibia. The Nam only settled in Namibia in the first century BCE and were the first cattle breeders in the region. They were joined by the Herero, another cattle-rearing nomadic people, in the seventeenth century. The language of the Herera people is unrelated to Khoikhoi. Herero is a Bantu language, a language group that contains around six hundred languages, the most well-known of which is Swahili. It belongs to the Niger–Congo language family and has several dialects. In common with all other Bantu languages, Herero is agglutinative and has a huge number of affixes to denote gender, tense, case, and so on. Thus, 'OmuHerero' means 'a Herero person' in Herero, where the prefix 'Omu-' indicates the singular class for human beings.

Again, as with most Bantu languages (not all – there are a small number of exceptions), Herera is a tonal language. It has several tonal patterns, including high tones, low tones, and rising or falling tones. So, the lexical tones high high on the word '-hórá' give the meaning 'to ripen', high low '-hóra' means 'to remove hair', and two low tones '-hora' is 'be stiff'. These tonemes (like phonemes but instead words that are distinguished by tones) are a common feature of Herero.[4] Herero has a distinction between aspirated and unaspirated consonants, which affects the pronunciation and meaning of words. Aspirated consonants are pronounced with a slight puff of air.

Earlier in the fifteenth century, Portuguese colonizers had interacted with the native people but, discouraged by the challenges posed by the Namibian desert, had not encroached further. However, with the arrival of European colonizers in the seventeenth century, the linguistic landscape of southern Africa began to change significantly. European powers, such as the Dutch, British, and Germans, established colonies and exerted control over the region.

In the late nineteenth century, Germany began establishing colonies to compete with other European powers and gain access to resources and trade routes. Namibia, then known as German South West Africa, became an area of interest due to its strategic location and potential economic opportunities. Namibia's geographical location on the south-western coast of Africa provided access to the Atlantic Ocean. It offered potential as a maritime base for Germany, allowing for trade, naval operations, and access to global shipping routes. Namibia was also rich in various natural resources, including diamonds, copper, gold, and other minerals. The German government saw the potential economic benefits of plundering these resources for industry and trade. Despite the desert, many areas of Namibia were fertile and suitable for agriculture, particularly in the central and northern parts of the country, and Germany sought to establish agricultural settlements and exploit the region's potential for food production and economic gain.

Strategically, Namibia's location provided Germany with a hinterland that extended into present-day Angola and South Africa, offering an opportunity for further expansion and control over neighbouring territories and offering a larger sphere of influence for Germany in the region. This, coupled with its vast and sparsely populated landscapes, allowed Germany to establish military outposts and bases. Missionary zeal combined with colonialism, and new Christian arrivals launched into evangelizing the country, largely by promoting German religious texts while denigrating native languages and customs as savage and pagan.

In 1884, German Chancellor Otto von Bismarck declared German South West Africa a protectorate under German colonial administration, and the German government took control of the region. Under German rule, the use of indigenous languages, including Khoisan languages, was discouraged and devalued. The German authorities enforced the use of German in administration, education, and the legal system. Indigenous languages were marginalized, and speakers faced pressure to abandon their mother tongues. A growing number of German settlers demanded the land, cattle, and labour of the Nama and the Herero.

So the displacement of the indigenous peoples began, but not without opposition. Faced with land seizures, forced labour, increasing debt to resettle lost herds, low wages on white-owned farms, racial inequalities, and an attempt at obliterating their culture, the Herero and Nama people resisted. The growing tensions between the German colonial administration and the Herero and Nama communities grew, leading to clashes and escalating violence. Then, in 1904, the Herero launched an uprising against German forces. The German response was swift and brutal. The Herero were defeated in the Battle of Waterberg, resulting in the displacement and scattering of Herero communities. In the aftermath of the battle, German General Lothar von Trotha issued extermination orders against the Herero people, calling for the suppression and elimination of the Herero population.

The few surviving Herero and Nama people were placed in concentration camps, subjected to forced labour and inhumane conditions. Many died from starvation, disease, or mistreatment. The Herero and Nama genocide is now widely recognized as one of the first genocides of the twentieth century. The exact number of casualties is a matter of debate, but it is estimated that tens of thousands of Herero and Nama people were killed during its unfolding. The Herero population, estimated at around eighty thousand at the time, was severely depleted, with somewhere between 50 and 70 per cent of the entire population lost.

The attempts to obliterate these languages and culture did not end with World War I. Afterwards, the League of Nations granted a mandate to South Africa to administer the territory of German South West Africa. The mandate was intended to oversee the development and well-being of the local population. Namibia was then governed as a de facto fifth province of South Africa, which established a system of apartheid – a policy of racial segregation and discrimination. The South African government implemented land policies that favoured the white settler population and marginalized the indigenous communities. Land was forcefully taken from indigenous people and allocated to white settlers, resulting in dispossession and loss of livelihood for many indigenous groups.

The apartheid policies of the government imposed strict racial segregation. Indigenous people were subjected to discriminatory laws that restricted their movement, employment opportunities, and access to resources. Separate schools, hospitals, and amenities were established for different racial groups. These oppressive apartheid policies led to resistance and calls for independence. Several political movements, such as the South West Africa People's Organization (SWAPO), emerged to fight against South African rule. Armed struggle and political activism increased throughout the years as Namibians sought self-determination and freedom. The international community, including the United Nations, condemned South Africa's occupation of Namibia and called for its independence. Pressure mounted on South Africa to end its control over the territory, leading to negotiations and diplomatic efforts. Finally, in 1990, Namibia gained independence from South Africa and became the Republic of Namibia.

But the influence of German, and later English and Afrikaans, had led to a language shift among Namibia's native populations. Younger generations grew up in an environment where European languages were dominant, and they increasingly adopted these languages as their primary means of communication. Proficiency in their ancestral languages declined, and intergenerational transmission was limited – the words that had bound and built their communities were in danger of being lost. We can see this today in the threat that the global dominance of English, and Spanish in South America, poses.

After finally winning its independence, Namibia took steps to address the effects of colonization on its linguistic pluralism. The newly formed government recognized the importance of preserving and promoting local languages, but were also faced with a challenge: the sheer number of languages spoken in the country.

Namibia's small population is extraordinarily diverse, with approximately nine ethnic groups: the Owambos, the Ovaherero, the Kavangos, the Caprivians, the Bushmen, the Namas, the Damaras, the Rehoboth Basters, and the Whites, most of whom speak more than one language. It was not only Khoikhoi, the language that had brought me a change of fortune by way of its dictionary project, that had to be nurtured back to health, but a huge number of other languages too, including that of the decimated Herero people. The differences between them were marked too. Khoikhoigowab (Khoikhoi language) is an umbrella term for both the Damara and the Nama language. Yet even these two languages have some marked differences in vocabulary. For example, the phrase 'ha re' (used largely by Damaras) means telling someone to come, while 'khî re' has the same meaning for Nama speakers. The Damara dialect of Khoikhoi has a simpler phonetic inventory than the Nama dialect, as well as fewer click sounds and a reduced set of consonants overall.

The threat to all of the languages in the group was palpable, and was not only limited geographically to Namibia. In March 1990, the newly independent government of Namibia was faced with an immediate decision. The country would have an official language, but they had to decide which of the country's many spoken languages it would be. In a surprising move, a decision was made to make English, spoken by only 0.8 per cent of the population, the sole official language, and not one of the thirty other languages of the country. The choice of English as the official language aimed to provide a common language for communication and administration in a multilingual society, facilitating national unity and efficient governance. English was spoken only by a small minority of the population but would be the medium of instruction in schools and the official language for government, religion, and bureaucracy. SWAPO removed Afrikaans, a language regarded as the 'language of the oppressors', while the prime minister, His Excellency Hage G. Geingob, defended the idea of English as the first language of the country, with the explanation that 'Namibian people had been restricted in their capacity to communicate with the outside world' for a long time, saying, 'There should be a switch-over to the use of English at all levels and this is now the time'.[5]

The choice of English as a neutral language would, Geingob reasoned, despite its colonizing associations elsewhere in the world, present the new independent Namibia as a more international country, engaged and in communication with the world.

Six criteria had led to the selection, the first of which was unity. Selecting one of the African languages as primary was seen as directly detrimental to this and likely to cause ethnic divisiveness. Afrikaans and German, which bore the weight of colonial memory for too many, were rejected too as being against the spirit of unity, while conversely English was deemed best 'because of its special role as the language already chosen and used by the Liberation Movement' (UNIN 1981). However, this unexpected linguistic policy brought its own problems. More than 90 per cent of non-Arabic African countries are still linguistically dominated by the language of their colonizer.[6] The effect of this has been described as 'linguistic inequality' by academics, with the language of the colonialist still being used for higher-status processes and communication, related to government and law.[7]

Namibia had attempted to circumvent this problem by using a third language, one that was spoken, albeit patchily, in the country but was completely dissociated from its colonial past. But in doing so, they encountered a lack of exposure to English, a dearth of teachers with good enough English proficiency to make it the primary language of study, and the detrimental effect of English-based education on the other Namibian languages in terms of status and preservation.[8] A newspaper report in November 2011 claimed that 70 per cent of all secondary school teachers in Namibia were not proficient at either reading or writing in English. However, there was also a policy to introduce native languages into the primary school curriculum for the first three years, based on local languages, with English used as a second language. This has led to local primary schools in Nyae Nyae, for example, where San children are taught in Jul'hoansi with textbooks and numeracy primers, as well as, most recently, traditional stories illustrated by San adults in the community.

Other government-supported initiatives include community drama and theatre productions in a wide variety of indigenous languages, including Damara, Nama, Herero, and Hoansi. These have included performances in Windhoek with translations to open the languages to much wider audiences.

Language activism

In South Africa, the story of Khoikhoi is still one blighted by the lingering effects of colonization, and a language that was once spoken by thousands has just a handful of speakers left in the Northern Cape. Language activist and advocate Denver Toroxa Breda writes:

> Khoikhoi can be heard across South Africa in three everyday words, dagga ('cannabis'), nai ('pan flute') and kak (slang for 'faeces' or 'rubbish'). The influence of place names, such as karoo ('dry place'), is also a reminder of the language's history in the country.[9]

He advocates for the inclusion of Khoikhoi as one of the recognized official languages of South Africa. At the time of writing, South Africa has eleven languages, nine of which are in the Bantu group; the other two, English and Afrikaans, are those of colonizers. Using social media, Breda challenges institutions that he sees as being guilty of perpetuating language inequity and discrimination:

> Kakapusa ('erasure,' 'amnesia' or 'forgetting') is one of my most used words, that really encapsulates the kuru ('work') that I do as an advocate for the officialization of Khoikhoi and N|uu, two of southern African's first languages.

I am not hoaragase ('complete') until I take full possession of my heritage. Sadly, though being Khoikhoi, I am
forced to think in and speak the language of tsu-khoen
('oppressors') who dehumanised my people.

Africa is my home, but I cannot commune with my
ancestors. How can I ever know vkhîb ('peace') when
foreign words echo within my soul? The vuru ('healing')
of my being will only start with the kawakawas ('restoration') of my nam ('mother tongue').[10]

I met Denver online in the middle of a Scottish heatwave
on a sunny June day. We had no visuals because, even without
his camera on, the internet connection was shaky and intermittently cut out. I asked him about his work, the position of
Khoikhoi in South Africa, and what he thought the reasons
behind its systematic exclusion might be. One of the first
things he told me, and I found this deeply poignant, was that
two of the Khoikhoi words still used widely in South Africa
are 'kakapusa', which means 'erasure', and 'nai', the word for
'speechless'. Even within the Khoikhoi communities in South
Africa, and Denver believes this is a problem in Namibia still
too, there is a reluctance to learn or use the language because
it has been so successfully denigrated and devalued by colonizers, a practice that he feels continues today in South Africa.

The problem comes from the historical violence against
our people that South Africa does not want to acknowledge. If you acknowledge the Khoikhoi story and

people you must admit that colonisation led to our land being stolen and our language and culture destroyed.

I asked what his thoughts were on the nine Bantu languages recognized by the government.

The Bantu story is one of convenience. By acknowledging the Bantu languages, South Africa appears to be doing something. But this is about land. Khoi place names are found widely across South Africa, 40 per cent of South Africa is referred to as the 'Karou', a Khoi word meaning dry land. When you start to think about all those words for places and the language, you have to ask yourself, what about the people whose land it was, who gave the land its names. There are Khoi words on the South African coat of arms, but it's not one of the eleven official languages … one problem is the idea of 'coloured' identity, created by our colonisers, a single group, that erased our Khoi consciousness within it. There is no 'coloured' identity. We are many unique peoples.

What Denver wishes, what he fights for, is for the language to become one of the official languages. In our conversation, he consistently refers to it as his own language, although he freely admits he is only now, as an adult, starting to learn it. His identification with the language is unrelated to his current ability to know it. Denver also wants investment to create spaces for the language and to promote it. It's not 'all doom and gloom', he reassures me. He's working with Khoi people in other countries, including Namibia, and they are sharing stories and histories. There's a network of people, a linguistic arterial crisscross of nationalities, ages, education, and economic status, impelled to share what they know and learn what they do not. Originally it was older people, but now, he tells me:

> Younger people are waking up to the importance of the language and realising it's not just words but our connection to our roots and our culture and our ancestors. It makes us part of this land. We are working together now to win back what was taken from us. We organise events and find support for them.

So as freed nations recover from their histories, as interest and support for the local languages grow in myriad ways, there may be hope for those that remain. With increased international popular and academic interest in these languages, perhaps we can all learn a little more from the tongues that may well be able to speak to us about how the very first ancestors of all of us communicated with each other.

3

—◄◦►—

Lost and Reclaimed

'The death of a language. The word has the same kind of
reluctant resonance as it has when we talk about the death of a
person. And indeed, that's how it should be. For that's how it is.
A language dies only when the last person who speaks it dies.'

– David Crystal, *Language Death* (2000)

WHEREAS THE FUTURE offers some hope for
Khoikhoi, that doesn't at first appear to be the
case for many other languages, those which may
already be lost to us or that very soon might be. A butterfly
flits across a scientist's path. The woman sees it, registers
surprise, photographs and writes details of her find. An
announcement is made that a new species has been discovered. It is given a name. A Western name, in a dead language
that is no longer spoken. But there was already a word for
those coloured wings, that fragile fluttering creature. It is
not that a human being has seen it for the first time, but
rather that it now officially exists in a catalogue kept in an

agreed language. The other names, those dusty, uncategorized things, are forgotten, set aside, written over by the language of the colonizers. Even the creatures are given a new identity.

Suppressing or banning a language is not only an attempt to wipe out individuals but also aims to destroy the culture they represent. The language we first learn is our home language, our mother tongue; these labels to describe it refer to kinship and belonging. It is so inextricably linked to our humanity that when a language no longer exists, we say it has died. When languages cease to be used, either naturally or because of an act of war against them, we speak of linguicide; and when a language has been systematically eradicated, we refer to linguistic genocide, regarded by the United Nations, along with physical and cultural genocide, as a crime against humanity.

Palumatu (Indonesia), Kansa (Sioux, United States), Welsh Romani, Pitta Pitta (Australia), Sened (Tunisia) – a symbolic list of words, many of which are not easily recognizable, the names of languages that are no longer spoken, no longer heard, or have such a paucity of speakers that their demise is imminent. Their story is of forgotten ways and unremembered sounds. There is also Pazeh, an Austronesian language spoken by the Pazeh people, an indigenous group in Taiwan. The last fluent speaker, Pan Jin-yu, died in 2010. Wukchumni is a Native American language that belongs to the Yokutsan language family. It was traditionally spoken in the San Joaquin Valley of California. In 2018, there were only about six elderly speakers of Wukchumni. Marie Wilcox, its last native speaker, died in 2021. It is now officially extinct, although due to Wilcox's efforts three family members remain with good knowledge of the language. Ubykh was a Northwest Caucasian language spoken by the Ubykh people in the Caucasus region of Turkey. It had a complex consonant system and was known for its large number of phonemes. The last native speaker, Tevfik Esenç, passed away in 1992, marking the extinction of the language. Livonian is a Finnic language that was spoken by the Livonians, a small ethnic group in Latvia. By the late twentieth century, there were only a handful of elderly speakers left. Today, there are no known native speakers. Eyak was a Native American language spoken in Alaska. By the twenty-first century, there was only one known fluent speaker, Marie Smith Jones, who passed away in 2008. And these, too many, so many, are only a few languages from a list of hundreds.

From the suppression of the indigenous languages of Australia and North America, Kurdish in Turkey, Ainu in Japan, forbidding a language, or restricting it, is a means of retaining control. Enforced homogeny enables unification and domination; diversity is the enemy of dictators. In a monolingual country you always know what someone is saying about you. Even among this litany of loss, one country has lost more of its languages than any other, so much so that it is now dubbed the linguicide champion of the world. A staggering 93 per cent of Australia's native languages are extinct or soon will be.

In the 1990s, when I was writing my PhD thesis, I won an award from the Robert Menzies Foundation to go to record and study Kunjen, a language with only a handful of speakers in Cape York, Queensland. My principal PhD supervisor refused to let me go, citing arguments that it might then take me too long to finish and that he didn't get the chance to go off to Australia when he was a postgraduate student. I never really understood what he meant by that; did he mean he got his PhD without travelling to Australia or that it wasn't a relevant experience? Regretfully, tearfully, if I'm honest, I turned down the opportunity and have harboured some resentment ever since. I looked it up from time to time, this language I've never heard. I worried about it, imagined its speakers. In my mind they were a pair, speaking to each other in words that only they remembered the meaning of. By 2005 there really were only a handful of speakers left – most projects researching critically endangered languages numbered them as just seven – and I even thought, ridiculously, impractically, of garnering some academic help to go to northern Queensland and meet them. Ludicrous though the trip would have been, and ill-informed, part of me still wishes that I had. In 2023, there are no known speakers of Kunjen recorded by any agency any more, none at all. I imagine, at some time in the past fourteen years, a last remaining couple dying. I wonder if they died together, or if, at the end, one speaker was left alone, no longer able to communicate in their first language because there was no one left who shared it. I mentioned my abiding interest to Christine, an indigenous Australian from New South Wales whom I met when researching a different book.

'It's a pity,' she wrote to me, 'there will be words in that language for plants and recipes that aren't in mine, and they will all be gone now. There will be songs that have been passed on and on from mother to daughter, father to son, through hundreds of years, and they'll all be quiet now, made quiet by the colonizers. But even a white person, like you, no offence, or those academics that come from time to time, taking note of some of them, is better than nothing at all. A bit ironic maybe that non-native people are trying to catalogue something they helped make vanish. I wish I had more time, but I'm trying to get back my children so I can teach them my language and my ways, and my mother's too while she's still alive, so they don't get forgotten too.'[1]

There's very little about Kunjen even on the internet any more. Most sites are out of date regarding the number of speakers, and many that do mention the language are Christian sites, highlighting the number of people following that religion. Christine's words come back to me, and I too find it sadly ironic that the lingering traces of the language are now tied to part of the social system that hastened its demise in the first place.

The death of a language

Many linguists recognize two kinds of language death: sudden and gradual.[2] Sudden death is caused by natural disaster, when all remaining speakers of a language are killed, or by genocide, as has been the case with many languages of indigenous people. This has been especially true in Australia, where the creation of urban centres led to native Aboriginal peoples being wiped out.[3]

In so-called gradual death, a language wastes away, the number of speakers diminishes, and then those speakers that are left may use the language less frequently or be less fluent than their antecedents, until only a few words remain.

In my twenties, my original interest in indigenous Australian languages was wholly thanks to the work of Australian linguist Professor Bob Dixon, whose books on the languages of Australia opened a world to me. His book on the Dyirbal language of North Queensland, for me, presented a different view of the world as much as it did a different language.[4] There were twenty different kin categories a person could belong to. So, for example, the word 'uncle' is four different categories: 'muqu' (mother's elder brother), 'qaya' (mother's younger brother), 'bimu' (father's elder brother), and 'nquma' (father's younger brother).

In Dixon's study in the 1970s, Dyirbal speakers could alternate between two different languages, a Djalnuy (translates as mother-in-law language) and a Guwal or everyday language. This former language was used in the presence of relations regarded as taboo. These relatives were a parent-in-law or child-in-law of the opposite sex, or a cross cousin of the opposite sex (father's sister's or mother's brother's child).

The vocabulary in Guwal is wider and more specific than that of Djalnuy. Three or four words in the former may correspond to a single piece of vocabulary in the latter. So, for example, 'bala mura' (semen) and 'bala dumbal' (the bump on a shield), 'balan ŋamun' (breast or breast milk), 'bala milgi' (cow or goat's milk) can all be understood by the Djalnuy word 'ŋuŋun'. The ŋ symbol represents the sound you get at the end of the English word 'sing'.

Dixon's study also looked at noun classes, the way words are grouped together. In Dyirbal, these look random to the non-speaker but are actually constructed according to cultural and mythological factors, as well as natural habitat.

So Noun Group 1, known as 'bayi', includes: men, kangaroos, most snakes, most fishes, some birds, most insects, but also the moon, storms, rainbow, boomerang, and spear.

Noun Group 2, 'balan', includes: women, dog, platypus, some snakes, some fishes, most birds, anything connected with fire, water, sun, and stars.

Noun Group 3, 'balam': all trees with edible fruit.

Noun Group 4, 'bala': meat, parts of the body, most trees, grass, mud, stones, noises, and language.

To see how these belong together, it's necessary to know that everything associated with entities in a group will join them in their class.[5] Fish are with men in Group 1 because they are seen as animals, while birds are with women in Group 2 because they are believed to be the spirits of dead human females. In their mythology, the moon and sun are husband and wife, so the moon belongs in the male noun class, whereas the sun belongs in the class for women. A study just over a decade later, in the mid-eighties, found that this information was already lost. Younger people who did not know the mythology behind the word groupings simplified them in their version of the language, so only two remained: one for animate objects and one for inanimate ones.

Similarly, the vocabulary itself has simplified and grown smaller. The English word 'big' used to be represented by several equivalent words – an eel that was big was 'qunuii' but a scrub turkey would be 'waqala'. Young speakers use only one word now, just as they use the term that would refer to a particular kind of spotted eel to mean all eels. Dixon recorded over six hundred different plant names in his study, but by 1985 younger speakers, who were able to identify several species by their English name, knew only the single Dyirbal word 'yuqu' (tree) for all of them.[6] The road to extinction has been rapid. The numbers dwindled quickly; a whole language atrophied into just scattered words. There are no fluent Dyirbal speakers any more.

The endangered languages of India

While Australia may be dubbed the linguicide capital of the world, UNESCO reports that India now has the highest number of endangered languages in the world. Perhaps most surprisingly of all, some of these languages are the official tongues of the states they are spoken in. There are currently 600 languages that are endangered in India; fourteen years ago, there were 196. Of these, 33 are critically endangered.

Since the 1950s, nine languages have been labelled as extinct. These are Ahom, Andro, Tolcha, Rangkas, Sengmai, Chairel, Kolhreng, Tarao, and Aimol.[7] The first five of these are from the Himalayan region and are no longer spoken by any living person at all.

One contributing factor is that Hindi, the official language of the Union of India, is only spoken by two-fifths of the population, yet it has the greatest support for literacy. In India, female literacy rates are notably lower in areas where minority languages, many of which are endangered, are spoken. This correlation is not coincidental but is rooted in the intersection of linguistic marginalization and socio-economic constraints, which disproportionately affect women. The traditional educational framework in India, primarily centred around dominant languages like Hindi and English, and regional languages like Bengali or Tamil, often overlooks the linguistic range of its population. This oversight manifests in a lack of educational resources, teachers, and infrastructure supportive of minority languages. The very lowest rates of female literacy are typically found in rural regions, particularly in the states of Bihar, Rajasthan, Jharkhand, and Uttar Pradesh. Many rural areas lack adequate school facilities, especially at the secondary level, and the long distances to schools and lack of safe transportation are major deterrents for parents when it comes to sending their daughters to school. The situation is further compounded for women due to societal norms and economic conditions. In many rural and tribal communities, where endangered languages are predominantly spoken, girls are less likely to receive education compared to boys. Factors such as poverty, child labour, and early marriage exacerbate this gender disparity in education. When educational opportunities are limited or are offered in languages alien to their mother tongue, it creates an additional barrier for these women. Unfamiliarity with the language of instruction not only hinders their learning process but also affects their willingness to participate in educational programmes.

Two languages in India that exemplify the intersection of low female literacy rates and the lack of support for endangered languages are Santali and Kui. These languages, spoken by tribal communities, can offer a poignant insight into how linguistic marginalization and gender disparities in education are interrelated. Unusually for tribal languages, Santali and Kui both have a written script. Santali uses a script known as the Ol Chiki, which was created for the language by the poet and writer Pandit Raghunath Murmu in 1925. Kui commonly uses the Odia script, the official language of the Indian state of Orissa, which is over a thousand years old.

Santali is predominantly spoken by the Santal tribe, one of the largest tribal communities in India, mainly residing in the states of Jharkhand, West Bengal, Bihar, and Odisha. It belongs to the Austro-Asiatic language family. Despite being one of the major tribal languages, Santali has historically lacked institutional support. Its inclusion in the Eighth Schedule of the Indian Constitution in 2003 was a significant step, but the ground reality in terms of educational and media resources in Santali is still lacking. Kui is spoken by the Kondh tribal community, primarily in Odisha. It is a Dravidian language, closely related to other tribal languages in the region. In Kui-speaking regions, just as in the Santali areas, women face significant barriers to education. The lack of educational resources, combined with socio-economic challenges typical of tribal areas, results in low literacy rates among both groups of women. They often find it challenging to engage with education provided in dominant languages like Hindi or Bengali, leading to higher dropout rates. This situation not only limits their personal and economic develop-ment but also hinders the preservation and continuation of both languages.

While languages such as Gondi, predominantly spoken in Central and southern India, are showing marked improve-ments both in terms of endangerment status and in women's literacy, because of rapidly growing school-based educational programmes in the language, others are less fortunate.

The Leco language of Bolivia

Much can be learned from these languages that we are losing so quickly. One of them even offers clues to our earliest human history. The Leco language of Bolivia has no more than twenty very elderly speakers remaining. There are no dedicated programmes currently in place to protect it. There may be no speakers left in a handful of years. They primarily inhabit the Beni Department in the north-eastern region of

Bolivia, near the border with Brazil, and have been described, until recently, as an isolated community, self-sufficient and contained. But a study of the language structure shows that at some point in the distant past there was contact between the mountain-dwelling Leco and the peoples of the Amazonian basin, that their lives were interlinked, possibly by trade, perhaps even by familial links.[8] With the demise of the language, the possibility to understand more about this unexpected travelling will be lost.

Leco belongs to the Tacanan language family, which is a small language family consisting of several languages spoken in the Amazon rainforest region of Bolivia and Brazil. Tacanan languages are considered to be part of the larger Panoan language family, which includes other indigenous languages spoken in the Amazon basin.

The Leco language is currently classified in some places as critically endangered and in others as extinct. If there are speakers, it's a tiny and rapidly decreasing number. But the exact number is uncertain. UNESCO currently lists between just ten and ninety-nine speakers remaining in its World Atlas of Languages. The Endangered Languages Project, however, numbers the native speakers at zero. So how did it happen? Again, colonization, followed by a concomitant language shift towards Spanish, the dominant language in the region, has sped the decline of the Leco language.

In the sixteenth to eighteenth centuries, the arrival of Spanish colonizers in the region that is now Bolivia marked the beginning of Spanish influence on the indigenous languages, including Leco. Spanish was imposed as the language of administration, religion, and education, which led to the marginalization of indigenous languages and cultures. This was compounded by Christian missionaries, right up to the late nineteenth century, who tried to convert the local populations to Christianity while further promoting the use of Spanish by prohibiting or discouraging the use of indigenous languages, on the grounds of them being unchristian. Yet, ironically, the only reason we have a record of this isolated language at all is due to the work of a missionary, Andres Herrero. His early-nineteenth-century Christian doctrine in Leco brought the language to the attention of the linguist Lafone Quevado, who published it in 1905 and used it to compile the very first grammar of Leco.

The advent of formal education systems for indigenous children in Bolivia that might have been progressive were not because of how they were implemented linguistically, so instead they further accelerated the decline of local languages. The new opportunity for education was primarily conducted in Spanish, and indigenous children were often discouraged or prohibited from speaking their native languages in schools. This led to a stigma against their use, of the kind described throughout this book, making the younger generation reluctant to learn or use a language that marked them as inferior or uneducated.

Traditional Leco culture is deeply connected to the natural environment, particularly the rainforest and rivers. The Leco language would have reflected this relationship fully, with vocabulary related to flora, fauna, and ecological knowledge. But by 2009, research linguists noted:

'Los lekos han logrado sobrevivir como grupo indígena, aunque han perdido su lengua' [the Lecos have managed to survive as an indigenous group, although they have lost their language]
    'Siguen viviendo unos semihablantes' [only some semi-speakers are still alive][9]

When natural habitats are destroyed, the lives that they sustain die or change too. So as developed nations destroy rainforests, repurpose land, steal resources, and alter the face of the planet through climate change, the languages of those lost civilizations and the people who speak them have their way of life subsumed to that of another culture. Colonialism strips the world of nature, but also smothers ways of being, drowning out the words to describe them, under a blanket of conformity and sameness.

The decline of Penan

North-eastern Sarawak in Borneo is home to the Penan people. Their number is not in decline, but their language is. Once again, a dominant culture has put another under threat. Logging, sanctioned by the Malaysian government, has led to pollution of water supplies, the loss of sago palms – an essential staple of their diet – and far fewer wild animals. Even the monkeys, which were a vital source of food, have been frightened away by loggers. As the Penan people's way of life becomes less sustainable, the language seems less relevant to its speakers and has become supplanted by Malay and English, the languages provided in their state education. Formerly bilingual people are using just the acquired language, the only one they can use if they want to proceed to higher education. As they lose the language that was native to them, the creatures that its words named disappear from the environment. Traditional lifestyles are dismissed as uncivilized, out of tune with a rapidly developing world. Former Minister for Environment and Tourism Dato James Kim Min Wong, a timber tycoon, encapsulated these views in one of his poems:

O Penan – Jungle wanderers of the Tree
What would the future hold for thee? …
Perhaps to us you may appear deprived and poor
But can Civilization offer anything better? …
And yet could Society in good conscience
View your plight with detached indifference
Especially now we are an independent Nation
Yet not lift a helping hand to our fellow brethren?
Instead allow him to subsist in Blowpipes and clothed in
Chawats [loincloths]
An anthropological curiosity of Nature and Art?
Alas, ultimately your fate is your own decision
Remain as you are – or cross the Rubicon![10]

A people best known for their cultural practice of 'molong', which means that the Penang never take more than is needed from the forest, find the land around them stripped by others who have no such regard.

The Ainu language of Japan

Ainu is the language of the people of that name, an indigenous ethnic group mainly situated in Hokkaido, the northernmost island of Japan, but also with smaller pockets in some parts of Sakhalin and the Kuril Islands. Ainu is considered a language isolate, meaning it is not related to any other known language, although many researchers believe it is Neolithic in origin. Ainu history is characterized by a complex relationship with the dominant Japanese culture, marked by assimilation, discrimination, and a struggle for recognition. The effects of colonization, assimilation policies, and societal pressures mean that the Ainu way of life is now on the verge of extinction. The Ainu people's origins go back thousands of years. Their unique culture, reflected in their language, is characterized by hunting, fishing, and animistic beliefs.

The Ainu in Tohuku, the northern region of the largest island in the Japanese archipelago, found their language and culture already under threat as early as the fourteenth century, because of pressure from the central government. By the seventeenth century, those in Hokkaido were controlled by the powerful Matsumae clan, regarded as serfs and subjects, forced to make tributes and fulfil labour obligations. Within a few decades, the Japanese government began to implement assimilation policies. The Ainu language and customs were banned, and land was taken away and redistributed. In the late nineteenth century, Japan's Meiji Restoration period brought even more significant changes. The Japanese government abolished the feudal system, and Hokkaido was officially incorporated as a Japanese prefecture. Ainu land rights and cultural autonomy were even further eroded. Assimilation policies continued to intensify. Ainu children were forced to attend Japanese schools where, in common with so many of the children in this book, they would be punished for speaking their own language.

From the 1960s onwards, the Ainu began a cultural and political resurgence. Activists worked to reclaim their identity, language, and land rights. But official recognition of the issue only came in 1997 when the United Nations' Special Rapporteur on the Situation of Human Rights and Fundamental Freedoms of Indigenous Peoples visited Japan and acknowledged the discrimination faced by the Ainu.

Eleven years later, the Ainu were officially recognized as an indigenous people of Japan for the first time, and the Ainu Cultural Promotion Act was enacted, aiming to preserve and promote Ainu culture and heritage. Then in 2019, the Ainu Language Act was enacted, recognizing Ainu as an official language of Hokkaido alongside Japanese. However, it was too little and far too late; the current amount of fluent speakers at the time of writing is estimated by UNESCO as just five and by the Endangered Languages Project as two.

The Ainu language features a unique phonology and grammar. It is characterized by a rich system of vowel and consonant sounds, as well as complex agglutinative grammar. Traditional Ainu culture and language are closely intertwined, with many aspects of the language reflecting the importance of the natural world and their spiritual beliefs. The Ainu's presence, like that of the Khoikhoi, is reflected in the place names of the parts of the country they inhabit. In Hokkaido, 80 per cent of all place names are from the Ainu, rather than Japanese.

One distinctive feature of Ainu is its classification of plants. The nuances of the uses of different parts of individual plant species are reflected in Ainu words (but not in Japanese). Ainu names of plants are often given to the parts that are useful for the Ainu, and sometimes there is no word at all that refers to the whole tree or herb. On the other hand, if we consider the Ainu words associated with mugwort (*Artemisia montana*), we find 'noya' (leaf), 'noya-ikkeu' (literally noya's spine) for the stalk, and 'noya-shinrit' (noya's root). The plant's name is also 'noya' but 'noya-ikkeu' indicates the veins as well as the stalk.[11]

And specific vocabulary indicates not only parts of the plant, but also the differences in ecological characteristics, such as habitat, colour, size, shape, or smell, as well as its uses. Thus the evergreen shrub *Rhododendron aureum* is called 'riyahamus', which can be broken down as riyaham-us and means 'stayed over the winter/leaves/attaching', while the Japanese spicebush, *Lindera sericea*, a tree that is very rich in oil, is 'sumnas', sum-nu-has, which translates as 'oil/having/branch'.

Cowbane is a poisonous herb if eaten indiscriminately, with seeds that are carried by the water. It grows in swamps and is known as 'tokaomap' – syllabically, to-ka-oma-p – and means swamp/on/existing/one. Cowbane is used by the Ainu as a cure for backache, while *Urtica platyphylla*, a plant similar to a nettle, has a thick fibrous stalk that can be made into thread and fabric. It causes itching and stinging when touched and is, in Ainu, 'ipishiship', i-pishishi-p, meaning 'us/irritating and itching/one'.[12] The natural information contained within the language is only part of its great value. There are also words relating to an animistic belief system, Ainu folk stories, and songs that are historical clues to a civilization that has existed for thousands of years.

But even though the number of fluent speakers is listed as less than five by the Endangered Languages Project, and despite the long past of discrimination, for the first time in recent history the future is looking hopeful for Ainu. Not only is there a popular Ainu conversation channel on YouTube, but also, perhaps most surprising of all, because of a project aimed at introducing Ainu back into daily life, some Hokkaido bus routes have announcements in Ainu as well as Japanese.

In 2019, an act 'Promoting Measures to Achieve a Society in Which the Pride of Ainu People is Respected' was passed by the Japanese government. Voice recordings of folk stories and narratives in Ainu have been made and archived in the past decade; these are now being digitized. A national centre for the promotion of Ainu language and heritage was opened in 2020 and named the Symbolic Space for Ethnic Harmony; there will soon be a searchable corpus of Ainu words and grammar. It may be too late for the language to fill again the huge geographical spaces where it was once spoken freely, and many Ainu feel that until it's part of the school curriculum in Ainu regions and made an official second language no real progress of any kind will happen. But there is enthusiasm and pride, especially among the younger generation, who are learning to regard their identity as 'cool' after teen years spent hiding their ethnicity. Language classes and learning materials are beginning to change the demographic. It seems that for this critically endangered language a future may not be lost after all.

The rarest language in Europe

Closer to home there are endangered languages too – perhaps none more so than Wymysorys. Wymysorys or Vilamovian has roots that stretch back to the Middle Ages. It is believed to have been shaped initially by settlers from either Germany or Flanders who arrived in southern Poland in the thirteenth century.[13] The town of Wilamowice, where the language is spoken, became a melting pot of cultures, creating a language that reflected this in its borrowings and its variation.

The language shares features with Middle High German but also exhibits traces of Latin, Polish, and Dutch. Linguists often classify it as a micro-language of the Germanic language group, but Vilamovians consistently trace their ancestry from Flemish settlers.

This linguistic diversity is a reflection of the people who have populated the town throughout its history. Unlike other regional languages or dialects that can be firmly placed within a specific language family, Wymysorys is an example of what some linguists refer to as a 'mixed language' – that is, one where the grammar and lexicon have come from different source languages.[14]

From the seventeenth to the nineteenth centuries, Wymysorys served as the primary language for the inhabitants of Wilamowice. Its usage was not restricted to informal settings but extended to the local administration and churches. This period saw the language at its peak, marking a time of significant literary output. It functioned not only as a medium of communication but also as a marker of local identity. While the language itself was inherently pluralistic, the effect of its cumulative influences made it distinct. But the twentieth century brought significant upheavals to the speakers of Wymysorys, and not always in the ways you might predict. Because of its strong German influence, during the Nazi occupation of World War II the language enjoyed a special position, while Polish was actively forbidden across much of the country. The repercussion of this was that under post-war communist rule the inhabitants of Wilamowice were deemed to be Germans. Many were arrested for what the Soviets called Nazi sympathies; people

lost their livelihoods and property; many were forcibly re-
located in 'Regained Land' – territory given back to Poland
after the war – where populations were now sparse. It was
also the beginning of a Soviet-imposed homogenization
process that aimed to eradicate or severely limit the use of
minority languages. State control is easier when you can
control the words people use. Wymysorys was stigmatized as
a 'foreign' element that had to be purged to pave the way for a
cohesive Polish identity, and in 1946 it was banned outright,
as was the traditional costume worn by its speakers. Fear of
reprisal brought an end to the teaching of the language; it
was rarely heard on the streets and confined solely within
family homes. By the beginning of the twenty-first century
the number of fluent Wymysorys speakers had dwindled to
alarmingly low numbers of predominantly elderly people.

Wymysorys has seven vowels, a number consistent with
its Germanic roots, but also features phonemes that are more
Slavic in nature. Looking at just a few examples of Wymysorys
words and their English equivalents immediately gives you a
feel for these different influences within the language:

asa (to eat)
Der arpul (potato)
S'blimla (flower)
Kniag (book)
Ny olys ej guld, wos zih fynkly, glanct oba liöeht? (All
that glitters is not gold)

Recent years have seen an attempt at language revival, thanks to the campaigning of the remarkable Dr Tymoteusz Król, a native of Wilamowice who has become the language's leading advocate. Tiöma, as he asks me to call him in our first email exchange, is an adjunct professor at the Institute of Slavic Studies. He is the joint author of 'Awakening the Language and Speakers' Community of Wymysiöeryś' as well as the youngest native speaker of the language.[15] I met Tiöma in person in his town on a blistering day in May, having driven there from Krakow. It was a beautiful drive, past nesting storks and lush greenery, alongside fields where farmworkers tended crops, and made me think briefly of my mother as a ten-year-old child with my grandmother, moving from farm to farm to pick potatoes and rhubarb back in Scotland in the late 1940s and early 1950s. But the signs for Oswiecim were a dark reminder that I was also heading towards Auschwitz-Birkenau and one of the most moving museum testaments of humankind's inhumanity. I had also expected Wilamowice to be isolated – I think because of the distinctiveness of its language – but instead found it to be one in a chain of similar townships, all with occasional architecture that showed they too had been here for centuries in some form or another.

The May celebrations for Roman Catholic first communions made finding somewhere to sit down and chat much more difficult than we had anticipated, so we ended up in a garden centre in a neighbouring village, where my very first question for Tiöma was about the nature of the geography of Wilamowice and its contrast with what I had imagined. He explained by telling me a little of the history of the Vilamovians over the centuries.

> We were weavers, historically, we arrived here, we made cloth and then sold our cloth to other nearby towns. But Vilamovians soon realised they could make a lot more money by buying cloth from other places and trading it across the region, and eventually even in other big cities, like Vienna, across Europe. We are just six or seven kilometres from the border of the Hapsburg Empire, so even without travelling far they could sell over the border for far more money.

He explained that the townspeople became wealthy merchants, surrounded by predominantly poorer agrarian communities, and with their economic status came prestige, which in turn brought respect for their language.

> Wymysorys was essentially a language of rich people. While people might ridicule them locally for their different ways, there was also a desire to be one of them. So, if you married into the village, say, of course you learned the language because it meant prestige.
> But World War II brought a terrible choice. The inhabitants of Wilamowice, and other surrounding villages with German dialects, were considered a German colony by the Nazis and obliged to sign the Volksliste to

show they were of German origin. Many did and were then drafted into the Wehrmacht. But those who refused were sent off to concentration camps.

Tiöma's grandfather was one such person, being transported first from his Upper Silesian village to Dachau, and then to Mauthausen-Gusen, where he died.

During the communist decades, the Vilamovian language and cultural practices were banned altogether. This was in part because of the Germanic association, but also due to the greed of the communist authorities, who could then possess the houses of the wealthy Vilamovians. Some of the residents of Wilamowice were sent as far away as Siberia; others were transferred to Auschwitz, which had been repurposed as a Soviet labour camp. Fear meant the language fell silent, and children who knew only Wymysorys were sent to live with relatives.

Tiöma only learned the language as a child because his bilingual grandmother was one of the few remaining people to use it, conversing often with a neighbour who was a monolingual Wymysorys speaker. When Tiöma was just thirteen, he wrote to the Library of Congress asking that Wymysorys be recognized as a language, and years later, in 2007, it finally was. His youthful interest grew into a life of scholarship and enthusiasm, and he drew on this to create classes in the language, attended not only by Vilamovians but also by language buffs from countries as far away as Japan and Australia. 'We meet regularly online,' he tells me, 'to speak the language, yes, but now also as friends.' Tiöma warns against the dangers of only cataloguing to preserve.

When I first worked on revitalising Wymysorys, I focused on the language. The other elements of Wymysorys culture seemed safer. I thought, for example, that you could collect traditional costumes and lock them in a museum in order to preserve them. When I was a child, I wanted to document everything 'Wymysorys'. It was a good thing to do, but it didn't keep the language alive. Now I'd like the language to be part of a counterculture, that's my hope, my dream.

On a tour of the town, Tiöma points out some faded graffiti from the 1990s, a now-illegible scrawl of red on a building opposite the main church. He tells me, 'That was in Wymysorys. It insulted a local public figure. The kids that wrote it wouldn't have known the language, it was banned then, but words were used as a protest, the language was part of their rebellion.' The local priest at the time would go on to ban the Way of the Cross in Wymysorys and, as recently as 2013, the reading of a Wymysorys poem at the funeral of a poet who wrote in the language. Tiöma speculates if perhaps this insult, in the language he worked to suppress, was directed at him.[16]

Like so many of the language revitalization projects around the world, results have come with intergenerational collaboration. As we've seen, language is constantly evolving and in flux – if it doesn't have space to develop and interact with its environment, it will fall out of use. Old and young Vilamovians come together to share knowledge about traditional customs, and in doing so have generated activities that not only perpetuate community identity but also improve the quality of life of many of the town's elderly. And for Wilamowice, Tiöma's passion has brought even more. Since 2016, Wymysorys has been offered as a course at the University of Warsaw, and several programmes focus on revitalizing its legacy. In the town itself, there is money from Norway, which will establish a new museum on Vilamovian culture, signs on the town's historic buildings in both Polish and Wymysorys, and for Tiöma, most importantly of all, his slowly growing worldwide community of speakers, with their weekly discussions, friends now, who share his language and his hope.

The language of Jesus

The language spoken by Jesus Christ, Aramaic, once the lingua franca of the Near and Middle East, has an endangered ancestor. Used predominantly by Assyrian diaspora communities, Assyrian Neo-Aramaic, also known as Suret, is categorized as 'seriously endangered' by UNESCO. Although the number of speakers is estimated to be around 200,000, their scattered distribution – the effect of migration – makes it almost impossible to maintain any infrastructure or growing community for the language, except those which spring up online, across great distances.

Aramaic belongs to the Northwest Semitic group of languages and came into prominence around the twelfth century BCE. Over the centuries, it evolved into nineteen dialects and forms, including Assyrian Neo-Aramaic, which became the predominant language among Assyrian Christians residing mainly in parts of modern-day Iraq, Iran, Turkey, and Syria.

The Assyrian community has a deeply rooted history linked to the Assyrian Empire, one of the major Mesopotamian empires. The empire fell in 609 BCE, but the Assyrian people, culture, and language persisted. During the medieval period, Aramaic continued to be spoken and written in various forms and served as a bridge between Arabic and Greek worlds, particularly in the translation of scientific and philosophical texts, and thus facilitating the Islamic Golden Age. Meanwhile, Assyrian Neo-Aramaic thrived within Assyrian communities. Its usage was widespread in religious contexts, especially within the Church of the East, which grew to be a major intellectual hub and left a rich legacy of theological debate, liturgy, and hymnody.

But the twentieth century was a turning point in its fortunes. The Assyrian genocide of 1915 during World War I, inflicted by Ottoman Turkey and its Kurdish allies, decimated the Assyrian population and forced many into exile, thus disrupting the natural transmission of the language to younger generations. Later, anti-Assyrian policies under Baathist regimes forced mass migrations and disruptions, while ethnic strife and the Iran–Iraq War further dispersed Assyrian communities, leading to a substantial decline in native speakers.

The isolation that had once helped to preserve the language now proved detrimental, as dispersed communities adopted other languages, primarily Arabic and Turkish, to adapt to new environments.

The distinctive linguistics of Assyrian Neo-Aramaic

Assyrian Neo-Aramaic shares a lot of its structure and vocabulary with other Semitic languages like Hebrew and Arabic but has many distinct features. It is written from right to left, usually using the Syriac alphabet. While the language is rich in consonantal sounds, it has a restricted set of vowel sounds. The twenty-two consonantal sounds include unique phonemes like the uvular plosive /q/ (a sound made by stopping the air briefly then releasing, like you do with the sound /k/, for example, but instead of the tongue meeting the soft palate, the closure is formed by the back of the tongue and the uvula) and the pharyngeal fricatives /ħ/ and /ʕ/. In Neo-Aramaic, the construction of verbs involves the combination of prefixes and suffixes with base roots. This modular approach allows for a rich variety of verb forms, enabling the expression of various tenses, moods, aspects, persons, and numbers.

Thus, if we take the root 'QRB' (to come) and add the prefix 'Qa-' and the suffix '-ib', 'QRB' (to come) becomes 'Qarib' (he/she/it comes). Qrabe (they come) indicates the plural. And if we take the root 'ZKR' (to remember), add the prefix 'Za-' and the suffix '-ar', 'ZKR' (to remember) transforms into 'Zakar' (he/she remembers).[17]

Despite its uniqueness and long history of survival, Assyrian Neo-Aramaic continues to face the challenges of assimilation, lack of institutional support, and the digital divide. Assimilation into dominant cultures, especially in diaspora communities, has led to a decline in intergenerational language transmission; and a lack of any state backing in the regions where it is natively spoken, due to political marginalization and conflict, has impeded formal educational opportunities for the language. But once again, the twenty-first century is bringing change, albeit slowly, in the shape of online forums for diaspora communities, especially in Australia, the United States, and Sweden. Distance and forced or convenient linguistic integration may gradually be defeated by the internet-afforded ability to communicate easily and inexpensively with other disparate groups who speak the same language.

Language reclamation: decolonizing the language of extinction

Increasingly, academics are beginning to rethink the long-established terms of 'dead' and 'dying' for languages that have no living speakers. Is this labelling really another act of oppression? This can be exemplified by looking at the case of the Kariri-Xocó language of north-east Brazil. In July 1873, a Brazilian government ministry announced that the indigenous languages of that region were extinct. Yet 146 years later, in 2019, the Brazilian author Idiane Kariri-Xocó addressed an international conference of linguists speaking her revived Kariri-Xocó language, and publicly attested to its existence.[18] As is often the case with indigenous group members in Brazil, she took as her surname the name of her people to emphasize the collectivity of the community. In the mid-1990s, Nhenety Kariri-Xocó began to reconstruct the language. When a word was missing from any of the sources he was able to gather together, he adopted words from other nearby indigenous languages. He shared the compiled lists with his community via WhatsApp, as well as publishing them on a blog. For him, this communal act was because

Getting involved with our language is a way of affirming our identity, bringing our own history into perspective, and reappointing our way of being. Our language brings us autonomy, freedom, power, pride, belonging, identity; it anchors us in our community, it strengthens our culture.[19]

This reclamation of a language is seen by linguist activists as a fight against the effects of colonization. Because colonization is the cause of most linguistic decline and disintegration, the act of reviving an indigenous language, or of reintroducing one that's no longer spoken, is active decolonization. It goes beyond the cataloguing and monitoring of languages that are under threat and instead offers an alternative possibility: a future where the effects of colonization are diminished, rather than just described. Some indigenous peoples too are now rejecting the terms 'extinct' and 'dead' and adopting instead the words 'sleeping' or 'dormant'.[20] Kaurna, spoken around Adelaide, South Australia, once had no fluent speakers, the result of colonization. Yet today, it has a vibrant multigenerational community learning and using the language. The revival is seen as 'an act of identity', a concerted, triumphant surge of resistance against the label of extinction. It is also a step towards recovering the ecological awareness that was almost lost.

Other native people, while acknowledging a major problem is being identified and highlighted by organizations such as UNESCO, categorically reject the endangered-language narratives that are being used to do so. One activist who takes this view is Wesley Leonard of Oklahoma's Miami tribe. His language, Myaamiaataweenki, almost fell into disuse in the sixties, having been displanted by English. Nowadays, as the result of textual reclamation work in the 1990s, there are many speakers and the language is a vital and integral part of the Miami community. Leonard argues that terms such as 'extinction' to describe a language suggest that the language in question is beyond hope. Therefore, any programmes or funding to support it are pointless and highly unlikely to be supported. The term itself becomes not only a label, but also a mechanism of oppression. Instead of this categorization, he argues that it's time for a reclamation of language. Perhaps if the term 'dormant language' becomes more widely accepted, we will speak about awakening languages within communities, and the context that often ignores the peoples who speak them and the colonial injustice that caused their situation can be acknowledged more in discussion.

4

—◄○►—

Languages and Ecosystems: An Environmentalist Vocabulary

'As the ecological crisis is also one of communication mani-
festing itself specifically in language, ecolinguistics may
justifiably be expected to play an important role in the
mastering of the crisis. A vision and a conviction shared by
most ecolinguists is that research findings should contribute to
sustaining diversity and the protection of animals.'

—Dr Wilhelm Trampe, *The Ecolinguistics Reader* (2001)

'Language endangerment is significantly comparable to –
and related to – endangerment of biological species in
the natural world.'

—Michael Krauss, *World's Languages in Crisis* (1992)

W HEN WE REFLECT on ecologically important
languages, we are confronted with the realization that languages do much more than facilitate
human communication. They also serve as warehouses of

traditional ecological knowledge and as conduits for the intricate relationships between humans and nature. Many represent systems where language and landscape are intertwined, each informing and shaping the other over generations. Let's consider an example of one such language, Hawaiian. For Hawaiians, vocabulary is not just a set of labels but a bridge to their ancestral understanding of the ecosystem. In addition to tangible objects, words and phrases in Hawaiian can describe subtle natural phenomena, seasonal cycles, and even what Hawaiians perceive to be sacred connections between land and sea. They can give us a glimpse at a thoughtful relationship with the environment that is increasingly pertinent in an era marked by climate crisis.

The notion of ecologically significant languages offers a compelling counterpoint to the often reductionist views of nature that are deeply rooted in industrial societies. In these languages, each term and idiom is interconnected and manifold in its meaning, contributing to a greater whole. Their rich lexicons often include nuanced classifications of flora, fauna, and weather patterns, information that has been gathered and refined through centuries of observation and may offer invaluable insights for modern-day conservation efforts. When we listen to, when we understand, the vocabulary of ecologically significant languages, we're benefiting from a collective wisdom about sustainable coexistence that may not be replicable, even by scientific knowledge.

Looking at these languages invites us to see language as a prism through which we can observe humanity's multifaceted relationship with the natural world. And, as we will discover here, losing an ecologically significant language is far more than a loss of vocabulary: it's a severing of an age-old bond between a community and its natural habitat, a disconnection from a wellspring of ecological knowledge. In a time when we are grappling with unprecedented environmental challenges, perhaps traditional knowledge can offer us an urgent lesson in survival.

The World Wildlife Fund conducted a survey in 2014. Using the scale they would normally use to track the loss of animal species around the world, they tracked the threat to indigenous languages in the same geographic areas. What they found out was that the two appear to be related and to have very similar occurrences. It's not surprising, really. All languages have a lot of specific local knowledge built into them, and, while the oft-reported story of the fifty Eskimo words for snow is nothing but a myth, studies of Finnish and Sámi have shown them to have a huge number of words relating to specific snow-related tracks and conditions that we just wouldn't find in a country that didn't have those weather events every year. Local names for plants may also tell us what they can be used for. Thus, a stubby yellow-coloured grass found in Mongolia is called 'togon shugur ebes' in the local language, which means 'pan cleaning brush grass', and is used for exactly that purpose. Indigenous languages have been used to pass down traditional ecological knowledge and have evolved to represent it. When the language dies, the knowledge vanishes too. When children no longer speak it, they also lose some of the secrets it contained. And the more isolated the community, and the more unusual or individual its ecosystem, the more the local language becomes the sole repository for its understanding.

Hawaiian

Hawaiian, once under threat, is now recognized as an ecologically significant language. We must preserve and fully comprehend Hawaiian if we are to have any chance at all to halt the degradation of the island's fragile ecosystem. The new process of re-education and awareness is crucially linked to gaining a better understanding of local flora and fauna. Hawaiian tree snails were important as a symbol of high rank and believed to be part of the 'realm of the gods'. Hawaiian royalty created edicts and decrees to protect them from over-harvesting, and the wearing of the beautifully coloured intricate shells was allowed only if you held a high enough rank. The snails are not only lovely to look at, but also essential for the health of native trees, because they eat fungi from the bark and help prevent diseases. But now the snails are under threat, with certain subspecies already extinct. The Hawaiian tongue possesses the knowledge of their feeding and mating habits, and only recently have scientists begun working closely with native speakers to try to better understand the snails' life cycle as well as the beliefs and cultural importance that used to protect them.

Many Hawaiian words and phrases describe specific land formations, types of rain, wind patterns, and other natural phenomena. The fact that the language has such detailed terminology demonstrates the significance of these elements in daily life and cultural practices and shows an informed awareness of and connection to the natural world. Let's look at two words relating to land formations.

'Ahupua'a': a traditional division of land that extends from the mountains to the sea, including resources from both the uplands and the coast. It emphasizes a system where all resources, freshwater, forests, and fishing grounds, are interdependent.

'Kīpuka': an island of land surrounded by lava. During volcanic activity, these patches of land remain untouched and often become oases of life.

The very concept of the ahupua'a showcases how Hawaiians visualize and organize their relationship with the land. This division isn't merely geographic: it is functional and ecological. Within each ahupua'a, the flow of water connects several distinct ecosystems, from the upland forests down to the cultivated terraces and fishponds, then finally out to the sea. Such a system inherently emphasizes the importance of balance and ensures that resources are used sustainably. The interconnectedness of the ahupua'a system promoted a variety of cultivation practices. The uplands, or mauka regions, are typically home to crops like taro, when there is sufficient water, or sweet potatoes and yams in drier areas. Moving towards the coast, or makai, you might find fishponds and salt beds. This assortment not only ensures a varied diet but also allows different parts of the land to rest and regenerate, preventing over-cultivation of one particular crop or area.

The 'kīpuka', can be equally invaluable in crop management. The knowledge of where amid the lava flows these islands of fertility are located enables Hawaiians to cultivate areas that might otherwise be overlooked. By understanding the nuances of different rain patterns, Hawaiians can determine when and where to plant specific crops. A sudden heavy downpour, or 'Ua Loku', might be ideal for replenishing aquifers and irrigating terraces, but not as conducive for certain delicate crops that might be damaged by torrential rains. Conversely, the gentle 'Ua Liʻi' rain can provide a light touch for nurturing young seedlings.

Wind patterns, too, inform agricultural practices. Recognizing the direction and behaviour of specific winds, like the 'Āpaʻapaʻa' of Lahaina or the 'Mumuku' of Kaʻū, can help Hawaiians decide where to plant crops that might be wind sensitive. Some areas protected from strong gusts might be ideal for crops that require still air, while other zones might be selected for plants that benefit from the aerating effects of a steady breeze.

This awareness can only be achieved through a good knowledge of the language; environmental stewardship becomes impossible without the words that teach us how.

Hawaiians see themselves as stewards, or 'malama 'āina', of the land. This isn't regarded as a burdensome obligation but rather as a privilege and an extension of familial ties. In Hawaiian thought, the land is an ancestor, a family member to be cared for with the same tenderness one would show to a beloved elder. This stewardship mindset manifests in sustainable practices, ensuring that resources are cared for and will continue to provide for future generations.

At the heart of this traditional Hawaiian belief system is the understanding that everything in the universe is connected, just like the Chinese proverb: 'The flapping of the wings of a butterfly can be felt on the other side of the world'. This is a perspective that doesn't compartmentalize the world into separate entities but rather sees them as interrelated and interdependent parts of a greater whole. This worldview extends to the land, the sea, the sky, and all their inhabitants, as well as to the invisible forces and energies that influence them. In a holistic Hawaiian worldview, the trees are not just trees, and the birds are not merely birds. They are ancestors, carrying the memories and essence of those who walked the lands before. Every element, from the smallest leaf to the vast horizon, is alive with 'mana', or spiritual power. This energy flows through everything, binding them all.

This sense of interconnectedness extends to human interactions as well. The 'aloha' spirit, often simply translated as love or affection, carries deeper meanings rooted in this worldview. It's an expression of respect, care, and recognition of the intrinsic worth of others and the environment. When Hawaiians greet with 'Aloha', they are acknowledging and honouring the divine essence in another human. The word 'ohana' is most often translated as family or kin but has a meaning that extends far beyond those concepts, encompassing not only extended family, but also community, and even the broader environment that sustains them. The idea is that everyone and everything is bound together and relies on one another. This interdependence brings responsibility, and the nature of that obligation is also carried in the vocabulary. So 'Pono', which is often translated as righteousness or balance, is more correctly interpreted as living with moral rectitude and integrity, in harmony with those around you and the natural world. The way to this is 'Lōkoahi' – again, often equated to unity, agreement, or harmony, but which is the principle of striving for balance and unity in relationships, community, and with nature.

Unsurprisingly, this view also shapes their understanding of health and well-being. Health isn't merely the absence of illness; it's a state of balance and harmony with the natural and spiritual worlds. Traditional healing practices, or 'lā'au lapa'au', do not just address physical symptoms but also consider the emotional, mental, and spiritual dimensions of well-being. Increased environmental awareness has in part driven the revival of the Hawaiian language, garnering it widespread championing and support. By accessing the ecological secrets of the ancient vocabulary, present-day concerns can begin to be addressed.

One clear example lies in the restoration of traditional fishponds or 'loko I'a'. Historically central to Hawaiian aquaculture, these systems had been mostly abandoned in the wake of Western colonization. As linguistic revival brought back terms and descriptions related to fishpond management, communities could reconstruct and rehabilitate these aquaculture systems. Prior to James Cook's arrival in 1778, there were 488 loko iʻa throughout the Hawaiian archipelago. These could have produced about 300 pounds of herbivorous fish per acre each year.[1] Most of these are degraded and useless now, but newly restored loko iʻa, such as those at Heʻeia and Maunalua, are beginning to function both as sustainable food sources and as hubs for imparting knowledge about traditional aquaculture practices.

In agriculture, the revitalized use of Hawaiian has facilitated the return to traditional farming methods. Taro cultivation, or kalo, has particularly benefited from this revival. Taro corms are a food staple in many regions of the world, including Oceania. Historical Hawaiian linguistic resources detail specific irrigation methods and pest control and crop rotation strategies emphasizing sustainability. Modern Hawaiian farmers, informed by this language-derived knowledge, are now deploying these techniques in regions like Waipā and Waianae. This shift has resulted in improved soil quality, enhanced crop yields, and reduced dependence on artificial pesticides and fertilizers.

Forest conservation in Hawaii also illustrates the environmental impact of the language's resurgence. The Hawaiian language delineates specific names for diverse plant species, each bearing its cultural narratives. As these terms re-entered

common parlance, there has been a reinforced focus on refor-
estation, with a marked prioritizing of culturally significant
native species. Let's take the 'iliahi', or sandalwood tree, previously over-exploited; recent efforts, driven by a linguistically
informed community, are now in place to replant and conserve
this species.

Above all, the linguistic revival has equipped communities
with tools for environmental advocacy. With chants, songs,
and speeches in Hawaiian, protesters have been gaining
international attention for the spiritual and ecological importance of the extinct volcano Mauna Kea since 2014 until the
time of writing. The protestors argue that the development
of the site of one of the Mauna Kea observatories threatens
already endangered native species, impacts essential ground-
water aquifers, and disregards the spiritual importance of the
mountain. Hawaiian is reaping the benefits of the knowledge
it carries and today is a language in resurgence, with one of
the most successful language-recovery programmes in the
world. Other languages are at a far earlier stage in the fight
for their worth to be recognized.

The Nuxálk language

Like Hawaiian, the Nuxálk language, spoken in British
Columbia, Canada, holds a plethora of information about the
coastal and rainforest environments of the region. The Nuxálk
Nation has detailed knowledge of local fish species, forest

resources, and traditional sustainable management practices. But this awareness is not part of large-scale Western fishery management systems in North America. It's reported that indigenous knowledge is 'drowned out, marginalised and, at times, worse, forgotten'.[2]

One of the essential species in the Nuxálk cultural and ecological system is the eulachon, a small anadromous fish. The eulachon holds significant economic, cultural, and nutritional importance for the Nuxálk people. Sometimes referred to as 'candlefish' due to its high fat content, which allows it to be lit like a candle when dried, eulachon has historically been a vital resource for many indigenous communities along the Pacific Northwest, including the Nuxálk. Beyond being a direct food source, eulachon is processed to produce eulachon oil, or 'grease', which is a prized product traditionally used for trade and ceremonial purposes.

However, in recent years, there has been a noticeable decline in eulachon populations in many rivers along the Pacific coast, including those in Nuxálk territory. Several factors have been cited as possible causes, including overfishing, habitat degradation, predation, and changes in oceanic conditions due to climate change. The decline has been so significant that eulachon has been listed as a species of concern in Canada. The Nuxálk eulachon project aims to address this by decolonizing fishing practices and returning land-management leadership to the Nuxálk and other First Nations people.

The Nuxálk historically never ceded the right to inhabit or manage their own territory; instead, their history is one of dispossession and occupation, with the accompanying mismanagement and misunderstanding of their territory. While the government is legally obligated to consult with them, the suggestions of the Nuxálk are often ignored and seen as incompatible with its priorities.[3] State management did not help to preserve eulachon stocks, as overfishing and commercial enterprise threatened the species with extinction. But the Sputc project aimed to reinstate the Nuxálk Nation's authority over the land by articulating and introducing their knowledge and using it as an integral guide for fishing management. This is a relatively new initiative, but part of a much wider movement among First Nations peoples. The Haida, Heiltsuk, and Nuu-Chah-Nulth nations have campaigned successfully to close exploitative and environmentally damaging commercial herring fisheries, while crab and sea-cucumber fisheries that did not comply with local laws have been closed by other First Nations campaigns. [4]

In *Landmarks*, Robert Macfarlane explores the loss of certain words from modern vocabulary, especially those that describe specific aspects of the natural world. He mourns the fading of these words from contemporary dictionaries and, more broadly, from our combined consciousness.

Drawing inspiration from Old English poetic traditions, Macfarlane uses the term 'word-hoard'. Essentially this refers to a store or collection of words and phrases, like how one might hoard treasures or memories. For Macfarlane, the word-hoard is more than just a poetic device: it is about our ability to 'shape our own sense of place'. These are words that constitute 'a vast vanished, or vanishing, language for landscape' in Britain and Ireland.[5]

But Macfarlane's exploration doesn't stop at lamentation for loss. Listening to regional dialects and minority languages, he gathers words that capture precise sensations, phenomena, or features of the land, from 'warp' in Northamptonshire ('the mixture of fine sand and mud left on meadowland after the receding of floods') to 'feevl' in Shetland ('snow that falls in large flakes').[6] These words, he argues, offer more than definitions, but rather a way of seeing, a prism through which the natural world can be better understood.

The idea of the word-hoard also intersects with Macfarlane's advocacy for a renewed relationship with nature. He suggests that by reclaiming and celebrating this rich vocabulary, we can foster a deeper, more nuanced understanding and appreciation of the world. Words have power; they shape perceptions and evoke emotions. By expanding our linguistic reservoir, we can reconnect with the landscapes we often take for granted. We discover a broader metaphor for memory, heritage, and cultural preservation.

Just as landscapes bear the imprints of history, so does language. I spent almost two years in Finland, much of it researching Finnish morphology and the way that changing the morphology of a word causes certain phonological changes to regularly occur too. During my studies, I discovered some similarities with the Sámi language and, as a result, spent time with Sámi speakers in the north of the country. While I was familiar with some of the structures of their language, I was, at that time, completely unaware of the ecological significance of Sámi vocabulary and the way that its changes could also reflect environmental shifts.

The ecological significance of Sámi

The Sámi are the indigenous people primarily found in the Arctic areas of Sweden, Norway, Finland, and the Kola Peninsula within the Murmansk Oblast of Russia. This region, known as Sápmi in the Sámi languages, consists of vast expanses of tundra, mountains, forests, and coastal areas. The cultural and linguistic heritage of the Sámi offers insights into the Arctic and subarctic environments, landscapes that are particularly vulnerable in the context of global environmental changes. Moreover, Sámi communities have also suffered from oppression and colonization. It's only recently that children are once again able to learn the language in local schools, and a whole generation still recall a time when the language was banned.

The Sámi languages, part of the Uralic family, are a closely related linguistic group, and, although they share the name 'Sámi', these languages can differ considerably from one another, to the extent that speakers from different regions might not understand each other.

The richness of the Sámi languages in terms of ecological lexicon is staggering in its range and scope. The languages encompass an elaborate vocabulary related to snow and ice, essential for survival and for the most mundane of daily activities in the Arctic regions. Words in Sámi can distinguish between the texture, depth, and condition of snow, reflecting its significance in their daily lives. Whether it's the kind of snow suitable for reindeer grazing or the type that indicates the onset of a particular season, this range of linguistic possibility offers important insights into local environmental conditions and changes.

Reindeer herding is a traditional Sámi livelihood, and there are words that classify reindeer not only based on age or gender but also based on their roles within the herd or their suitability for different tasks. Such detailed classification signifies the symbiotic relationship between the Sámi herders and their reindeer, where understanding every nuance of an animal's behaviour, health, and position in the herd ecosystem becomes crucial.

Climate change has direct and profound implications for the Sámi way of life. Changes in snowfall patterns, ice melting rates, or vegetation have immediate consequences for reindeer herding, fishing, and other traditional activities. The Sámi languages, with their keen emphasis on ecological indicators, can serve as barometers for such changes. For instance, shifts in local environmental conditions could be indicated by certain terms related to specific snow conditions or reindeer behaviours becoming less frequent in everyday conversation. Beyond particular words, or differentiated vocabulary, there is also the inherited wisdom present in Sámi oral traditions, folklore, and yoik (a unique form of Sámi song). These encapsulate millennia of observational data on the environment, climate patterns, animal behaviours, and plant cycles, and together they form a cultural and linguistic archive that is invaluable for researchers aiming to understand historical environmental conditions and changes in the Arctic region.

Languages of medicine

Most medicinal knowledge relating to plants is found only in one language, thus meaning that every indigenous language represents the sole repository of information on a given set of plants and their uses. A recent study across three different regions with markedly contrasting biodiversity – Amazonia, North America, and New Guinea – demonstrated that over 75 per cent of the more than 12,000 plants investigated were linguistically unique. In the Amazon, that percentage was even greater, with 91 per cent of medicinal plants having their uses encoded on only a single language.[7] While the plants themselves were not endangered, the languages that carried information about their intrinsic properties often were. And the range of medical categories relating to the healing properties of the fauna were astonishingly wide-ranging, including everything from blood and cardiovascular to dental health, the digestive and endocrine systems to infections and infestations, and from the nervous system and mental health to poisoning, pregnancy, birth, and puerperium, and the respiratory and sensory systems. With the demise of each language the usage of the plants within its biosphere is lost, so while the plants remain, the benefits they afford are forgotten, despite having been part of a collective knowledge for hundreds or thousands of years.

The language of the itinerant healers of Bolivia

In the Andes of Bolivia, a linguistic minority group resides that perfectly illustrates the relationship between healing and biodiversity. It's a group with knowledge that has been handed down for over five hundred years and is so extraordinary that UNESCO deemed it a 'Masterpiece of the Oral and Intangible Heritage of Humanity' in 2003.[8]

The number of Kallawaya (their name comes from the Quechua 'kolla', for healer, and 'waya', for wanderer, and they are Quechua speakers) who speak the language Machaj Juyai now number fewer than two hundred and are primarily found in the Bautista Saavedra region. Historically recognized as itinerant healers, they are custodians of a vast repository of knowledge concerning the medicinal properties of plants. But the language that carries this knowledge is a secret language, used only by a small subset of the Kallawaya – those who are itinerant ritual healers. It is learned first as a second language as part of an initiation into the group, but then used for daily conversation between its members once acquired. The speakers are almost exclusively men; women are only inducted into the secrets of healing when an existing male practitioner has only female offspring to pass the knowledge to. However, it is predominantly women who gather and dry the herbs and prepare them for medicinal use. The knowledge has been passed down orally through generations, and the Kallawaya's proficiency in diagnosing and treating a variety of ailments using natural remedies has earned them a reputation that extends well beyond their territory and into other parts of the Andes. Their ability is so respected within Bolivia that more than 80 per cent of the population will visit one at some point in their life, while 30 per cent will never use any other kind of medicine.

The linguistic heritage of the Kallawaya is as rich and intriguing as their medicinal traditions. They communicate their specialized knowledge to some within the group but also keep their skills secret from others in the community by using their own specialized language. Machaj Juyai is replete with terms that not only identify various plants but also encapsulate their healing properties, preparation methods, and the ailments they treat. The vocabulary often provides direct cues to the plant's medicinal usage, allowing practitioners to quickly identify the right remedy for a particular ailment. In most cases, the name of the plant in the Kallawaya language will have some connection to at least one of its uses, so that learning the language as an inductee into the role of healer is inextricably linked to learning the craft itself.

The Andean region, with its varied altitudes and microclimates, hosts a vast array of flora. The Kallawaya have catalogued and utilized this botanical range in their healing practices. They recognize that plants from different altitudes have distinct properties. For example, plants from higher, colder regions might be used to treat inflammatory conditions, given the colder environment's potential anti-inflammatory properties. Conversely, plants from warmer zones might be employed for conditions requiring improved circulation or warmth. There is also a wealth of vocabulary pertaining to the life cycle of the plants, the stage at which they should be harvested, what climactic factors need to be mitigated, and what type of land best sustains each different cure, and this makes their practice sustainable. When newly introduced exotic species of plant are found to have medicinal properties, they too are added to the pharmacopoeia. And plant applications are not limited to their medicinal properties: they are also used as food, for decorative purposes, as hallucinogens, and as dyes, timbers, and perfumes, with many of these uses known only by the healers and the small armies of women foragers who gather and prepare the plants for their purposes.

African indigenous knowledge systems

In 2016, a group of academics conducted research that focused on African indigenous languages and their huge role in African indigenous knowledge systems. Crucial to this work was 'the realization that language and culture cannot be separated from the articulation of environmental issues including the local knowledge systems associated with them'.[9]

As with the other ecologically important languages in this chapter, there's a central concept that defines this relationship and gives rise to the vocabulary. Ubuntu is a philosophy that embraces a relational sustainability between people and their environment. It's applicable not just to the local or even regional sphere, but globally, emphasizing that people must value the good of communities more than self-interest, with human responsibility to sustain and nurture natural life portrayed as an essential part of all ecosystems. The communication of these ideas informs indigenous languages.

So in the South African indigenous language IsiZulu, there is a saying: 'Umuntu Ngumuntu Ngabantu', which means that 'a person is a person through other persons, that is, we, as human beings, affirm our humanity when we acknowledge that of others including other forms of creation'.[10] While in Kiswahili, 'Mtu ni watu' indicates 'a human being is other people, that is, without other people one cannot realize his/ her humanity'.[11]

In continental Africa many of these communities, especially rural ones, depend on the natural environment around them for food security and, therefore, are immediately affected in the worst possible ways by environmental issues. The indigenous understanding and experience of the causes and consequences of these issues often lead to conflicts between the indigenous ethnic groups and the governing authorities who might have contradicting opinions or policies. One example of this is the continued conflict in the Niger Delta, initiated by tensions between major oil companies and exploited local ethnic groups.[12]

The intricate ties that exist between rare languages and ecological knowledge offer glimpses of a community's accumulated wisdom regarding its environment and the health of its people. Through the words of languages like Hawaiian, Nuxálk, and Kallawaya, stories emerge that underscore the depth and breadth with which many communities can understand, interact with, and respect their natural surroundings.

By juxtaposing these languages, we note thematic similarities: the specificity and granularity of linguistic terms usually correlate with the cultural or ecological significance of the described entity or phenomenon. Such linguistic precision, shaped by centuries of lived experiences, highlights a kind of adaptive expertise. Communities develop detailed vocabularies because they have identified the aspects of their environment that are crucial to their well-being and survival. But the commonalities among these languages, in their nuanced categorization of flora, fauna, and natural phenomena, also serve as a testament to our universally shared human ability to observe natural environments closely and to forge symbiotic relationships with nature. Every language carries secrets about caring for the land, every person can glean some of these from observation, from trying to live more harmoniously with it, but much of contemporary society has forgotten how to do so. Some of the rare tongues, with their centuries of acquired knowledge, may be able to teach us how to do so once more.

5

—◁◦▷—

Plains Sign Talk –
The Sound of Silence

'They signed to us that they thought that we had
rained down out of the clouds.'

—*Lewis and Clark Journals* (30 October 1805)

L ANGUAGES NEED NOT be whistled or spoken or sung:
they can also be silent. The story of the sign languages
used within almost all the language families of Native
North America is one of how silence once triumphed over
sound. And the best-documented and -researched remains that
of the Great Plains.

The Great Plains span five US states and two Canadian
provinces and make up one of the largest expanses of prairie
and grassland in the world. It is a vast area, stretching from
north to south for over two thousand miles, from Canada to
the Rio Grande in Mexico. It's one-third of the land mass of the
United States, equivalent in size almost to the area covered
by the EU member states. But just as we have seen with the

languages of Australia, the tongues are diminishing. Today, there are thirteen endangered languages spoken by a handful of speakers. Just over a century ago, there were over forty; historically, there were hundreds of languages in an area of extreme linguistic diversity. For more than two centuries, there was also one language that dominated them all, for trade, for inter-tribe communication, and for dealing with colonizers; that language was signed, not spoken, and became known as the 'Hand Talk' or 'Plains Indian Sign Language', now also sometimes referred to as Plains Sign Talk (PST).[1]

The development of Plains Sign Talk

The origins of PST can be traced back to pre-colonial times, when many different Native American tribes inhabited the Great Plains region. The vastness of the plains and the nomadic lifestyles of the tribes necessitated effective means of communication over long distances. PST emerged as a visual and gestural language that transcended linguistic and cultural barriers, enabling tribes with distinct spoken languages to communicate with one another. Its exact origin is obviously impossible to pinpoint, as it predates written records and has likely evolved over thousands of years. However, it is believed to have been influenced by the natural gestures and signs used by Plains tribes for hunting, warfare, and other daily activities. Over time, these gestures were systematized and expanded to encompass a wide range of concepts and ideas.

The first historical record we have of the language was made by Spanish colonizers among tribes in Florida in the sixteenth century. On 14 April 1528, three hundred Spanish soldiers landed on the west coast of Florida. Panfilo de Narvaez, a one-eyed, red-bearded conquistador, led them, with seasoned campaign veteran Alvar Nuñez Cabeza de Vaca by his side. Only a day after landing, one of their first actions was to announce to the natives they had encountered that any land they occupied now belonged to King Charles V, by order of the pope.

But the bluster and bombast of this initial encounter came to nothing. A series of misjudgements by Narvaez combined with starvation, the disease-ridden swamps of Florida, and the angry, retaliating natives, until finally just four survivors remained, barely able to return to Spain after seven years of living as labourers and captive slaves and a journey of several thousand miles.

One of the survivors was De Vaca, and his published account of their adventures, *La relación y comentarios (The Account and Commentaries)*, is the first time that the sign talking of the Plains tribes was observed and recorded.

Initially De Vaca noticed how it was used to overcome the language barriers between the colonizers and the natives:

We came across a great variety and number of languages, and God, our Lord, favoured us with a knowledge of all, because they always could understand us and we understood them, so that when they asked they would answer by signs, as if they spoke our tongue and we theirs; for although we spoke six languages not everywhere could we use them, since we found more than a thousand different ones.[2]

Later he discerned that it was also frequently used as a kind of common language between different tribes. He noted that there were some native groups that spoke the same language, others that spoke different tongues but communicated through a shared understanding of a third, distinct tongue, and those that did not understand each other at all, except through the use of sign language.

Thirteen years later, another Spanish expedition force, led by Francisco de Coronado, a notorious conquistador whose expeditions had devastating effects for the indigenous population, set out to look for the gold and minerals of Quivira. Again, the invaders observed the hand talking between tribes, and Coronado reported on their great aptitude, writing that the Plains natives in what is now north-western Texas 'were so skilful in the use of signs that it seemed as if they spoke. They made everything so clear that an interpreter was not necessary.'[3]

The use of PST became particularly prevalent during the eighteenth and nineteenth centuries, when the Great Plains became a major crossroads for trade and intertribal interactions. Tribes such as the Lakota, Cheyenne, Arapaho, Blackfoot, and Comanche, among others, embraced PST as a lingua franca for communication with other tribes. This was especially important during large intertribal gatherings, such as powwows and trade fairs, where PST served as a means of establishing alliances, conducting negotiations, and sharing cultural knowledge. Fluency and skill in using PST were highly respected within Native American societies, and individuals who excelled in its use were revered as skilled communicators. Its prevalence and use became even more apparent in the early nineteenth century, with the Lewis and Clark Expedition of 1804.

In 1803, President Thomas Jefferson, eager to expand American territory, negotiated the Louisiana Purchase from France, doubling the size of the United States. Jefferson saw an opportunity to explore and survey this vast, uncharted land and turned to Merriwether Lewis to lead the expedition group, which would come to be known as the Corps of Discovery.

Lewis was born on 18 August 1774, near Charlottesville, Virginia, to William Lewis and Lucy Meriwether. His family were well-known in the state, with deep roots in Virginia's colonial society. Growing up on the frontier, Lewis developed a keen interest in nature and exploration, spending countless hours in the wilderness, learning about plants, animals, and survival skills. This curiosity drove him to acquire knowledge in various scientific fields, including botany, zoology, and astronomy. Lewis's education began with private tutors, but he later attended the College of William and Mary in Williamsburg, Virginia, where he studied natural history, mathematics, and the classics.

In 1794, Lewis served with William Clark during the Northwest Indian War. Lewis's intelligence, resourcefulness, and passion for exploration impressed Clark, while Clark's calm demeanour, surveying skills, and familiarity with the frontier terrain resonated with Lewis. Their time together in the military had allowed Lewis and Clark to gain practical experience in dealing with Native American tribes as well as a knowledge of how best to navigate the rugged landscapes of the west.

When Lewis was given his commission by Jefferson, it was no surprise, given their shared history and the bond of friendship between them, that he immediately invited Clark to accompany him. Setting off from St Louis, Missouri, the Corps of Discovery first embarked on a treacherous voyage up the Missouri River. During the course of the expedition, they would suffer through the deprivation and bleakness of a Clatsop winter, be almost overwhelmed by the rapids of the Columbia River, encounter diverse wildlife, and attempt to engage with myriad Native American tribes. At times, their survival depended on the latter and was often only made possible by the sign language that their guide used to communicate with Native peoples.

The expedition's goals extended beyond geographical discovery and charting territory: it was also a diplomatic mission aimed at establishing peaceful relations with Native American tribes. Jefferson's instructions to Lewis included:

The commerce which may be carried on with the people inhabiting the line your will pursue, renders a knowledge of those people important. You will therefore endeavour to make yourself acquainted as far as a diligent pursuit of your journey shall admit, with the names of the nations & their numbers;

- the extent & limits of their possessions; their relations with other tribes of nations;
- their language, traditions, monuments;
- their ordinary occupations in agriculture, fishing, hunting, war, arts & the implements for these;
- their food, clothing, & domestic accommodations;
- the diseases prevalent among them, & the remedies they use;
- moral & physical circumstances which distinguish them from the tribes we know;
- peculiarities in their laws, customs & dispositions;
- and articles of commerce they may need or furnish & to what extent.
- And considering the interest which every nation has in extending & strengthening the authority of reason & justice among the people around them, it will be useful to acquire what knowledge you can of the state of morality, religion, & information among them.[4]

Lewis recruited George Drouillard (Drewyer in the journals), a part Shawnee Illinois man with extensive experience of hunting, trapping, and fishing. Crucially, he also knew several

Native languages as well as having the ability to sign. He was paid $25 a month to work as an interpreter for the expedition group, but his hunting skills would also prove invaluable and the deer, elk, and bison he caught just as crucial to the expedition's success. His knowledge of local customs and tribal differences meant that he was able to establish good relations with Native tribes as well as enlist their help with navigation. Fifteen months after the expedition had begun, on 14 August 1805, Lewis noted in his journal their encounter with the Lemhi Shoshones on the continental divide:

> The means I had of communicating with these people, was by way of Drewyer who perfectly understood the common language of gesticulation or signs which seems to be universally understood by all the Nations, we have yet seen it is true that this language is imperfect and liable to error but is much less so than would be expected the strong parts of the ideas are seldom mistaken.

Clark had already some skill in the language, presumably learned from Drouillard, and wrote earlier in the year:

Jan 8th, 1805, Clark

> I enquired of those people as well as I could by Signs the Situation, mode of living & Strength of their nation They informed me that the bulk of their nation lived in 3 large villages.

An understanding of sign also enabled the explorers a glimpse of understanding of how strange they appeared to the Native people:

Oct 30, 1805

they Signed to us that they thought that we had rained down out of the clouds.

By August 1806, other members of the group had acquired some signing ability. It was recorded that:

one of our men Spoke to them in Pania tongue and told them that we could not Speak their Language but Soon found that they were the Same band of Tetons that held our boat as we passed up the river Capt. Clark told them and Signed to them that they were bad Indians and treated the white people bad and they might keep from us for we would have nothing to Say to them nor Suffer them to come to our Canoes. they then Signed to the rest of the nation to keep back and Capt. Clark returnd.[5]

In the decades that followed, PST grew from strength to strength. It became the language of the fur trade, the major economic activity of the region, facilitating communication between Native American trappers and European American traders.

By 1870, more than a hundred thousand sign-language speakers were recorded. It was a language of trade, one that enabled transaction between tribes with no understanding of each other's tongues, one that united different peoples across a huge swathe of land, one that, at its height, was documented as the lingua franca for forty-one different spoken languages, used by both hearing and Deaf without distinction

William Philo Clark, also known as 'Handsome Lake' Clark, was born in 1845 and was of Seneca descent. He developed a deep interest in Native American languages and culture from a young age, becoming one of the leading authorities on PST, conducting extensive fieldwork and research. He collaborated with Native American speakers, including members of his own Seneca tribe, to collect and document PST vocabulary and grammar.

In the introduction to his book *The Indian Sign Language*, published in 1885, he observes: 'these Indians, having different vocal languages, had no difficulty in communicating with each other, and held constant intercourse by means of gestures'.[6]

Later, he elaborated: 'Vividness of description is secured by exactness, earnestness and vigor of gesture; a graceful execution can only result from long practice. Rapid and vehement signs have the same force in this language that such a manner of utterance would give in speech'.[7]

Clark also recognized the importance of context and cultural understanding in interpreting PST, emphasizing that gestures alone could be easily misinterpreted without considering the specific contexts in which they were used. In addition to his individual contributions, Clark collaborated with another influential linguist and ethnologist, Garrick

Mallery. Their joint project, 'The Gesture Language of the Plains', aimed to meticulously document and analyse PST. Together, they sought to create a comprehensive resource that would capture the intricacies of PST and provide a deeper understanding of its structure and usage. Unfortunately, the project was left incomplete at the time of Mallery's death in 1894. But their legacy was to begin to reveal the complex and sophisticated nature of PST. PST was not limited to simple gestures but encompassed a complex system of signs and facial expressions. It incorporated both iconic signs, which directly represented objects or actions, and abstract signs, which conveyed concepts or emotions. Additionally, the language relied heavily on non-manual markers, such as facial expressions, body movements, and spatial references, to convey nuanced meanings.

One of the most important features of PST is classifiers, also known as classificatory signs. These are used to represent categories of objects, people, animals, or actions and play a role in describing or referencing specific entities. Classifiers involve the use of specific handshapes, movements, and spatial relationships to represent objects or actions within the signing space. Clark presents an alphabetical list of these in his book. So, for example, we find:

RAIN Conception: falling from clouds. Hold closed hands, backs up, in front of body, about height of head, the hands near each other, equally advanced and same height; lower the hands slightly, mostly by wrist action;

at the same time open, nearly extend, and separate fingers and thumbs; in this position fingers point about downwards; repeat motion two or three times.[8]

Syntactically, PST employs a subject-object-verb (SOV) word order. This is also the case in, for example, Finnish, Japanese, or Turkish, where the subject typically precedes the object and both precede the verb. Thus the Turkish 'Adam elmayı yedi' (The man ate the apple) is, word by word, 'The man apple ate'.

However, due to the flexibility and fluidity of signing, word order variations are possible, allowing for emphasis or discourse-related purposes. Information structure, such as topic–comment constructions, can influence word-order shifts within PST discourse.[9] Signs are organized according to a spatial framework that represents the real or imagined physical space surrounding the signer. The signer's dominant hand serves as the subject marker, and the non-dominant hand functions as the object marker. The verb occupies the space between the subject and object markers, highlighting the syntactic relationships between the elements. There is extensive use of verb agreement to indicate various grammatical categories, including person, number, gender, and aspect. The agreement markers are produced near the signer's body, with handshape, location, and movement modifications to reflect the agreement features. For example, a signer may indicate the plural form of a verb by using a repetitive movement or a larger signing space. Non-manual markers play a crucial role in conveying grammatical and pragmatic information in PST. These markers include facial expressions, head movements, body postures, and eye gaze. They provide additional layers of meaning and help disambiguate the intended message. Facial expressions, in particular, can indicate emotions, negation, questions, or other pragmatic functions.

Negation in PST is typically expressed through specific non-manual markers, such as furrowed eyebrows or head-shakes, coupled with specific manual signs or modified signs. Interrogation is marked using question words, question facial expressions, or the inclusion of specific question particles within the signing space. PST also employs a range of aspectual and modal markers to express temporal and modal meanings. These markers convey information about actions, events, and states, including ongoing actions, completed actions, habitual actions, and potential or hypothetical situations. The combination of manual signs, non-manual markers, and body movements creates a rich system for expressing a variety of temporal and modal concepts.

Despite his unfinished joint project, Clark continued his work on PST, building upon the research and insights he had gathered. He dedicated his life to preserving and promoting PST, recognizing its cultural and historical significance. Clark's commitment to the language's revitalization extended beyond academia, as he actively engaged with Native American communities to teach and raise awareness about PST. In 1930, army general Hugh Scott set about filming what users referred to 'Hand Talk', after he had observed and learned it in the Western States. From these images, as well as from others taken by researchers over the decades, it's very clear that that there is a high rate of iconicity, meaning that the gestures have often been devised to physically resemble or replicate an aspect of what they represent. Thus, the sign for a buffalo is two curled forefingers held up at ear height, as if to represent horns; the sign for a wigwam is the fingertips of both hands touching with the hands angled away from each other to represent its shape; and the sign for a gun is a forefinger pointing, familiar to us all. Scott planned to make a film dictionary but died before completing the project. The footage remains, however, stored in the US National Archives, a pictorial archive and an invaluable tool in the recent revival of the language. Thirty years later, La Mont West submitted a PhD that comprised the most detailed of study of PST in its history. He noted that dialect differences in signing between different groups of natives was no barrier to their communication and that at the time of his research, in the late 1950s, PST was still used, both for inter-tribe communication and for storytelling and conversation.[10]

PST today

The language is still in use today too, but only by scattered groups and mainly for storytelling, rituals, prayers, and recounted reminiscences, having been replaced by English, Spanish, and American Sign Language in other contexts.

But I spoke to a horse-breeder friend in the United States about my interest in learning more, and through a chain, beginning with a Cherokee horse trainer she had known since childhood, was introduced to Singing Bird. He is part Crow, part Cherokee and was then, just before the pandemic, in his eighties. I met him in Oklahoma, on a horse ranch belonging to a friend of the friend who had originally found him for me. It's an amazing property on a flat plain so the view is more sky than land, with fields of beautifully cared for horses grazing, rolling in the grass, nuzzling. It was early summer and two colts, a palomino and a bay, shared one field with their mothers.

Singing Bird's grandmother had hearing loss and, as a result, he grew up in a house where PST was regularly used. Despite his age, his hands were remarkably fluid and graceful, with no signs of stiffness; when he gave the horses instructions, it was as if he was signing to them. Despite having been around horses intermittently throughout my life, I had never seen any-thing like it before, and I found it captivating, almost magical.

When he recollected his grandmother telling him about her youth, his voice became quieter, and I had to move more closely towards him to hear.

She was taken from her parents and put in a boarding school. It was common then, a way of ridding us of our barbarian ways, they said. The most uncivilized thing you could do, separate a family, was a means of civiliza-tion. My gran was older, already ten, and could sign, and she said she taught some other girls at the school to sign too so they could communicate with each other. They didn't speak much English and she wasn't allowed to speak Crow at school. They punished the girls for speaking their mother tongue by washing their mouths with lye. The signing was all they had, their secret language, a way to stop going mad with it all.

Singing Bird teaches PST now and says he feels he is not only reviving a lost culture but also performing a small act of defiance to commemorate his grandmother. He is understandably proud of the work he does with young people locally, both native and non-native, but also wants to stress that he sees the reclaiming of his language (he uses those exact words) as a 'tiny step towards the winning back' of the culture, land, and rights the colonizers stole from him.

Singing Bird's work was community based and local, but today there are many larger, officially recognized and supported projects and initiatives to document and revitalize the language. These offer hope for the language, working towards its continued use as well as its preservation. One such initiative, the Plains Sign Talk Project, is led by linguist Jeffrey E. Davis and focuses on documenting and analysing PST. It involves collaborations with Native American communities and elders who are fluent in the language. The project aims to create a comprehensive database of PST signs, grammar, and cultural context, which will serve as a valuable resource for researchers and educators.

The Lakota Language Consortium is focused on the

revitalization and preservation of the Lakota language, which includes PST. They develop curriculum materials, textbooks, and online resources that incorporate PST and promote its use in educational settings and offer workshops and training programmes for teachers, ensuring the transmission of PST to future generations.

The Native American Language Preservation and Documentation Program, funded by the Administration for Native Americans, supports various Native American language revitalization efforts, including PST. By providing grants to tribes, community organizations, and educational institutions, it enables them develop language programmes, create language-learning materials, and conduct research on indigenous sign languages.

Signalling

While PST signing was a lingua franca for the First Nation peoples of much of continental America, communicating across vast expanses of countryside required different methods entirely – other ways of signalling urgent messages that were not limited by the properties of sound and its ability to travel or visual proximity to decipher signs. Black smoke rising high into the atmosphere could be seen for great distances; smoke signals were one way of warning of danger or the need for help, gathering people together, sending news of births, deaths, victories, and defeats.

Wood-based fires made the thickest, darkest smoke, with added horse manure and certain kinds of cactus or leaves, depending on the region.[11] Woollen blankets, soaked in water, would temporarily be thrown over the fire and then lifted away so that huge bursts of black smoke, easily visible to other tribes, would rise.

Sometimes the message given by the number of puffs, or even their shape, was decipherable only to one recipient, following a prearranged code. These might show the outcome of a battle or, say, that one possible course of action was better than another. But other signals were universal, with two evenly spaced, similar puffs indicating that all was well, and three being a cry of help.

The journals of Meriwether Lewis and William Clark, again, provide a source of information and observation in their references to the sight of the baffling but teasing signals.

In his journal, Lewis recounts how

early one morning, he saw smoke up Potts' Creek. Unsure of the smoke's significance, the explorer thought it was either accidental or a message-carrying Native signal. According to his journal entry for the day, he learned later that some Shoshonis had seen either his or Clark's men, feared they were Blackfeet warriors, and fled from the river. Later the same day Clark's force, painfully working its way up a path filled with sharp rocks and prickly pear along Pryor's Valley Creek, saw a second smoke signal. Eager to let Indians know they were friends, not enemy raiders, Clark and his men took to scattering pieces of clothing, paper, and linen tape along their route. Despite these efforts, the Shoshonis seemed as tantalizingly out of reach as their smoke signals.[12]

The Yámana people of Cape Horn also used smoke signals, both to convey complex messages and to simply alert others. Four distinct billows, for example, would tell families in the greater vicinity that a stranded whale had been spotted. The whale would become a site of a great gathering, with families settling for as long as a month to enjoy the meat and blubber before it rotted and to perform sacred rites.[13] Ursula Calder, one of the two last surviving Yámana, described these events before her death in 2003: 'When the people saw the smoke, all the canoes gathered there, and they built the house [hut] for the ceremony and stayed there in the Chexaus [hut] until they finished eating all the whale.'[14]

For other communities, the difficulties of communicating across wide or dense landscapes was surmounted in a different way. There are languages scattered around the world that are whistled rather than spoken. Many are used to convey complex messages across great distances. These whistled languages are the subject of our next chapter.

6

—◁◦▷—

Whistled Languages

'It appears that the progenitors of man, either the males
or females or both sexes, before acquiring the power
of expressing their mutual love in articulate language,
endeavoured to charm each other with musical notes.'

– Charles Darwin, *The Descent of Man* (1871)

O N GOMERA IN the Canary Islands, almost three
decades ago, I heard an eerie sound, a whistling
noise that seemed to be travelling from a distant
place. I knew what it was. It was the reason I had travelled to
that rocky, mountainous region so often eschewed by tourists
in favour of neighbouring Tenerife. The shrill calls were the
whistling language known as El Silbo, which has been used
on Gomera since the fifteenth century but which was beginning to fall into decline.

Strangely, though, it wasn't as unfamiliar as I had expected
it to be. It reminded me of the gangs of my childhood who
used to call and gather their members across the seemingly

endless houses of our council estate with a mixture of whistling and something akin to yodelling. I never learned to
distinguish which gangs had which calls, although one of my
first boyfriends did try to teach me, so the recognition was
tinged with regret. You can't hear it any more. The streets of
North Lanarkshire are quieter now. There are no more eerie
calls across the two-up two-downs and the graffiti-covered
flat closes, because texting and social media have made them
unnecessary, but their memory persists, a ghost of a sound.

In both instances, two very different landscapes had
caused normal language to be adapted to better suit its
geography. And in both cases, the change had resulted in
sounds that could be heard across greater distances than just
shouted speech. The North Lanarkshire calls I'd heard carried
simple calls to meet or warnings about rival gangs being
nearby, but the whistled languages were far more complex
and sophisticated. There are languages, like that of Gomera,
scattered around the world, all whistled rather than spoken.
They are not exclusive to any language family or type, or to
geographic land masses, and they have been around for millennia. As early as the fifth century BCE, Herodotus became
the first writer to describe a cave-dwelling people in Ethiopia
who 'spoke like bats'.

In his book *The Descent of Man*, in 1871, Charles Darwin
posited the idea of a 'musical proto language'. This concept
was rooted in his broader view of the origins of language.
He proposed that human language, like other complex
traits, evolved gradually over time through a process of

natural selection. According to Darwin, this ancient form of language was characterized by simple melodic sounds and rhythms, akin to what we might consider musical elements. Darwin's hypothesis was influenced by his observations of various cultures around the world. He noted that even among societies with limited exposure to external musical influences, there were commonalities in certain musical patterns and expressions. This led him to speculate that there might be a fundamental, innate capacity for music within the human species. He further proposed that this musical proto language might have served as a precursor to spoken language. In this early stage of human development, musical sounds and rhythms could have played a crucial role in communication and social cohesion. Singing, or perhaps whistling, came first, with the melodies used to ward off predators and attract a mate, then gradually became more sophisticated in their range as our vocal apparatus evolved. Over time, as human societies became more complex, this proto language evolved into the diverse array of languages and musical forms we observe today.

Whistled languages are much less common now; those that survive have far fewer speakers than even just fifty years ago. Yet, it remains a global phenomenon; there are still people who whistle to share complex messages in Ethiopia, just as there are in China, Brazil, the Himalayas, and Europe. Julien Meyer, a world authority on whistled languages, describes them:

Whistled speech consists of speaking whilst whistling to communicate at a long distance. The result is a melody that imitates modal speech and remains intelligible for the interlocutors.[1]

The phonetics of whistling

The phonetic system of the language is simplified but the information of the utterance remains encoded in whistled sounds. People in whistled-language communities acquire the ability to reconstruct spoken words as whistled patterns from childhood. The whistled language is always based on or adapted from a spoken language, and the patterns used reflect the structure of the natural language. It is supplementary to everyday communication but sophisticated in its possibility and range. Because it has evolved to make communication easier between inhabitants of remote rural communities that are, or were historically, difficult to access, whistling languages are found only in these environments. They are almost exclusively recorded in dense tropical forests or high mountainous regions.

Astonishingly, all inhabited continents of the world have examples of whistled languages.[2] Reported incidences include those in such widely differing language groups as Yoruba in Africa, Totonac and Desano in Central and South America, Folopa in Australia, Hmong in the Himalayas, as well as Silbo in Spain, and Kuskoy in Turkey. The sheer variation and scope of these languages show that whistled forms can develop from any language in any language family, but that the properties of the languages, which we will explore with respect to some of those we discuss here, closely resemble that of the spoken language. Thus, the Hmong, who speak a tonal language, have complex tonality in their whistling, while those associated with non-tonal languages display different phonetic properties.

This correspondence between the whistled language and its spoken equivalent results in a clear distinction between those that are tonal (like Hmong) and those that are not (like Silbo). In non-tonal languages, the whistlers mimic the shape of the vocal tract during the articulation of the spoken form. The resonance of vowel sounds is mimicked in the changing whistling patterns and the consonants recognized from the length and type of the transitions between them. For speakers of tonal languages, their whistling focuses on the pitch, following underlying melodies of the sentence or phrase, with languages containing the most lexical tones being the ones most capable of expressing complex ideas with a high level of understanding.

The common factor is that, in each case where spoken communication is constrained by the geography of the land, whistling overcomes the limitation of speaking or even shouting; social isolation is prevented, and news can be shared across communities. It's incredible that full sentences in whistled speech are intelligible over distances ten times greater than if you were shouting the sentence instead.[3]

The reason for this is an acoustic one. Whistling, unlike shouting, doesn't strain the vocal cords, and it enables powerful production over a narrow range of frequencies. These frequencies are almost always higher than those prevalent in background noise and correspond to the best possible range for humans to hear and clearly discriminate them.

The differences between these languages can be as fascinating as their homogeneity, so let's look at some examples in more detail.

El Silbo of Gomera

The island of Gomera in the Canary Islands still seems as much a world apart from the tourism of Tenerife and Lanzarote as it did three decades ago. The tourist infrastructure is limited and its population mostly scattered in small groupings across dense forests and steep ravines, congregating around its highest peak, Alto de Garajonay, which is 1,500 metres high. Late in the twentieth century, roads were built to connect the bigger townships, but even now some parts remain remote and difficult to access. This perhaps in part explains why there are still, proportionately, a good number of whistlers on the island today, and El Silbo has the most proficient communicators of any of the whistling languages.

The origins of Gomera's El Silbo can be traced back to the indigenous inhabitants of La Gomera, the Guanches. The oldest historic record of a whistling language relates to

Gomera. Jean de Béthencourt, the Norman French explorer known as the conqueror of the Canary Islands, arrived on the island in 1402, accompanied by two priests, Pierre Boutier and Jean Le Verrier. The priests would go on to write the first chronicle of the conquest, 'Le Canarien', in which they described the local people speaking 'as if they had no tongue'. When the Andalusians conquered and suppressed the Guanche populations, the native people preserved their whistling technique but gradually adapted it to fit the language of their conquerors, so El Silbo is now a whistled language that replicates the tones, rhythms, and phonetic elements of Spanish, with just a few idioms from the original language of the Guanche.

As with the other whistled languages, its development was a response to the island's challenging terrain and the dispersed community, which necessitated a form of communication that could transcend these natural barriers. What differentiates it is the sheer distances over which it can be used.

Frequently used for exchanges over a kilometre, El Silbo was shown to be capable of communicating messages over an incredible distance of 8 kilometres in the late 1950s, although only when the climate and background noise from natural sources, such as the torrent of the river, was favourable.[4] Silbo Gomero relies on a set of whistled phonemes to represent the sounds of the spoken Spanish language, which serves as its foundation. The language employs variations in pitch, duration, and intensity to convey different phonetic elements. For example, a high-pitched whistle represents the vowel 'i', while a low-pitched whistle stands for 'o'. Just as in spoken language, the distinction between words isn't always expressed, and elision happens. Thus, in the Spanish sentence 'Tiene que ir', the /e i/ from 'que ir' is whistled as a diphthong similarly to the /i.e./ of the word /tiene/.[5] Consonants are created by modifying the pitch, duration, and intensity of the whistles.

El Silbo exhibits a simplified grammar that retains the fundamental structural elements of the spoken Spanish language. It maintains the basic word order of subject-verb-object, like Spanish. However, due to the nature of whistled communication, the order of words within a sentence can be altered for clarity and emphasis. The language also employs the conjugation patterns of Spanish verbs, adapting them to the whistled format, with varying pitch, duration, and intensity of whistles carrying cues to different verb tenses, aspects, and moods. It also utilizes whistles to express various grammatical features associated with nouns, such as number and gender.

However, unusually for whistled languages, El Silbo has dialectic variation. Academic research from the 1970s describes a marked contrast between the sounds made by inhabitants from the region of Chipude, high on the island, close to the Garajonay forest, where fogs are frequent and thick. These whistlers use a slower and lower-pitched whistled signal than their neighbours in the valley village of San Sebastian.[6]

This phenomenon has interesting parallels in birdsong and animal communication, where correlations between the natural environment of the species and their call or sound commonly exist. The 'environmental adaptation hypothesis' in bioacoustics considers the way unrelated bird species in dense forests use lower frequencies and avoid rapid repetition of notes compared to species in more open areas.[7] Residents of Gomera recall that when there were more whistlers, blackbirds frequently mimicked the whistling language sounds perfectly.

Silbo Gomero faced a decline in usage during the twentieth century, as modern forms of communication took hold. Middle-class Gomerans did not encourage their children to learn what was locally known as a 'peasant language'. But there were periods of recovery. On my visit there, a local, who described her knowledge of whistling as 'very basic', told me that her father had recalled a period in the 1950s when the language was popular as a way of warning each other about the presence of the Guardia Civil, who frequently forced villagers to join them in fire-fighting work. In the closing decade of the twentieth century, a group of traditional whistlers launched a campaign to preserve and revitalize the dwindling language. These initiatives by the 'Maestros De Silbo' led to Silbo being included in the compulsory curriculum of Gomera primary schools.[8] Then, in 1999, the cultural significance of Silbo Gomero was acknowledged when it was designated a Masterpiece of the Oral and Intangible Heritage of Humanity by UNESCO. These efforts have paid off. There's a little more tourism now than when I visited, with people making the trip, often for a day from Tenerife, because they've heard about the language. There are educational displays for the public as well as a pride in the language that has quashed the snobbery that used to see it as belonging to a world that was no longer relevant. Nowadays, there's an Instagram page for the Silbo Gomero Cultural Association, which holds regular shows on neighbouring islands to introduce tourists to the language and proudly displays photographs of a new generation of children who are already becoming proficient Silbo whistlers.

Hmong: the language of courtship

The Hmong ethnic group primarily reside in the mountainous regions of China, Vietnam, Laos, and Thailand. The language is spoken by 2.5 million people in this wide geographic area and has various dialects. The dominant dialect, known as White Hmong, is the one on which the whistled language is based. Unlike Spanish or Turkish, though, Hmong is a tonal language, with seven tones.

These are Tone 1 (level-high 55), Tone 2 (level-mid 33), Tone 3 (level-low 22), Tone 4 (low glottalized 21), Tone 5 (mid-rising 24), Tone 6 (high-falling 52) and Tone 7 (murmured falling 42). The numbers following the tones refer to the Chao system, a method commonly used for describing tonal languages. They refer to the level of the tones, where 1 is the lowest.[9]

The vowel system is simple, with just six vowels and five diphthongs, but there are fifty-eight consonants, including twenty-eight different nasal sounds (for perspective, English has just three, 'm', 'n', and the sound written phonetically as 'ŋ', which is what you hear at the end of a word like sing). The whistled language, however, appears to reproduce the tone melody, with only a very limited differentiation between consonant groups (those that are continuous, like 'l' or 'm', for example, and those that are not, such as 'p' or 't') rather than individual consonantal phonetic sounds.

However, for the Hmong, the whistling language has evolved not only to share news and information across the mountains, but also as part of their courtship. Young Hmong men stroll around their villages in the evening whistling poetry, waiting for a girl to respond. If she does, they then begin a whistled dialogue. Observers have noted the loveliness of the melodies, but there's also the advantage of clandestine exchanges because the whistled language makes it far less easy to identify individual speakers. As couples grow together, they even sometimes develop their own private whistling codes, used only by them, enabling them to exchange messages of love and endearment in public, with only the intended recipient able to understand them at all.[10]

The bird language of Turkey

In the Giresun province of Turkey, another such whistled language, known as the bird language of the Black Sea, Kuş dili, is still used by around 10,000 people.

Kuskoy, 'the village of birds', begins in the valley with straggled houses dotted up the steep mountain slopes towards the often-overcast sky. Even as late as April, snow can, at times, be glimpsed on the highest of the peaks. The language is known to have been in use for more than five hundred years, since the time of the Ottoman Empire, and there have been reports that the agricultural workers who gather peanuts or tea will whistle to each other throughout the day to share gossip, discuss the weather, and even tell jokes.[11] But today, Kuskoy is the last remaining bastion of bird language in the region – although, even as recently as the last century, just as with El Silbo in Gomera, it was much more widely spread. In the 1950s, it could still be heard frequently across all thirty-five villages of this Black Sea region and had an estimated 25,000 speakers.

Like the calls of gangs across my sprawling council scheme, its demise has been attributed, in part, to the increased use of mobile phones, which UNESCO name the 'key threat' to its survival. In 2017, they even took the step of adding the language to the List of Intangible Cultural Heritage in need of Urgent Safeguarding.[12] It wasn't just a question of common language for the last speakers, but, as UNESCO reported, 'The practitioners are mainly agricultural communities who spend most of their lives outdoors. The communities concerned consider this practice to be a key reflection of their cultural identity, which reinforces interpersonal communication and solidarity'.[13] In the village of Kuskoy, the older residents are keen to speak about their language and to demonstrate it. Metin Kocek, the mayor of Kuskoy, recalls how the locals welcomed the news from UNESCO, saying it was as if a dream had come true. Gonul Tekin, a local shopkeeper, now in her seventies, who sadly acknowledges how few people remember the whistles nowadays, says she feels it was a reward for all their efforts as a community.

She told me:

When I was a girl, my cousins as far as Rize could whistle. Now I don't know anyone there who can even make the sounds let alone have a conversation. But the festival helped us. It was just part of life for me. My grandparents taught my mother and father and they taught me. I could ask a friend for help when the babies were small, without leaving my front door, or I might hear of a wedding or even a funeral.

The festival she spoke of is an annual event in Kuskoy. There is both a bird-language festival and a bird-language cultural association. With more publicity and international awareness come increased numbers of visitors who want to hear and learn more about the language. Yet the threat remains that it may become 'an artificial practice', ripped from its environment and culture, used only to entertain. Gonul insists:

There are things I can say in the whistling language that I can't in Turkish, it's not just a translation, but an addition to it. I know the academics that come say it's just Turkish, but it really isn't. The tourists bring much to the village but what I really want is for my children and grandchildren to know the language and to use it, to see how it works for us in this place, our home. I don't want it to be something in a museum.'

I ask her for a demonstration and, using her forefinger to pull her lip to the side, she makes a sound that, to my uneducated ear, is like a very loud bird trill. 'What does it mean?'

She replies that it's for attracting attention but also lets the hearer know she's a bit down, perhaps lonely. There are some expressions peculiar to the bird language, the same ones that Gonul feels are lost in translation, but for the most part, like the other whistled languages, Kuş dili appears to be a whistled variant of Turkish. Each of the sounds in Turkish that make up a word have a different-sounding whistle, and practitioners of Kuş dili are easily able to differentiate complex meaning and sentences by using the pitch and volume of the spoken language.

Turkish is a non-tonal language, so during whistling the organs of articulation – the mouth, tongue, lips, hard and soft palate – roughly replicate the shape of the spoken sound counterpart, with the amplitude of different whistles also being used to contrast sounds. As early as 1970, researchers were able to illustrate, through spectrograms, the similarity between formants in a spoken and whistled word. Thus, a word like Turkish 'okul' (school) will, in Kuş dili, have a brief inaudible signal between the two whistled vowel sounds, which is perceived as a voiceless consonant sound.

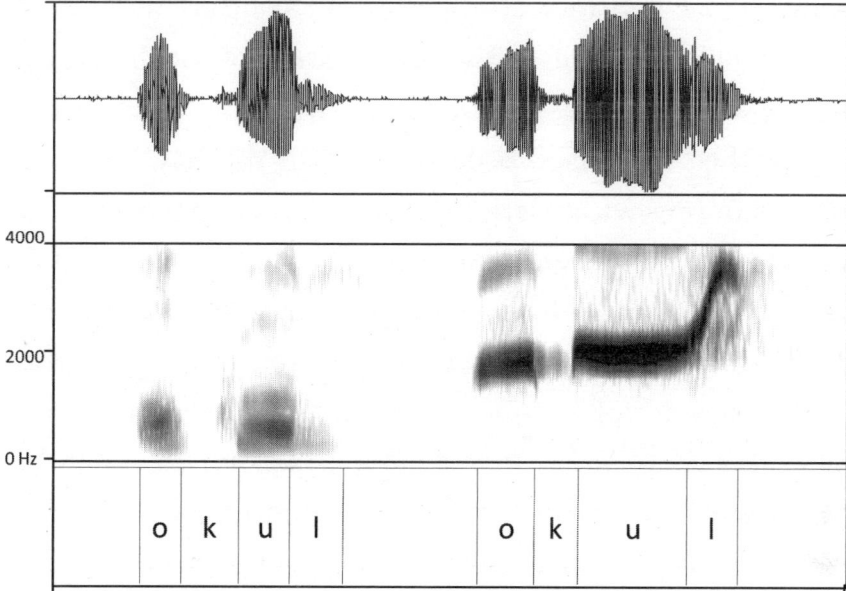

A spectrogram illustrating waveforms and spectrograms of, respectively, spoken and whistled 'okul' (school) in Turkish.[14]

Kuş dili whistling of consonantal sounds is achieved using the tongue and teeth; other whistled languages, like El Silbo, rely on the use of a bent index finger. This gives the Turkish whistled language a greater range of articulation for making labial sounds (sounds made with the lips, like /b/ or /p/) and it shows distinction between voiced and unvoiced consonants.

However, the scope of its extraordinary range doesn't end there. Turkish has a higher number of vowels and consonants than Spanish or Greek (both of which can be found in whistled forms). Following spoken Turkish, Kuş dili reflects these greater phonological and phonetic properties. The average number of vowels in a whistled language is somewhere between two and four (Silbo, for example, has five spoken vowels and three whistled ones). Whistled Turkish contains eight vowels, decreasing in frequency, with only some overlap.

Together, these factors mean that Kuş dili has one of the widest ranging vocabularies of expression among the different whistled languages. An academic study, conducted by Onur Güntürkun, a biopsychologist, used the language to explore brain function by explicitly exploring how the brain handles and deciphers a language that is more akin to music than other languages. Brain functions are not clear-cut, but it is generally believed that the left hemisphere is the most important in our understanding of any language, whether tonal or not, whether signed or spoken. The right hemisphere, however, is dominant when it comes to music and pitch, our processing of melody. His experiment with thirty-one speakers who were fluent in both spoken Turkish and the whistled language suggested a marked difference between the two, with the former showing the expected left dominance, but production and processing of the latter being much more evenly distributed between the two.[15] This similarity to music is very much in evidence with the Hmong whistlers, who even play poems on a mouth-harp instrument that replicates the meaning of the verses.

Technology in the guise of mobile phones is a threat to all the whistling languages, and we've noted that Kuş dili is no exception. But in Kuskoy it's also being used to its advantage. Villager Organ Civelek teaches the language of the birds to schoolchildren from the region in the summer. To do so, he uses a free app called Islık Dili Sözlüğü, the whistle-language dictionary. Choose a word, select it, and you can hear Mr Civelek whistling it on the app. Friends in Istanbul tell me that the publicity around its inception was the first they had ever heard of the language, and now, although far from the northern Turkish village, they too are interested in its continuity as part of their country's rich and varied culture.

The whistling of lullabies

Until 2013 there was no road to connect Kongthong, in the dense forest of the hills of Meghalaya, India, with the surrounding towns and villages. Today, it still retains that calm quietness that this isolation over generations brought, even though there's some scant eco-tourism and an inter-mittent international research presence. The hills of this north-east state earned it the nickname 'Abode of the Clouds', and the village of Kongthong is known as the 'whistling village' because many of its 700 inhabitants communicate over distance with a whistling language.

Only here, in this place, with the birth of each child, the mother composes a whistled lullaby, a 'jingrwai lawbei' – literally 'song in honour of the root ancestress'. It's wordless, a simple tune, but completely unique to the newborn. There are two versions, the short version or song title, which is the one that will be used most often, just five or six seconds long, and a longer one for calling across fields. In the early weeks, months, and years of the child's life, the adults close to them will constantly whistle the melody, usually between thirty seconds and one minute long. It must be the only one of its kind – even after someone dies, their tune cannot be passed on to someone else – and it must be distinguishable to the villagers, although the differences are often so slight as to be imperceptible to outsiders. Each mother gets her inspiration for the tune from nature, often from a bird call. The lullaby's title is the name by which a person will be known throughout their life. Some villagers say that the practice is more than a practical one, enabling someone to be called for over a distance. The melodic name might also offer protection against hidden evil spirits, living in the middle of the dense forests. Many villagers believe that when these spirits hear someone's spoken name, they can curse them and make them ill. The whistled songs can be used to call for the person but keep them protected too.

The whistled name also plays an important part in the courting rituals of the village. On a night with a full moon, a bonfire is lit in the middle of the village, and each man of marriageable age sings his lullaby. The women can then choose a groom according to how well they think he has sung.[16]

The forests are full of whistling

The Amazon forests contain one of the highest levels of language diversity in the world. Perhaps unsurprisingly, given its topology, the area also has one of the greatest numbers of whistled languages. The advantages offered by whistled languages in a place of dense vegetation, rivalries between near neighbours and the ever-present threat of loggers are manifold. Allies can contact each other and even send warnings of danger without fear of being overheard. When hunting, communication is possible and can go undetected even by animals because so many of their signals are similar. The latter is especially crucial because so many of the more isolated communities are dependent on hunting and fishing for food. The distances that the sounds can carry across are not those of the mountain peoples, because the thick vegetation and high trees absorb the sound far more, but the Amazonian whistling languages are still far better at carrying than a shout or a cry, as well as being far more nuanced in the messages they can send. The Mondé language family, which contains three different languages, all spoken in Rondônia in western Brazil, is one such example. All of the dialects and languages in the group that are still in active use can use whistled speech. It is used both for speaking within villages at medium distances and over greater distances. Not used solely for hunting, it's also an important way of sending out a warning of danger in the area and of calling people to come together for activity, or reminding someone to bring some-thing on a visit.[17] Despite all of this, possibly because it may have evolved originally for hunting communication, whistling is traditionally a male activity for one of the three, the Gaviao, whose women don't whistle but instead hoot and are able to communicate in this way.

In 2003, the Gaviao Indians approached the Museu Goeldi to create a collection of their whistled and instrumental speech, which they worried was becoming less used and thought important to save and record. With the collaboration of an academic, Julien Meyer, from the French National Centre for Scientific Research, a collection was made and is now accessible online.[18]

What can we learn from the whistled languages?

One of the most fascinating facets of whistled languages is what we can learn from them, and not only about humankind. A recent study suggests that whistled languages may hold a key to understanding some animal communication too.[19] Whistled languages are intelligible to their speakers despite the vast reduction in signal. In fact, the acoustic parameters are similar to those made by dolphins when they 'speak' to each other. Like the whistled languages, dolphin whistles are perfectly adapted to their natural environment, enabling them to communicate across great distances. Dolphins have more in common with humans than you might expect.

Bottlenose dolphins have large brains in proportion to their body size, a characteristic known as encephalization. Their brains are highly convoluted, suggesting a high level of neural complexity. In fact, dolphin brains are known for their large neocortices, which are associated with higher-order cognitive functions in mammals. They exhibit advanced problem-solving skills. They can understand and solve complex tasks, such as using tools, coordinating group hunting strategies, and manipulating objects. Dolphins have been observed using sponges as protective 'tools' when foraging on the sea floor, a behaviour unique to certain populations.

Their sophisticated communication system includes a wide range of vocalizations, body postures, and movements. They use distinct whistles, clicks, and burst pulse sounds for communication, social bonding, and navigation. Studies have shown that dolphins can use a complex series of clicks, known as echolocation, to navigate, locate prey, and distinguish objects underwater.

Especially relevant when thinking about their method of communication is that they exhibit intricate social structures and live in groups called pods, which can consist of a few individuals to several hundred members. Within these pods, dolphins form complex social bonds, engage in cooperative behaviours, and demonstrate cultural transmission of knowledge and behaviours across generations. Most interesting of all, like humans, they have distinct dialects and vocal traditions that vary among different populations. Signature whistles tell other members of a group who the transmitter is; these signature whistles can then be imitated by other dolphins in the group. Dolphins can then repeat another dolphin's signature whistle in order to communicate with that particular member of the pod, almost like a name. There's a lot of work still to be done to fully understand the similarities between human whistled communication and that of dolphins, but early research suggests that much can be learned about the information conveyed in dolphin whistling, including that its complexity is far greater than we currently realize, by better understanding human whistled languages.

Silbo Gomero in the Canary Islands, Kuskoy's 'bird language' in Turkey, and Kongthon's 'whistling village' in India clearly illustrate the adaptability and perseverance of human language. All the whistled languages serve as a testament to the versatility and resilience of human communication, its ability to adapt to geographical isolation, social context, and even suggest, when we consider the studies of the dolphin's whistled communication, the possibility of greater interspecies interactions. They challenge our conventional understanding of what we often assume language is and can be, expanding it beyond the realm of words and sentences to incorporate a range of tonal, melodic, and rhythmic elements, completely different from those with which we are familiar. Through these languages, we gain insight into how people use sound to navigate complex terrains.

Reflecting on whistled languages isn't just an exercise in linguistic curiosity, but a call to re-examine the ways in which we understand and categorize human and non-human communication. It may encourage us to question our preconceptions about the limitations of language, reminding us that it can evolve to meet specific needs and challenges. Whether it's the sheer cliffs that gave rise to Silbo or the jungle that created the need for the Amazonians to be heard and understood through thick vegetation, each account reinforces the existence of an unbreakable link between language, culture, and environment. We may be tantalized and intrigued by the dolphins, their sophisticated whistle-based communication making us ponder on our definitions of what language is, but they should also act as a reminder to us that the urge to communicate, to form social bonds and navigate the world, is not unique to humans.

7

---<o>---

Rare Tongues in Europe: Sicilian, Corsican, Catalan, and Monégasque

'The Sicilian language is the only one in Europe that has no future tense. The island's bitter legacy of conquest and revolt seems to have stunted its inhabitants' ability to conceive of a time outside this recurrent cycle.'

– Leonardo Sciascia, *The Wine Dark Sea* (1973)

I N EUROPE, AMID dominant languages like Italian, French, and Spanish, there are lesser-known languages that offer unique perspectives on culture and identity. One of these is Sicilian, which has a mixed linguistic heritage thanks to influences from Arabic, Greek, Latin, and Norman invasions. Another is Corsican, spoken on an island where the population has consistently sought to protect its unique culture and language from French influence. Then there's Catalan, the language of a region with a strong sense of identity and a history of striving for political autonomy. These languages aren't 'minority' languages or regional dialects:

they are full-fledged languages with complex grammars, rich vocabularies, and deep ties to unique traditions and ways of life. They carry the weight of entire communities who have fought for their preservation and legitimacy.

In focusing on these languages, we are led to reconsider what it means for a language to be considered 'minor' or 'regional'. The Italian philosopher Antonio Gramsci pointed out that when a language disappears, a unique way of understanding the world vanishes with it. Sicilian, Corsican, and Catalan each have specific qualities and are the result of different historical events that shaped them and brought about the ongoing struggles faced by their speakers. How has Corsican managed to sustain itself despite being part of France, a country known for its strong centralized identity? How did Catalan survive periods of being outlawed? And what does the complex linguistic history of Sicilian reveal about the history of the Mediterranean? By exploring these questions, we'll not only gain a deeper understanding of these languages themselves and the people who speak them but also learn more of the broader social and political forces that impact language survival and change. We'll also come to appreciate the diversity they bring to the linguistic landscape of Europe.

Sicilian

Sicilian took me by surprise. I speak Italian fairly well. We lived in Italy for several years, and with most Italian dialects, no matter how different they are, it's usually possible to find some glimmer of understanding in a word or a phrase. But it wasn't like that with Sicilian. It sounded to me far more like Arabic than Italian, but then I'd be surprised again by a word I thought of as Spanish. How did this language evolve? Is it really a language or is it a dialect, as it is so often called, just like so many of the other variations of Italian spoken in each region of the country?

Firstly, yes, it's a language, distinct from Italian and recognized as such by UNESCO and the European Charter for Minority Languages. As a language, it has different dialects of its own, which have particular characteristics local to geographic areas or communities. One of the difficulties of categorizing Sicilian, of describing it, is there isn't an agreed standard version because, within Italy, it has no official status. Most of the descriptions in this chapter are based on the dialect spoken around Palermo, the capital, because my two linguistic informants come from that region. But what makes Sicilian really intriguing to look at is the way in which it carries reminders of the other languages it has encountered through the millennia, and how these reflect the history and development of the language.

Sicily's history is astonishingly long in terms of sources. It is the only name of a western Mediterranean country that can be identified in Egyptian sources from 2000 BCE onwards. All languages carry memories of their roots and of the cultures and peoples that have coexisted in or dominated them. Take English, where a word like 'philosophy' comes from Greek, 'mouse' from German, and 'ego' from Latin, or Finnish, where the word for hangover, 'krapula', is taken from the Latin word 'crapula' meaning exactly the same thing! Sicilian, for me, shows these borrowings in a way that is flamboyant and fascinating, displaying grammatical and phonological traces of Arabic, Old French, Latin, Greek, and Castilian Spanish, because the strategic position of the island and its climate made it desirable to so many different conquerors and settlers. A close look at Sicilian, in the context of its history, shows the development of a unique and complex tongue, one that reflects the variety of the island's heritage, as well as its turbulence. What remains, the language still spoken in the markets of Palermo and the fields of Enna, is a seamless melange of origins, influences, and alterations.

In the eighth century BCE, Sicily was a fertile, strategically placed island when the very first colonizers, the Greeks, sailed toward its shores. Driven by a need to find agricultural land to feed their ever-expanding number of colonies, the Greeks landed on the island just north of the Alcantra River, with its dramatically beautiful gorge. The island was already inhabited by three peoples: the Siculi in the East; the Sicani, who had been in the mid-west since at least the Iron Age; and the Elymians in the extreme west. This latter group were probably not indigenous to the island but arrived from Turkey and, indeed, had themselves taken over some Sicilian settlements by the time of the Greeks' arrival. The two languages native to the island were Sicanian and Siculian. This latter was an Indo-European language, although, because it was never actually written down until the Greeks introduced their alphabet, it's difficult to trace a clear lineage. Numerous carved inscriptions have been found and identified, and these offer us our only clues, such as the jug from Centuripe that has over 100 characters scratched onto it or the carved spiralled epitaph found close to Enna, in the centre of the island.

Greek colonies in Sicily were typically established by groups of settlers known as 'apoikiai', which means 'home away from home'. These colonies often carried the name of their founding city-state and maintained close ties with their mother cities. The Greek colonies served as self-governing entities, maintaining their own political systems and social structures while interacting with the indigenous Sicilian populations. The Greeks founded numerous colonies across Sicily, with notable city-states such as Syracuse, Gela, Agrigentum (present-day Agrigento), and Selinus (present-day Selinunte) becoming major centres of Greek culture and power, their importance and elegance still obvious from the ruins that remain, even now. These colonies thrived economically, engaging in agriculture, trade, and manufacturing. They cultivated crops such as olives, grapes, and wheat, and established trading networks that extended throughout the Mediterranean.

The Greek-script transcriptions of the languages of Sicily are only one hint at the cultural interactions between the new arrivals and the Sicilians. While the Greeks had brought their own religion with them, they linked their gods to those of the Sicilians, often using existing religious sites and incorporating local ceremonies. The Temple of Diana, a plateau on a high hill that overlooks Cefalu on the coast, was the site of worship for the Siculian goddess of hunting before the arrival of the Greeks. They adapted their usual agricultural practices to fit with the new landscape and its climate by incorporating those that were already in place. Another important linguistic tell remains too. Other parts of mainland Italy that were also subject to Greek occupation have systems of dialects that are completely distinct from those of Sicily but related to each other. The Greeks recognized the distinction too: Siculian and Italian were regarded by the Greeks as different languages, with the former referring not just to the language of the previous inhabitants of Sicily but of all those who lived on the island.[1] A few words of Siculian origin remain still, words that are clearly unrelated to Greece or to the other languages that would later change the linguistic landscape of the island.

'*dudda*' – mulberry
'*scrozzu*' – not well developed
'*Sfunnacata*' – multitude, vast number[2]

There are, in contrast, many Greek words that are still easily recognized in the Sicilian lexicon and these borrowed words are not limited in their scope, but cover a wide range of fields, such as food, agriculture, trade, and mythology.

'*Meluni*' (Greek: μελούνι) – melon
'*Riganu*' (Greek: ὀρίγανον) – oregano
'*Archiulugghìa*' (Greek: ἀρχαιολογία) – archaeology[3]

There's a grammatical legacy too. So we find that Sicilian retains the ancient Greek practice of using a definite article before a person's name, such as 'u Giorgiu' (Greek: ὁ Γεώργιος), meaning George. The Greek presence in Sicily endured for several centuries, but eventually the island fell under the domination of other powers, including the Carthaginians and later the Romans.

When the Roman Empire arrived in Sicily in 241 BCE, Latin was introduced as the dominant language. As we've seen in an earlier chapter, Roman conquest led to Latin being used as the language of administration and trade in the occupied territories, and Sicily was no exception. Latin's domination meant the steady decline of both the original island languages and Greek, although some small Greek communities continued to thrive in the east.

Perhaps the most dramatic linguistic impact of all came in the ninth and tenth centuries, with the Arab conquest. Arabic become the only official language and was used for law, for all official and state occasions, and for commerce. What remains of this today is a substantial number of loanwords from Arabic in Sicilian. Around three hundred words related to agriculture, trade, and navigation can all trace their roots back to Arabic. Examples include 'aranciu' (orange), 'zagara' (blossom), and 'babbaluciu' (snail but also spiral staircase, or, literally, staircase like a snail), 'senia' (water irrigation, from the Arabic *saniya*, a water-lifting wheel), all words that originated from Arabic, as well as one of Sicily's most famous cakes, cassata (Sicilian ricotta cake), and cubbàita, a traditional sweet, a sort of nougat made with almond, walnuts, and honey, whose name comes from the Arabic 'qubbayta'.[4]

Arabic also influenced the phonetics of Sicilian, bringing new sounds and phonetic patterns into everyday speech. The presence of certain consonant sounds, such as 'h' and 'ʕ' (ayn), reflects its influence. Additionally, Arabic has a distinctive emphasis on vowel length and stress, which changed the phonetic patterns of Sicilian words. The adoption of vowel-length distinctions in Sicilian phonology, and the preservation of certain Arabic-infused vowel qualities, still attest to the enduring phonetic influence of Arabic on Sicilian. Arabic also influenced the syntax, resulting in the evolution of Sicilian's noun declension patterns, particularly in relation to gender and plural formations.[5]

The Norman conquest in the eleventh century introduced the French language to Sicily. Old French, spoken by the Norman ruling elite, began to influence Sicilian, leaving an indelible mark on the lexicon and introducing a large vocabulary of words that the language retains today. Many of these words were related to feudal administration, courtly life and literature, and chivalric traditions. For instance, terms such as 'castellu' (castle), 'barunu' (baron), and 'cavalleria' (knighthood) entered Sicilian directly from Old French. These words not only enriched the vocabulary but also reflected the cultural and social milieu of the Norman ruling class.

But Old French also influenced everyday language and brought a variety of words related to clothing, food, and household items. Words like 'furguni' (oven), 'mantellu' (cloak), and 'tavula' (table) originated from Old French. Sicilian grammar also began to change again, creating yet another layer in its complex development, leaving traces in both certain linguistic structures and syntactic patterns. Sicilian adopted elements of Old French word order and sentence construction, features that were most often used in more formal and literary contexts. One notable grammatical influence is the adoption of Old French possessive constructions. Sicilian borrowed the use of the preposition 'di' (of) followed by a personal pronoun to express possession. For instance, the phrase 'la casa di miu frati' (my brother's house) mirrors the Old French construction 'la maison de mon frère'. The Norman French dialect spoken by the ruling elite introduced new sounds and phonetic patterns to Sicilian. The nasalization of certain vowels is one of these prominent phonetic features that can still be heard in some regions of Sicily today and is particularly noticeable in the southern dialects. In Sicilian, vowels before nasal consonants, such as 'n' or 'm', are pronounced with a nasal quality, like their Old French counterparts. For instance, the Sicilian word 'munnu' (world) corresponds to the French 'monde'.

The influence of Old French on Sicilian extended beyond vocabulary and grammar. The literary traditions of the Normans, steeped in courtly romance and chivalry, permeated Sicilian literature. Sicilian poets and troubadours drew inspiration from the troubadour poetry coming out of the courts of Provence and incorporated elements of courtly love and knightly ideals into their own compositions. This was exemplified in the Sicilian School of poetry, which emerged in the thirteenth century, showcasing the fusion of Sicilian and Old French literary traditions. Heavily influenced by southern French troubadours, Sicilian poets such as Giacomo da Lentini and Guido delle Colonne developed their own unique poetic forms and styles, blending Sicilian language and themes with elements of courtly love and lyricism. But another domination was yet to come. When the Spanish took over Sicily from the fifteenth to the eighteenth centuries, they too brought about another significant linguistic change.

In 1469, when Ferdinand of Aragon married Isabella of Castile, they united their kingdoms and created a powerful Spanish state. This union also brought Sicily firmly into their sights. The island was already part of the Aragonese possessions, but under their combined rule they sought to solidify their control. Then, in 1494, Charles VIII of France decided to lay claim to the Kingdom of Naples, which included Sicily. This prompted a series of complex conflicts known as the Italian Wars. Amid this chaos, Ferdinand and Isabella saw an opportunity to further strengthen their grip on Sicily. In 1495, they sent an army led by Gonsalvo de Córdoba, a skilled general known as 'The Great Captain', to

Sicily. His forces clashed with the French and their Italian allies, resulting in a series of hard-fought battles. Gonsalvo's strategic brilliance and the tenacity of his troops gradually turned the tide in favour of the Spanish. Within a year, Gonsalvo had effectively pushed the French out of Sicily, solidifying Spanish control over the island. This marked the beginning of a new chapter in Sicilian history, with Spanish influence becoming deeply ingrained in the island's culture, politics, and society. Under Spanish rule, Sicily experienced many changes. The Spanish introduced their language and administrative systems, leaving an indelible mark on the island's identity. However, they also imposed heavy taxes and strict governance, which caused discontent among the local population.

Many phonetic characteristics of Castilian found their way into Sicilian during the occupation. This Castilian influence resulted in changes in the way certain sounds were articulated. For example, the Castilian 'j' sound, represented by the letter 'x' in Spanish, was adopted in Sicilian, replacing the original 'g' sound in words such as 'giardinu' (garden), which became 'xardinu' in Sicilian. The grammatical structure of Sicilian also shifted with the introduction of certain verb conjugation patterns that mirror those found in Castilian. In particular, the use of the preposition 'a' before an infinitive verb, as seen in constructions like 'vaju a fari' (I am going to do), is a direct influence from Castilian.

Castilian also influenced the pronoun system in Sicilian. The use of subject pronouns before verbs, such as 'io vado'

(I go), is reminiscent of Castilian syntax. It adopted certain object pronouns and their placement within the sentence structure from Castilian, as in the expression 'mi dica' (tell me), where 'mi' corresponds to the Castilian pronoun 'me'.

The influence of Castilian on the Sicilian vocabulary is still apparent in the adoption of numerous loanwords. Words pertaining to administrative, legal, and military matters, as well as terms related to agriculture, commerce, and urban life, were borrowed from Castilian. For instance, words like 'castidda' (chastity), 'capitanu' (captain), and 'giustizzia' (justice) entered the Sicilian lexicon directly from Castilian. Loanwords also began to permeate the vocabulary of daily life in Sicily, including vocabulary relating to food, clothing, and household items. Words like 'sartu' (stew), 'pantufola' (slippers), and 'mantellina' (cape) all reflect the Castilian influence. Many idiomatic expressions in Sicilian also bear the traces of Castilian. Phrases and proverbs borrowed from Castilian, translated into Sicilian, and adapted to the local context became integral parts of the Sicilian linguistic repertoire. The phonetic shifts, grammatical changes, vocabulary expansion, and the assimilation of idiomatic expressions attest to the lasting influence of Castilian on the linguistic fabric of Sicilian.

But a transformational political change was coming that would see not only Sicily but the whole of Italy altered forever. In the nineteenth century, the Italian Risorgimento dramatically changed the position and status of all regional languages and dialects, and Sicilian was no exception. The movement for Italian unification, led by figures like Giuseppe Garibaldi, Giuseppe Mazzini, and Count Camillo di Cavour, recognized the importance of language in fostering a sense of national identity. They advocated for the adoption and promotion of a standardized Italian language based on the Tuscan dialect, chosen because of its historical association with great literary works, particularly those of Dante Alighieri, author of the *Divine Comedy*. The plan was to create a common linguistic framework that could be understood and used across all the regions that aspired to be part of a united Italy. This standardized Italian, often referred to as 'Florentine-based Italian', became the language of the Risorgimento movement.

In 1861, with the proclamation of the Kingdom of Italy under King Victor Emmanuel II, the newly unified state set about establishing Italian as the official language. Government institutions, schools, and the media were encouraged to use Italian, and efforts were made to spread literacy in this standardized form. Many regions persisted with their local language or dialect and viewed the imposition of Italian as an affront to their cultural identity. This resistance was particularly strong in areas where dialects were deeply ingrained in daily life and culture and scant knowledge of Tuscan Italian existed. The Risorgimento's language policies did play a crucial role in fostering a sense of national unity, enabling the diverse regions to communicate and identify as part of a single Italian nation. But it was an uneasy alliance, and not without linguistic casualties.

Just like Sámi, and the now endangered languages of India, Sicilian was marginalized in official contexts and education. As part of the broader drive towards national unity, Sicilian was often stigmatized and considered inferior to Italian. The association of Sicilian with backwardness and lack of education fuelled negative perceptions, leading some Sicilians to distance themselves from their native tongue. Speaking Italian became a symbol of progress and modernity, while speaking Sicilian was often viewed as a marker of rural or provincial identity. The linguistic policies of the Risorgimento era had a profound impact on the usage patterns of the Sicilian. The promotion of Italian as the language of administration, education, and social mobility led to a gradual decline in the use of Sicilian in formal settings. As has happened throughout the centuries around the world with other languages, many Sicilians, particularly the younger generations, shifted languages towards Italian as a means of upward mobility and assimilation into the newly forming Italian nation. Yet during this, despite it all, Sicilian experienced a literary renaissance. A group of Sicilian intellectuals and writers, known as the Sicilian School, emerged, advocating for the recognition and preservation of the Sicilian language and its literary heritage. These writers, such as Giovanni Verga and Luigi Capuana, utilized Sicilian in their literary works, contributing to the revitalization of the Sicilian dialect in the realm of literature.

Giovanni Verga was born in Catania in 1840. But it was not until he moved to Milan, in his thirties, that he developed the technique of creating characters through dialogue that would make him renowned. His decision to write in the Sicilian dialect during a time when the dominance of standard Italian was unquestioned represented a literary revolution. He believed that language was deeply intertwined with regional identity and sought to capture the authentic voice and cultural richness of Sicilian society through his characters and narratives. He depicted the nuances of regional accents, idiomatic expressions, and grammatical features, providing readers with a genuine representation of his native Sicilian language. His commitment to linguistic accuracy lent credibility to his literary portrayals and resonated with audiences seeking to explore the miscellany of Italian linguistic heritage.

Through his books, such as *Cavalleria Rusticana*, best known now as the opera that was based on it, and *Little Novels of Sicily*, Verga shed light on the struggles, aspirations, and idiosyncrasies of the Sicilian people, offering a unique perspective on their way of life and their distinct cultural identity. His works reflected the complex realities of rural life, social hierarchies, and the impact of historical events on the Sicilian psyche. His writings in the Sicilian dialect gained national and international recognition, marking a significant step in the popularization of regional dialects within the broader Italian literary landscape. His works were widely acclaimed and translated into multiple languages, introducing readers worldwide to the richness and depth of the Sicilian language.

Verga's pioneering use of the Sicilian dialect influenced subsequent generations of writers, who drew inspiration from his works and continued to explore the linguistic and cultural aspects of Sicilian society. His linguistic legacy paved the way for authors such as Luigi Pirandello, Leonardo Sciascia, and Andrea Camilleri, whose literature carried on the promotion and preservation of the Sicilian dialect.

But resistance was not only literary. During the Risorgimento era, Sicily demonstrated its socio-cultural resilience, continuing to thrive in informal settings, within families, communities, and cultural traditions. The language was still used for oral storytelling, folk traditions, and every-day interactions, serving as vehicles for transmitting heritage and local identity. In recent decades, movements promoting linguistic diversity and cultural heritage have sought to reclaim the value and significance of the Sicilian dialect, challenging the language policies of the Risorgimento era. And of all the Italian regions, Sicily remains the region where it's easiest to hear the local language. In particular, the use of Sicilian idioms is still pervasive, and it is known throughout Italy for its colourful language. Some of these are particular to certain areas of the island, while others reoccur across it. Those which refer to character traits or a particular type of person are the ones my Sicilian travel companions thought of as being used by elderly people they knew in everyday speech.

So 'Chiddu è r'acqua, sutta vinu 'un va' (literally: 'He is like water, he doesn't go well under wine') describes someone who doesn't mix well with others or doesn't fit into a par-ticular social setting, comparing their compatibility to the inability of water and wine to mix. While 'acqua davanti e ventu d'arreri' (meaning 'water in front and wind behind') is said of a person for whom you at first feel sympathy but who turns out to be unbearable.

Despite sociopolitical challenges, the language is enduring, with hope that it's starting to be revitalized as a cherished emblem of Sicilian heritage. But there is a darker side to the persistence of the language too – one that is more about fostering secrecy and solidarity, and forging a distinct criminal identity.

The Sicilian Mafia has long been associated with the use of the Sicilian language as a means of communication within its ranks. The use of the Sicilian language by the Mafia serves as a linguistic barrier that contributes to the organization's secretive nature. By employing a language understood only by insiders, the Mafia creates a sense of exclusivity and restricts access to information, effectively shielding its illegal activities from law enforcement and the wider community. The Mafia employs various linguistic codes and jargon to further enhance secrecy and evade surveillance. This includes the use of slang, metaphors, and euphemisms specific to the Mafia subculture. Such linguistic devices allow members to communicate covertly, obscuring the true nature of their discussions from outsiders. But their use goes far beyond this: they also serve as a marker of cultural identity and solidarity. The adoption of the Sicilian language reinforces a sense of belonging and loyalty among Mafia members, fostering a shared cultural heritage and strengthening group cohesion.

The use of Sicilian dialects, regional accents, and idiomatic expressions further emphasizes the connection between the Mafia and its Sicilian roots. This use of language within the Mafia is closely tied to power dynamics. It has become a tool for establishing authority and respect within the organization. Mastery of the Sicilian language, particularly the use of complex linguistic codes and cultural references, can denote seniority and expertise, granting individuals a higher status within the Mafia hierarchy. But this reclamation of Sicilian has much wider implications for societal perception and stigmatization of the language itself. The association of Sicilian with criminal activities perpetuates negative stereotypes and creates prejudice against the language and its speakers.

I met Gianni Pacitti in the living room of my small B & B, close to the Palermo opera house. Gianni's in his early thirties and had got in touch after I asked a Sicilian friend to help me find someone to speak about what Sicilian means to locals of that generation. Gianni isn't his real name. He's part of the anti-Mafia group of activists, although when I say this to him, he tells me they're not really an organized group, more a collection of people, many of whom don't know each other but who have similar hopes and ideals for their island.

In part it's about reclaiming Sicily as a modern, vibrant, beautiful place, getting rid of the taint of criminality and corruption. In real terms, there's still a lot needs to change, but there's so many good things that just don't have the same international association with our culture as crime. All the television shows don't help. Yes, they do use our language, but it's reinforcing it as being associated with drugs and old-fashioned codes and secret killings. Those of us who care about the future of our reputation want the language to be part of that. My grandmother spoke it all the time, my mother not so much, but now it's coming back, you hear it in playgrounds, and not just when kids are trying to be tough.

Gianni turns towards a stuffed bookcase, inlaid with colourful ceramic tiles, so typical of the island, and gestures:

We are the place of Giacomo da Lentini [a Sicilian poet of the thirteenth century]. He invented the sonnet, you know? It wasn't your Shakespeare. Young poets are writing in our language again, but you don't see that on Netflix. There it's all gang wars, drugs, and criminals. We want to change the image of our language.

Another notable aspect of the contemporary revival of Sicilian that Gianni tells me about is its presence in music. Sicilian musicians and artists have embraced their native language, incorporating Sicilian lyrics and melodies into compositions, creating a vibrant fusion of traditional and contemporary sounds. Formed in Palermo in 1979, Agricantus is one such group, blending Sicilian folk music with various global influences, to create a unique sound. Their lyrics often feature the Sicilian language and address related themes of cultural identity, social issues, and historical events. Through their music, Agricantus has played a crucial role in bringing Sicilian language and culture to a wider audience, both in Italy and internationally. The singer-songwriter Rosa Balistreri, known as the 'voice of Sicily', was born in 1927 and dedicated her career to promoting Sicilian folk music. Her powerful and emotive voice, coupled with her heartfelt lyrics in Sicilian, resonated deeply with Sicilian audiences. Balistreri's songs, such as 'Abballati', 'Cu ti lu dissi', and 'Nesci Maria', are still regarded as icons of Sicilian musical heritage.

In addition to music, Sicilian language and culture have also found their way into contemporary Sicilian cinema. Filmmakers have embraced Sicilian as a means of capturing authenticity and the unique flavour of the region. The 2002 film *Respiro*, directed by Emanuele Crialese, set on the Sicilian island of Lampedusa, tells the story of a woman named Grazia, played by Valeria Golino, and her struggles within her traditional community. *Respiro* masterfully weaves Sicilian dialogue into the narrative, giving the film an authentic and immersive feel. The revival of Sicilian in music and film is a testament to the efforts of artists, musicians, and filmmakers. But Gianni's concern that it is also perpetuating a stereotype the next generation are keen to abandon lingers with me. Sicily is a rich, eclectic, diverse tongue; the seamless fusion of Latin, Greek, Arabic, French, and Spanish influences has given it a distinctive identity in terms of its linguistic make-up, but the criminal association of its past lingers, although perhaps more lightly than it used to, in the international imagination.

Corsican

Sicilian is not the only minority language in Europe to be stigmatized by perceptions of criminality. In wider French society, Corsican is viewed in a similar light. The Corsican language, or Corsu, is a Romance language spoken on the island of Corsica. Aside for a temporary truce in 2016, Corsica has been engaged in an armed political struggle for the right to be independent from France since the 1970s. Because Corsican nationalists have made the language such an integral part of their fight for independence, for many French people the language and the conflict, with its continuing violence and recrimination, are inextricably interdependent.

Corsican is part of the Italo-Dalmatian branch of Romance languages, closely related to the Tuscan dialect of Italian. It evolved from Vulgar Latin and, just like Sicilian, has been influenced by various languages throughout its history, including Italian, French, and Ligurian. The island has been inhabited since prehistoric times and has been under the control of the Greeks, Romans, Vandals, Byzantines, and several Italian city-states. Its volatile history is marked by the rule of various foreign powers, including the Republic of Genoa, the Kingdom of France, and the Kingdom of Aragon. All these different influences left their linguistic imprint on

Corsican, with Genoese and French playing the most significant roles in shaping the language.

In the eighteenth century, Corsica declared independence from the Republic of Genoa and became a self-governing entity under Pasquale Paoli's leadership. However, the French took control of the island in 1769, leading to an extended period of French rule. Corsica had not developed a literary tradition until the Renaissance, with the first written works appearing in the sixteenth century. However, due to political and cultural factors, including the dominance of French and Italian, Corsican literature did not fully flourish until the twentieth century. Notable Corsican writers such as Petru Giovacchini and Ghjacumu Thiers contributed to the development and recognition of Corsican literature. The history of Corsican language and culture is closely tied to the island's sense of identity and its struggle for autonomy. Corsican nationalism and the desire for independence have been significant forces shaping Corsican society. The independence movement re-emerged during the twentieth century as a response to perceived cultural and economic marginalization by the French government. Pro-independence political parties and organizations, such as the Corsican National Liberation Front (FLNC), have advocated for greater autonomy or full independence for Corsica. They continue to argue for the protection of Corsican language and culture, as well as the economic development of the island.

Corsican exhibits several distinctive features that set it apart from its linguistic neighbours and other Romance languages. These features encompass phonology, morphology, syntax, and lexicon.

Phonologically, Corsican is distinguished by its conservative retention of the Latin stress system, which is typically penultimate or antepenultimate, depending on the word's length and structure. This is unlike the fixed stress patterns observed in French or the dynamic stress in Italian. For instance, in the Corsican words 'cantà' (to sing) and 'telefunà' (to telephone), the stress falls on the penultimate syllable, reflecting this phonological conservatism.

Morphologically, Corsican retains a gender system, as is common in Romance languages, with masculine and feminine nouns. However, Corsican has a distinctive feature in its use of a definite article system that reflects the phonological nature of the subsequent word. The masculine singular articles 'u', 'un', and 'lu' can be chosen based on euphonic principles to ensure phonological harmony. For example, 'u libru' (the book) employs 'u' before a consonant, while 'l'omu' (the man) illustrates the use of 'l'' before a vowel for ease of pronunciation.

In its syntax, Corsican showcases a degree of flexibility in its word order, more so than in French. Subject-verb-object (SVO) remains the standard structure, yet variations are possible and sometimes necessary to convey nuances in focus or emphasis. For instance, object-subject-verb (OSV) constructions are employed for topicalization or to highlight the object, as in 'quellu libru aghju lettu' (that book I have read), where the object 'quellu libru' is fronted for emphasis.

The rich vocabulary of Corsican reflects its historical inter-actions with various cultures. While it is primarily Romance in origin, there are notable influences from Italian, Genoese, and to a lesser extent French. These influences are evident in loanwords and calques. For example, 'guvernà' (to govern) is clearly of Italian origin, while 'mercatu' (market) echoes both Italian 'mercato' and French 'marché'.

Intriguingly, Corsican, like Italian, has developed a distinctive system of diminutives and augmentatives, which are prolific and convey subtle shades of meaning or affec-tion. The diminutive suffix '-ellu' can transform 'cani' (dog) into 'cagnellu' (little dog or puppy), while the augmentative suffix '-one' can change 'pani' (bread) into 'panone' (big loaf of bread), each inflecting the base word with nuanced connotations.

The future of Corsican

The Corsican village of Pigna is home to a unique language experience. Pigna is situated at altitude, in the Balagne region of the island, with views over the beaches of Ile Rousse. In the summer it throngs with tourists, but the project dubbed the 'poeticizing of the economy' by one of its primary supporters is aimed not only at the many tourists who visit in the summer months but also at locals. This multifaceted experi-ence includes events, Corsican signage and QR codes that tie places to Corsican music, and multilingual texts with Corsican always included as one of the languages.

The aim is to integrate traditions, both those of the village itself and of the wider island, with the Corsican identity through a sophisticated use of modern technology and thus create a unique way of sharing and understanding them. This new approach has been the subject of much academic interest, as well as proving popular and lucrative for the tourist economy. It's about language promotion but shifts from the usual focus on educational and official contexts and, instead, projects integration into a commercial economy. The Corsican language becomes not just a feature to be used in the promotion of the region, but rather an integral part of the process itself.[6]

Catalan

I first encountered the simmering tensions between the languages of different Spanish regions in Catalonia at a linguistics conference in Girona when I was still a graduate student. In retrospect, it was an odd venue for a meeting where academics attempted to look at language in a scientific rather than an emotive or cultural way. At that time, I was interested in acoustic correlates – that is, looking at the wave patterns of different sounds in many languages to see if there were commonalities across them. If you think, for example, about the sound /s/. Pause for a second, now just make a long /sssss/. You will feel the friction between your teeth. On a spectrogram – a picture of the different sound waves that make up speech – this looks like lots of activity in high frequencies. This is something our brain is capable of hearing and recognizing as significant to our understanding of the word /sun/, for example. But even more than that, these high frequencies also can, in English, let our brain know we have made a plural, so /suns/ will have that same pattern again, at the end, and we will know there is more than one. I arrived with my pictures and calculations and theories but on the first morning had already, at breakfast, met a Catalonian student who attempted to teach me some Catalan, saying that my Spanish would give entirely the wrong impression – not because it was poor (it was) but because it wasn't the local language. Did I really want people to think I wasn't sympathetic to the independence movement? I was Scottish – surely, I could empathize better than most? So began my education into the Catalan independence movement and what would become an abiding interest in identity, language, and power, and the interaction between them.

Catalan is a Romance language spoken primarily in Catalonia, the Balearic Islands, and Valencia in Spain, as well as some parts of France and Sardinia. It presents a fascinating array of linguistic features that underscore its unique position within the Romance language family. While sharing commonalities with its neighbouring languages, Catalan, like Corsican, possesses distinctive phonological, morphological, syntactic, and lexical characteristics that merit close examination.

One phonological feature that sets Catalan apart is its use of the 'vocal neutra' or neutral vowel, also known as schwa [ə]. This is the most common vowel sound in the English language and can be heard, with some dialectic exceptions, in unstressed syllables. However, it isn't typically found in Romance languages. In Corsican we can hear it in a word such as 'parella' (couple), where the second 'a' is pronounced as [ə].

Morphologically, Catalan retains the use of the definite article derived from the Latin 'ipsum', a feature it shares with some Occitan dialects but which is otherwise rare in Romance languages. The masculine singular definite article 'el' becomes 'l'' before a vowel, as in 'l'amic' (the friend), and pluralizes to 'els', as in 'els amics' (the friends). This retention points to the historical development of Catalan and its ties to older Romance forms.

In the realm of syntax, an especially notable feature of Catalan is its use of periphrastic verb constructions to express the future tense. Rather than conjugating the verb in the future tense as in Spanish or Italian, Catalan often uses the present tense of 'anar' (to go) followed by the infinitive of the main verb, akin to the English 'going to' construction. For example, 'aniré a comprar' (I am going to buy) employs this periphrastic future.

Another interesting syntactic feature is the use of 'pronoms febles' or weak pronouns. These clitic pronouns, which are attached to the verb, can be quite complex due to their place-ment and the multiple forms they can take depending on factors like case, number, and gender. For example, 'La dona me l'ha donat' (The woman gave it to me) illustrates the use of weak pronouns 'me' (to me) and 'l'' (it).

Lexically, Catalan, like Sicilian, showcases a fascinating blend of influences from its Romance neighbours, reflecting its historical and geographical position. It has vocabulary that is shared with Spanish, Occitan, and French, yet it also retains its own unique words and expressions. For instance, 'espardenya' (espadrille) is a type of shoe particular to the Catalan-speaking regions.

Again, like Sicilian, Catalan is distinguished by its colourful idiomatic expressions, so we can find 'Estic en els núvols', an expression that translates literally as 'I am in the clouds' and is used to describe someone who is daydreaming or not paying attention to their surroundings – just like the English 'head in the clouds'. And the common Catalan saying 'Bufar i fer ampolles', which in English translates to 'Blow and make bottles', is used to say that something is very easy to do, similar to describing a task or an activity as 'a piece of cake' in English.

Some background on the Catalan language

The Catalan language emerged from Vulgar Latin, the colloquial form of Latin spoken by the settlers of the Roman Empire that we discussed in an earlier chapter. In this case, it was the form used by settlers who colonized the Tarragona region. In the ninth and tenth centuries, as the Kingdom of Catalonia and Aragon began to take shape, Old Catalan started to develop more pronouncedly as a distinct language. It was heavily influenced by the Romance dialects spoken in the region, as well as by the Mozarabic language, a Romance language spoken in Muslim-controlled territories.

During the twelfth and thirteenth centuries, Catalan experienced a golden age of cultural and literary growth. The troubadour tradition, influenced by Provençal poetry, thrived, leading to the development of a rich body of lyrical and narrative works. The 'chansonniers' (songbooks) containing the poetry of the troubadours, such as the *Cansoneret de Ripoll*, were highly regarded. Ramon Lull, the philosopher, theologian, and writer, made significant contributions to Catalan literature during this period. His works, written in the language, explored topics of theology, philosophy, and love.

When the Crown of Aragon expanded its influence, the Catalan language enjoyed prestige and official usage, even becoming the language of the royal court. However, the marriage of Ferdinand of Aragon and Isabella of Castile in 1469 led to the union of the crowns and the subsequent centralization of power in Castile. During the sixteenth and seventeenth centuries, Castilian emerged as the dominant language of administration, culture, and communication across the Spanish territories. This was partly due to the expansion of the Spanish Empire and the centralizing policies of the Habsburg monarchy. Catalan, while still widely spoken, started to lose its prestige and was increasingly confined to private and local use. The War of the Spanish Succession had a profound impact. Catalonia supported the

Habsburg claimant, Archduke Charles, against the Bourbon claimant, Philip V. When the war ended with the victory of Philip V, the subsequent Treaty of Utrecht (1713) marked the beginning of a new era. In 1716, Philip V issued the Decrees of Nueva Planta, which abolished the traditional institutions, privileges, and autonomy of the Crown of Aragon, including those of Catalonia. These decrees imposed Castilian laws and language on the administration and legal system. Catalan was significantly suppressed in official domains, and Castilian became the language of the ruling elite and government, promoted as the official language of administration, education, and culture.

In the nineteenth century, Catalan cultural and linguistic identity experienced a revival known as the Renaixença (Renaissance). Catalan intellectuals, writers, and scholars, such as Bonaventura Carles Aribau and Jacint Verdaguer, played instrumental roles in the resurgence of Catalan language, literature, and culture. During this period, various cultural organizations and institutions were established to promote Catalan language and identity. The founding of the Institut d'Estudis Catalans (Institute for Catalan Studies) in 1907 and the publishing of literary works, newspapers, and journals in Catalan were crucial in fostering a sense of pride and preserving the language. From 1939 to 1975, during the dictatorship of Francisco Franco, the Catalonians faced severe suppression and repression – just like many of the speakers of other languages discussed in this book. Franco's regime aimed to centralize power, promote a unified Spanish identity, and suppress regional identities and languages, including Catalan. The suppression of Catalan was part of a broader policy to enforce Spanish nationalism and eliminate any perceived threats to Franco's authority. Under his regime, the use of the language in public and official contexts was strictly prohibited. Catalan was banned from schools, government institutions, and the media. The regime sought to promote the exclusive use of Spanish (Castilian) as the language of administration, education, and culture throughout Spain.

The education system was a key target for Franco's language-suppression policies. Students were forbidden from speaking Catalan on school grounds. Catalan-language textbooks and materials were replaced with Spanish-language ones. Teachers who insisted on using Catalan or promoted Catalan culture and identity were often dismissed or punished.

The Franco regime exerted strict control over the media to suppress the use of Catalan language and culture. Publications in Catalan were heavily censored, and any content deemed politically subversive or against the regime's nationalist ideology was strictly proscribed. Newspapers, magazines, and books in Catalan were subjected to government scrutiny, and many publishers were shut down or forced to publish exclusively in Spanish. Catalan cultural expressions, including literature, theatre, and music, were heavily targeted. Works in Catalan were censored, and cultural institutions that promoted Catalan culture faced strict restrictions and scrutiny. Many cultural figures were forced into exile, and their works were banned within Spain.

Politically active Catalans who advocated for regional autonomy or resisted the regime's centralization efforts were targeted. Many politicians, activists, and intellectuals were imprisoned, exiled, or executed. The regime aimed to dismantle Catalan political structures and suppress any form of dissent. Yet despite the harsh suppression, there were efforts to preserve and promote the Catalan language and culture clandestinely. Underground networks, known as 'Els Grups de Llengua', secretly organized Catalan language classes, cultural events, and publications. These initiatives were risky, as those involved were subject to persecution and punishment by the regime's authorities.

With Franco's death in 1975 and the restoration of democracy in Spain, there was a gradual reversal of language policies. The new Spanish constitution of 1978 recognized the linguistic diversity of Spain and the right of regional languages, including Catalan, to coexist with Spanish. The restoration of democracy in Spain led to a renewed focus on regional autonomy and cultural difference, and Catalonia was granted a significant level of self-government within Spain, including the recognition and official status of the Catalan language. Since this transition to democracy, Catalan has experienced a remarkable revival. It has gained official status in Catalonia, the Balearic Islands, and Valencia, and is widely used in education, media, government institutions, and cultural expressions. In the 1980s, an educational programme called 'linguistic normalization' played a pivotal role in revitalizing the language as well as restoring its reputation. It ensured that children in the Catalan-speaking regions would be proficient in both Spanish and Catalan, thus fostering bilingual competence but also consolidating the equal status of both tongues. Today, Catalan is spoken by over ten million people, with over nine million of those living in regions of a country where it was once illegal to do so. It has largely overcome the trials of history, thanks to activism, advocacy, and international recognition by bodies such as the EU, who recognize it within their minority languages of Europe policies, while a plethora of bilingual and multilingual programmes mean that younger generations are once again proud to speak their national language.

The language and the prince

'Thus, teaching our language to young Monégasques is one of the surest means of safeguarding our identity. To let a language die is to forever tarnish the deep soul of a people'

—Prince Rainier III (1982)

For three years, my husband and I lived in Ventimiglia, on the Italian–French border. For most of that time, we worked in Monaco, taking the train on weekdays from Italy, past the French coastal town of Menton, to the Principality of Monaco. It's a tiny country, just 1.95 square kilometres, and the second smallest independent state in the world (Vatican City is the first). It's also the wealthiest country, with a GDP per capita that significantly exceeds that of any other. Yet its native language almost didn't exist any more, and possibly wouldn't at all if not for a concerted campaign by its monarchy.

The very first time we arrived in Monte Carlo, there was an odd sense of familiarity, although neither of us had ever been before. The luxurious modernity of the high-rise flats, their contrast with the elegance of the old district of Monaco-Ville, and the bright glinting turquoise sea were familiar from movies and sporting events, a place of dreams and glamour. The first time I heard the language in Monaco, I had a similar sensation – of something familiar that I thought I should be able to understand, only to find I could not.

The Monégasque language is a Romance language spoken only in the Principality of Monaco. The official language of Monaco is French. Yet the traditional language is Munegascu: 'a lenga d'i nostri avi' (the tongue of our ancestors). It is listed by UNESCO as having between just ten and ninety-nine remaining speakers and is classified as endangered/unsafe.[7]

Monégasque belongs to the Gallo-Italic branch of Romance languages and is closely related to Ligurian, which was spoken in the neighbouring region of Liguria in Italy. Historically, the Monégasque language has its roots in Genoese, as the Genoese took possession of the Rock of Monaco in June 1191 and settled there in 1215. Over time, the language spoken in Monaco would gradually move away from Genoese, as it absorbed influences from migrants from the valleys of Nice, Piedmont, and Liguria, especially with the creation of Monte Carlo in 1860. Each brought their own dialect, enriching the common language, which became a veritable 'patois' associated with a clear identity.

Monaco was a bilingual country. In the fifteenth century, popular Monégasque existed alongside Italian, which was the language of political power (generally used in official documents, in the same way as Latin), and also briefly Catalan, at the time of the occupation by the Spanish armed forces. It was not until the annexation of Monaco by France in 1793 that the French language began to establish itself, as Napoleon imposed French as the dominant language, restricting the use of other tongues. When the Grimaldis once again established the principality in 1814, they retained French as the only official language, but with a more liberal position on Monégasque and Italian. In 1860, the French annexation of Nice brought an outright ban on Monégasque, which was derided as a type of slang, and it was not taught again in schools until 1976.

Today, French remains the only language used in documents and sovereign ordinances in the principality. Indeed, the 1962 constitution recognizes it as the country's sole official language, while Monégasque is recognized instead as the national language.

Until the twentieth century, Monégasque was principally spoken, with only a couple of early eighteenth-century documents showing any kind of written version. But in 1924, the National Committee for Monégasque Traditions, founded by representatives of the old Monégasque families whose roles include preserving and promoting Monégasque, made it a written language. In 1927, Louis Notari became the father of Monégasque literature with *A Leganda de Santa Devota*, the first literary work written in the language. Its success heralded a flurry of literature, poetry, and plays, as well as stories. In 1960, Louis Frolla codified the language with the publication of his Monégasque grammar, followed by the first-ever Monégasque–French dictionary.

To preserve this distinctive heritage, Prince Rainier III ordered that the teaching of Monégasque be mandatory in public primary schools from 1976. The requirement was extended to include private schools from 1988 onwards. The language is now taught until middle school level, and pupils may opt to study it as part of the French high school baccalaureate. The establishment of cultural associations aimed at promoting the language and governmental support for the use of Monégasque in public signage and communications has further consolidated the language's position, although it remains endangered.

Monégasque syntax and phonology demonstrate its Romance-language heritage while also showcasing unique features that distinguish it from other Romance languages. Syntax-wise, it follows typical patterns, such as SVO word order and adjective–noun agreement, so 'I love Monaco' is 'Mi amo Múnegu'. The phonology is simple, in comparison to many Romance languages, with five vowel sounds, which can be short or long:

Short vowels: /a/, /e/, /i/, /o/, /u/
Long vowels: /aː/, /eː/, /iː/, /oː/, /uː/

Monégasque consonants follow typical Romance patterns, but with some unique features as well. The consonant /ʒ/ (like the 's' in 'measure') is common, as in the word 'mə'ʒu' (meaning 'apple') and the consonant /k/ can be pronounced as /tʃ/ (like the sound at the beginning of the word 'church') before front vowels (/e/ and /i/), as in 'tʃo'zɛː' (meaning 'cheese').

There are still very few native speakers. Monaco's population is largely made up of immigrants drawn to its climate, lifestyle, and tax-status advantages. Only around a fifth of the population is native to the principality. Monaco, as well as being densely populated, has one of the most cosmopolitan populations on the planet. This does not make revitalizing a native tongue any easier.

I meet Claude Passet, the secretary general of the Académie des langues dialectales, in a small building that seems more like an informal library than an academy. It's early April but already unseasonably hot, and I'm glad to sit in the cool room amid piles and piles of books and chat, mostly in Italian, but with odd smatterings of French when he says a word I don't quite understand.[8]

Claude was born in the 1940s and remembers the years when the language was banned, when a whole generation was 'forbidden from using it'.

My generation did not learn Monégasque. We couldn't speak it at school – it was considered a vulgar, popular language. I was given lines to write over and over, 'I must not speak in dialect'. But in Monaco-Ville, occasionally people would still speak Monégasque in the street in the 1960s. The kids repeated what they heard and we learned, if not the language, then at least some vocabulary from it.

He says the challenge now is to bring it back to life. He agrees that it's good that it's once again taught in schools, 'but it's not enough, two hours a week just isn't enough to make the language seem anything but a kind of relic'. A small number of phrases persist in everyday use among those who don't speak the language. He gives me an example: 'If you want to say someone is tight-fisted, we say that he has "a sea urchin in his pocket".'

In 2021, there were only two students taking the Monégasque option up to the baccalaureate. 'It's not much,' Claude laments, 'but it's inevitable. These days everything is English, even in Europe, but especially here. In a country with so very many nationalities, with languages that are all different, the common one is always English – it makes it impossible.'

In one sense, the passionate attempts to rekindle interest in an old language seem anachronistic in today's Monaco, a place of high-rises and a futuristic eco development reclaimed from the sea, but in another, it isn't at all. Old Monaco towers above Monte Carlo, cobbled streets with colourful houses give way to expansive views, the elegant palace with its stubborn history remains, the street signs are in Monégasque. A sense of the principality and its traditions and people is all-pervasive.

It is easy to imagine, the day following our interview, as I descend the Rampe de la Major to the flower market, that one morning these narrow winding ways of Old Monaco might once again eavesdrop on a casual conversation in easy Monégasque, even if the gleaming metropolis below does not.

8

———— ◇ ————

Language in Conflict

'Non-linguistic conflicts are often projected on to language
differences, and may be played out in the language policies of
governments and other holders of power.'

—Louis Jean Calvet, *Language Wars and Linguistic Politics* (1998)

W**HEN WE TALK** about conflict, we often think
of political upheavals, civil wars, or border
disputes. Yet, one dimension that frequently
gets overlooked is the battlefield of language. As we've
seen throughout this book, languages are vessels of culture,
identity, and historical memory. This chapter focuses on
situations where languages themselves become part of the
conflict, examining the cases of Euskara (or Basque) in
Spain, the linguistic divides in Sri Lanka, and the complex
language politics in the former Yugoslavia. In the Basque
Country, Euskara serves as both a symbol of regional identity
and an expression of political aspirations, challenging the
uniform identity proposed by the Spanish state. Sri Lanka

offers a case study in how linguistic divisions can fuel long-standing ethnic and political conflicts, as seen in the tension between the Sinhala and Tamil communities. The dissolution of former Yugoslavia left a linguistic landscape as fractured as its political one, forcing us to confront questions about how languages are defined, divided, or even created for the purpose of national identity.

Each of these cases offers unique insights into the role that language plays in conflicts and how these battles, in turn, can shape the destiny of languages. Language is not merely a passive element subjected to larger forces; it actively contributes to the formation and crystallization of group identities, sometimes becoming a tool for both unity and division. How did Euskara survive decades of suppression under the Franco regime, and what role does it play in the modern Basque identity? What are the consequences of Sri Lanka's decision to prioritize Sinhala over Tamil, and how has this contributed to civil unrest? How did the Serbo-Croatian language splinter into several 'new' languages in the aftermath of Yugoslavia's break-up, and what does this say about the interplay between language and nationalism? As we explore these questions, we'll see that language wars are more than just a byproduct of social and political discord: they are often at the very heart of these conflicts, shaping and being moulded by them in a complex interplay of history, culture, and power.

Basque and Bertsolaritza

A few years ago, just before the pandemic, I was in Pamplona for a guest talk on my novel, and a graduate student, Irina, asked me if I was interested in going to what she described (in English) as a 'Basque poetry slam' one evening. Of course, I was. She drove me to a hall just on the outskirts of the town. There were competitions, big events, Irina told me, but this was just a local gathering. There might, however, be some good people there to practise or people performing just for the love of it. But the hall was packed. I estimated there might have been a couple of hundred people, a lot of young men and women of an age with Irina, but many older people too. To me, it was more like a musical performance than a slam. The art form 'bertsolaritza' is part of the Basque oral tradition. The performers are given a prompt and must create a bertso – a kind of short poem – on the spot. It has to fit a particular rhythmic structure, which is traditional and strictly observed. Then, selecting a traditional melody, or improvising one as they go, they perform their creation. The performers were as varied as the audience, and, although I couldn't understand any of the language at all, I was caught in the sheer magic of the creativity of the event. Its spontaneity, yet quite rigidly specific requirements, left me in awe of the musical poets. The time taken from receiving the prompt to performance was never longer than a few minutes, and the silence from the audience, during that time, was part of the spell.

And this, I was reminded by my host, was a small amateur gathering and part of an ancient tradition, one of many happening regularly across the Basque Country. Not in the same league, Irina assured me, as the bertsolaritza championships that were so quickly gaining popularity in a growing movement of language nationalism.[1] The event stayed with me, long after I had returned home to Scotland, and I decided to investigate its history and its links to language identity.

The Basques are an ancient ethnic group with a distinct culture and language, Euskara, and history that predates the formation of modern nation-states. Euskara is the most unusual of European tongues – like Ainu, the Japanese language we looked at earlier, it is considered an isolate language, meaning it has no known linguistic relatives. Many linguists believe it predated the arrival of Indo-European languages in Europe. This makes Euskara/Basque one of the oldest living languages in the world.

Historically, the Basque people enjoyed a degree of autonomy within the Kingdom of Navarre and only later became part of the Kingdom of Spain. Largely rural in nature, Basque society maintained its own legal and political institutions. Their oral tradition, which would eventually develop into bertsolaritza, combined song and storytelling and was first noted in the fourteenth century, when travelling 'female improvisers' were described as narrating the historical highlights of the previous two centuries.[2] The 'profazadoreak' were female singers who went singing from village to village, but there were also balladeers and epic minstrels.

In 1801, the first bertsolaritza, a direct ancestor of my own experience, was held. More than four thousand spectators crammed into a village square to hear a competition between two locals. There were strict rules around what meter could be used, and the two men performed improvised songs for a prize of five ounces of gold. The result was a tie, and the event ushered in a phase of many other such events – some competitive, some just for entertainment. Largely rural based, with practitioners who displayed their strong regional dialects, the art form became a symbol of Basque identity.

But the suppression of Spain's multiple identities under Franco took its toll on Euskara, just as it did on Catalan, as we discussed in the previous chapter. During the Spanish Civil War (1936–1939), the Basque Country was republican, but fell under the control of General Francisco Franco's nationalist forces. Under Franco's dictatorship, Basque culture and language were suppressed, and Basque political institutions were dismantled. The language ban lasted until 1975. For thirty-six years, it was illegal to speak Euskara or to write it. But just five years after the ban was enforced, a group of parents had set up a secret language school in Bilbao, the biggest city of the region. By 1970, there were many such clandestine schools and more than eight thousand students learning in secret. Irina told me stories of her father and his own account of a basement school when he moved from the mountains to the city as a young teenager. 'He spoke mostly Euskara anyway,' she said. 'In the mountains it [the ban] wasn't so enforced but in the cities, even in the sixties, there were people who would report you to the police. That could mean imprisonment, worse. There was bertsolaritza even then. My dad told me about one in the cellar of a pub when he was growing up. It was our defiance. Our way of making our language sing.'

In 1959, Euskadi Ta Askatasuna (ETA) was founded as an armed separatist group aiming to establish an independent Basque state. The organization used both political and violent means, carrying out bombings, assassinations, and acts of terrorism throughout Spain, with the goal of achieving independence and social revolution. But it was not until Franco's death that nationalist parties and movements were able to emerge and to demand recognition of Basque identity, language, and self-governance.

The Spanish constitution of 1978 recognized and granted significant autonomy to the Basque Country, just as it did to Catalonia. The Basque region would have its own government and a devolved degree of legislative and executive powers. It wasn't enough for ETA, who refused to settle for anything less than independence and continued its campaign of violence and terrorism, targeting Spanish security forces, politicians, and civilians. The conflict resulted in numerous casualties, until ETA finally declared a permanent ceasefire in 2011, renouncing the use of violence as a means to achieve its goals. Basque nationalist parties, such as the PNV, have played a prominent role in regional politics, advocating for greater autonomy and Basque identity within the Spanish framework. But many still believe that anything short of independence is untenable. The bertsolaritza events too have evolved. The one I witnessed had elements of rap, and I could understand why Irina had likened it to slam poetry. It seemed urban, somehow, a city cousin to the rural tradition with its village tales and accounts of farming. The performances are a coming together of those who believe that the language is what unites them as a people, within their own culture. I asked Irina if they were mostly very political events these days, and she replied that in some senses, yes, they were, because they were about Basque autonomy and difference, but they were also one of the few spaces where people who believed the goal should be independence came together with those who did not. The language, its new-found freedom, was a celebration that bridged their differences.

The declaration of a common language

Violence and terrorism can be enacted over the right to speak a language; war and genocide kill languages and cultures, or attempt to. But language can also be an implement of peace, of bringing peoples together. In the country that was formerly Yugoslavia, most of the states spoke a language known as Serbo-Croat. The main difference between the regions was that while Croats wrote in the Latin alphabet, Serbians commonly used Cyrillic. Tito's death brought the end of communism to the country and a move from central control to autonomously run regions. With the dissolution of the Soviet Union in 1991, a drive for independence coupled with a further upsurge in ethnic nationalism among its former members spread across the wider continent and led to the Balkan Wars. The long and bloody conflict lasted from 1991 until 2007 and led to the fragmentation of the country into distinct ethnically based countries: Serbia, Montenegro, Bosnia, Croatia, Slovenia, Kosovo, and Macedonia.

Afterwards, each of the newly formed countries renamed their language to echo and reiterate the nationalist sentiment of the area. The regional variations of the language were renamed as new languages according to country: Bosnian, Serbian, Croatian, and Montenegrin, in the former Serbo-Croatian regions, and Macedonian and Slovenian (whose languages had always been distinctive). An area with three languages now had six.

In 2016, a group of linguists got together. They met over the course of twelve months at four conferences, one in each of the countries of the former Serbo-Croat regions. On 30 March 2017 they concluded their discussions by signing an agreement, 'The Declaration of Common Language'. The four languages, Bosnian, Serbian, Croatian, and Montenegrin, were all really variations of the same language. The declaration was drafted by thirty experts, half of whom were linguists. It also had over two hundred signatories from the four different countries. When the declaration was opened to signing by others, the signatures rose to over eight thousand. The agreement stated that because the four distinct peoples could communicate effectively without needing an interpreter or translator, the variations were, in fact, of a common polycentric language, one that had developed differently in different states but which remained similar enough in these different versions to still be classified as a single language. Just like French, for example, which is spoken in France, Canada, Switzerland, and Belgium, but where each variation does not represent a language on its own. The purpose of the declaration was clearly laid out too. It would counter 'the negative social, cultural, and economic consequences of political manipulations of language in the current language policies' of the four countries.[3]

The policy of marking linguistic distinctiveness as uniqueness had led to divisiveness, to each language being seen as an expression of ethnic nationalism. Each country could have its own version of the common language, but there would be no difference in status, no discrimination made between the forms, and each would enjoy equal rights in terms of education and public use. It stated:

Therefore we, the undersigned, call for
- abolishing all forms of linguistic segregation and discrimination in educational and public institutions.
- discontinuing the repressive and needless practices of language separation that are harmful to the speakers;
- terminating the rigid definition of the standard variants;
- avoiding the superfluous, senseless and costly 'translations' in legal proceedings, administration and public information media;

- the freedom of individual choice and respect for linguistic diversity;
- linguistic freedom in literature, the arts and the media;
- the freedom of dialectal and regional use;
- and finally, the freedom of 'mixing', mutual openness and interpenetration of different forms and expressions of the common language, to the benefit of all its speakers.[4]

One issue remained, however: what would the newly recognized language be called? It still varies. When I travelled in the region, I heard many people refer to it as Serbo-Croat and Croat Serbian, but the term BCSM is also popular in the media (Bosnian, Croatian, Serbian, Montenegrin) and, of course, many people still use the old distinctive terms. But it was a step towards unification, a different approach, where celebrating similarity in language, rather than championing differences, might begin to help heal the scars and wounds of a bloody war.

Sri Lankan language wars

Conflict and language are common bedfellows, though, and it was again the unbreakable connection between ethnicity and language that marked the civil war in Sri Lanka. I went to Sri Lanka in a calm moment between the waves of war. I had a string of introductions for a book I was writing at the time that was nothing to do with linguistics, yet so many of my interviews and discussions returned to it as a subject. The Tamil people I met were impassioned, almost desperate, in their descriptions of injustice and inequity. Many Singhalese people empathized with the history of oppression but found it impossible to forgive or accept what they saw as retributive, terrible acts. It was a cycle of bitterness, and as a mere onlooker I could do little but listen.

There have been Tamil speakers in Sri Lanka since the second century BCE. The Sri Lankan Tamils (a distinct group from Indian Tamils) are one of the two main ethnic groups on the island. The Singhalese are the majority group and primarily inhabit the southern and central parts of the country; the Tamils are concentrated in the north and the east. The two languages are markedly different, even belonging to different language families: Sinhala is classified as an Indo-Aryan language and Tamil is classified as a Dravidian language. As is so often the case, the origin of the conflict lies in colonization.

During colonial British rule, English was established as the administrative language, which created a divide between those who could access education and opportunities through English and those who couldn't. This linguistic division continued even after Sri Lanka gained independence in 1948.

One of the most significant events that fuelled the language conflict was the introduction of the Sinhala Only Act by the newly elected government led by Solomon Bandaranaike. This act made Sinhala, the tongue of the majority of the population, the sole official language of the country, effectively sidelining

Tamil. This move was seen by the Tamil minority as a discriminatory measure that marginalized them from government jobs, education, and other opportunities.

The Sinhala Only Act, officially known as the Official Language Act No. 33 of 1956, was a pivotal piece of legislation that played a significant role in the language conflict in Sri Lanka during the last century. Enacted on 22 June 1956, this law displaced English and effectively marginalized the Tamil language-speaking minority. Government functions, official communications, legal documents, education, and other important aspects of public life would be conducted exclusively in Sinhala. Prior to the Sinhala Only Act, Sri Lanka had been operating with both Sinhala and Tamil as official languages, along with English. This bilingual system was intended to ensure equal treatment and representation for both Sinhalese and Tamil speakers. The act eliminated Tamil as an official language at the national level. Tamil speakers faced insurmountable challenges in accessing government services, education, and employment, as proficiency in Sinhala became a requirement for these opportunities. Schools that were previously bilingual shifted to teaching primarily in Sinhala. This led to difficulties for Tamil-speaking students, many of whom did not have a strong command of the Sinhala language. There were economic and political implications. Tamil-speaking individuals faced barriers to government employment and other economic opportunities due to their lack of proficiency in Sinhala, and this led to deep resentment from feelings of disenfranchisement and unequal representation in various sectors of society.

The act became a catalyst for Tamil nationalism, with the demand for greater autonomy and rights for the Tamil-speaking minority leading to the formation of political parties and movements advocating for the rights of Tamil speakers, including calls for a separate Tamil state. The Tamil community's demands for linguistic and cultural rights evolved into broader calls for political autonomy and self-determination. This gave rise to political parties like the Tamil United Liberation Front (TULF) and militant groups like the Liberation Tigers of Tamil Eelam (LTTE), which pursued separatist agendas, sometimes by bloody means. In a downward spiral of act and retaliation, in 1958 anti-Tamil riots brought further death and devastation. The Tamil Language (Special Provisions) Act in the same year reintroduced Tamil as a language for some administrative functions and of school-level education – but it was too little too late for the Tamil community and did little to assuage the tensions.[5]

In 1983, anti-Tamil riots erupted in Colombo, resulting in significant loss of life and property. This event marked a turning point, leading to the formal outbreak of the Sri Lankan Civil War. This war, characterized by brutal violence and human-rights abuses on both sides, lasted for nearly three decades and resulted in a staggering loss of life. The LTTE used suicide bombings, assassinations, and guerrilla warfare tactics, while the Sri Lankan government launched military campaigns to defeat the insurgency.

During my own travels across the country, the conversations where language was raised were almost exclusively with

Tamils. With Singhalese, the stories were of atrocities and missing children. But, of course, my experience was limited; my conversations were in English and were no more than a handful of views.

Tarika is a young Tamil woman who was working in Colombo as a receptionist when I met her. She speaks English, Tamil, and Singhalese and freely volunteered that the only reason she spoke Singhalese was because her mother had been forced to learn it during the period of the Sinhala Only Act. I was there to speak to her about childlessness, but we ended up speaking about the wishes and hopes she had for a yet unborn child: 'I'm proud to be Tamil. I'm proud of my identity, my religion, my ethnicity. I can express myself differently in my own language.'

It was immediately noticeable that, despite being raised bilingually, Tarika made very explicit distinction between Tamil as her 'own' language' and Singhalese as a 'useful' language to have learned.

If we have a child, she can learn Singhalese for her work prospects, although I wish that still didn't have to be the case, it just is, there's no other way about it. But we will always speak Tamil in our home, it will always be the language she belongs to.

She paused to offer me some tea in a small delicately painted porcelain cup in an oddly recurring ritual of my trip. In the burning early summer heat, I was repeatedly offered tea in fragile vessels that looked like they belonged in an old English country house. I thanked her and she smiled, then continued:

> It's an uneasy peace here, for us. More like two countries than one, and the one where most people speak my language is home, whereas the other will always be foreign, and I will always be different there. But the different one, the foreign one, is where I need to be to give my child the best life she can have when she comes. I hope in her lifetime, if not in mine, she will be able to be all she can be with only Tamil, but I can't take the risk that it will ever be so.

The Tajikstan language conflict

In Tajikistan, a language conflict has also been the precursor to years of bloodshed. Before the arrival of Russian and then Soviet influences, the lands of modern-day Tajikistan were part of a Persianate world. Tajik, essentially a variant of Persian, was the dominant language. But in the mountainous region of Gorno-Badakhshan, there were exceptions. Populated mainly by the Pamiri people, this area had its own set of Eastern Iranian languages, such as Shughni, Rushani, and Wakhi.

When Tajikistan became part of the Soviet Union, in 1929, an initial policy of 'Korenization' (Russian коренизация) to integrate non-Russian nationals into the Soviet government, or 'nativization', encouraged the use and development of local languages. This was in marked contrast to the Russification of the preceding century, which had forced non-ethnic Russians to give up their cultures and languages. However, as Stalin consolidated power, this policy was rolled back. Russian again became the lingua franca, promoted as the language of the future, of science, and of culture. Tajik and Russian were taught in schools, but knowledge of Russian was a requirement for any kind of upward mobility. The Pamiri languages, meanwhile, were relegated to domestic use and received very little official attention or support.

The Russian language became further entrenched in all aspects of life. It was the language of the military, bureaucracy, and higher education. Russian-language media dominated, and people who were fluent in Russian had better job prospects. Meanwhile, Tajik remained significant but was confined especially to rural areas and within Tajik families. Pamiri languages were still used in Gorno-Badakhshan, but they had no official status and were not part of any formal education. The Soviet government began a campaign of resettlement. Vast amounts of Pamiris – reported numbers vary between 40 and 70 per cent – were deported against their will to farms at lower altitudes; traditional crafts were discouraged, as were the crops the Pamiri had grown for centuries. Gorno-Badakhshan became one of the poorest regions in the country.[6]

A language law introduced in 1989 aimed to make Tajik the only language of business by 1996, thus preventing the

Pamiris from using their language at all in business or education. Tajikistan's independence in 1991 was followed by a devastating civil war, from 1992 to 1997, that had complex ethnic, regional, and political dimensions. Gorno-Badakhshan became a stronghold for opposition forces, led by the Lali Badakhshan Party, further isolating the Pamiri community from mainstream Tajik society. And after the war was over, with a victory for the Tajikstani government, discrimination against the Pamiris continued, resulting in continual outbreaks of violence and fighting.

In the wake of the civil war, the Tajik government pushed hard to promote the Tajik language as a way to forge a unified national identity. A policy of 'Tajikization' started to take form. Russian loanwords were replaced by native or Persian alternatives, and Tajik became more prominent in official and public settings. However, Russian still retained its prestige and utility, especially for international business and diplomacy. Once again, the Pamiri languages were excluded from any kind of official recognition, status, or support.

They remained marginalized, and although there were sporadic efforts to document these languages and even to introduce them into local schooling, they were unsuccessful in gaining any widespread support outside of the community. The Minority Rights Group charity (MRG) reported widespread discrimination and extremely limited language rights. In 2012 and 2015, violent clashes broke out between the Pamiri and the Tajik government. The Tajik government responded by refusing to acknowledge the distinct language or ethnic identity of Pamiri and instead promoted the view that they were closely associated with Islamic fighters. The position of Pamiri speakers continues to deteriorate: there are no national programmes on television or radio; even in Gorno-Badakhshan, there's a belief that regional broadcasting has become little more than a Tajik propaganda machine. MRG has recently reported on the shutdown of civil society and the detention and torture of leading Pamiri figures. Frequent internet blockades mean that even the linguistic internet communities that have proved so vital for other language communities under threat and in conflict are not viable, either for the education of Pamiri youth or for language perseverance.

Pamiri girls and young women have long enjoyed more freedom and less pressure to marry early than Tajik girls. But these small triumphs are now being eroded, along with their individual identity and the language that carries it.[7] In the midst of this decline, some Russian academics offer up papers about the vocabularies of the Pamiri languages, attempts to gather the words that are significant for those activities where local communication is essential, for agriculture and the medicinal uses of plants, the protection and understanding of sacred sites and the values they represent. The value of the ecological knowledge within the Pamiri languages is recognized, albeit sparsely. They note that the different language communities, denied access to other such groups in the region and to any form of media, are often unaware that the language they use every day is under threat.[8]

And in a final irony, one of the most important traditional activities, that of performing religious poetry – 'maddoh' (maddāḥ) or 'maddohkhoni' (maddāḥkhāni) – flourishes in the dominant language, Tajik Persian. It is unique to the Pamiri, who are Ismaili rather than Sunni Muslims. Yet it is regarded by the Pamiri people as one of their most powerful expressions of unique identity.

The stark disparity between languages deemed to be a symbol of education and progression with those regarded as lesser is at its most pronounced during conflict and colonization. Yet despite derogation, these banned and discriminated tongues can hold crucial information for our understanding of the planet, as well as cultural understanding of geographic spaces and diverse peoples. As wars wage on, languages may always be among their victims, but there is hope in the recognition of the inherent value of multilingual societies and what that gives to all of us.

9

———◁◦▷———

Language Revival

'Ma te rongo, ka mohio
Ma te mohio, ka marama
Ma te marama, ka matau
Ma te matau, ka ora.'
(Through listening, comes awareness,
Through awareness, comes understanding,
Through understanding, comes knowledge
Through knowledge, comes life and well-being.)

—te reo Māori proverb

SOMETIMES THE ENDURANCE, even flourishing, of a language through diverse historical and geographical contexts serves to underscore its linguistic robustness. Te reo Māori is one such case, having navigated the perils of colonial history to emerge as a language that not only survives but also thrives in a contemporary world. Hebrew is another, an ancient tongue that was brought back to life, recreated by determination, drive, and dedication to be a language for its people. Their stories not only shed light on the unique attributes of both of these very different languages but can also offer us some understanding of linguistic evolution and resilience in the face of ever-changing socio-cultural landscapes.

Hebrew: creating a new language for a modern world

The Hebrew language can be traced to the second millennium BCE, where it emerged as a Canaanite language in the region corresponding to modern-day Israel and Palestine. The earliest extant texts in Hebrew are the Gezer Calendar, a small limestone tablet that wasn't discovered until the early twentieth century, twenty miles to the west of Jerusalem, and five lines of text on an ancient floor – the Qeiyafa ostracon – in Israel's Elah Fortress. Both date from the tenth century BCE. However, it wasn't until the period between the twelfth and sixth centuries BCE that Classical Biblical Hebrew became prevalent, primarily as a literary and liturgical medium. This period saw the composition of large portions of the Hebrew Bible, including the Torah, and consequently this form of Hebrew became deeply embedded in Jewish liturgical and scholarly tradition.

Following the Babylonian exile in the sixth century BCE, there was a marked shift in the linguistic landscape of the Jewish community. Aramaic, the lingua franca of the Near East, began to exert influence, leading to the emergence of

Late Biblical Hebrew, which showcased a significant Aramaic substrate. By the end of the Second Temple period (around 70 BCE), Aramaic had substantially displaced Hebrew as the everyday language of Jews in both the Land of Israel and the diaspora. Hebrew did continue to thrive, but now primarily as a language of religious scholarship, prayer, and literature.

Throughout the Middle Ages, while Hebrew was not the daily spoken language of most Jews, it remained a vibrant channel for literary, philosophical, and poetic expressions. Eminent Jewish scholars like Rashi (1040–1105), Maimonides (1135–1204), and Judah Halevi (1075–1141) composed significant works in Hebrew, reinforcing its status as the language of Jewish intellectual and spiritual life. In parallel, the diasporic Jewish communities developed a variety of Judeo-languages such as Judeo-Arabic, Yiddish, and Ladino, which integrated Hebrew elements into the local vernaculars of their respective regions.

During the Renaissance, Europe experienced a renewed interest in classical languages and antiquity. As a result, Hebrew, along with Greek and Latin, began to be studied by Christian scholars eager to access biblical texts in their original form. This period of revival witnessed the establishment of Hebrew chairs in European universities, such as the University of Wittenberg in 1502. The driving force behind this movement was primarily Christian Hebraists, such as Johann Reuchlin in Germany and Guillaume Postel in France, who advocated for the study of Hebrew as an essential component of a deeper understanding of the Christian Bible.

These years were also marked by dynamic interactions both within Jewish communities and between Jews and the broader European intellectual milieu, and saw Hebrew positioned not merely as a liturgical language but also as a bridge to the ancient world, a symbol of Jewish continuity. It was the foundation for what would later see it transformed into a medium for national resurgence. But this introduction belies the fact that the story of Hebrew isn't just one narrative but is about the ways a language came to evolve and be used in very different parts of the world.

North Africa, the expanse from Egypt's Nile Delta to Morocco's Atlantic coast, is a region with a richly diverse assortment of cultures and languages. And amid this mosaic, the Hebrew language found a significant, albeit often overlooked, niche. The presence of Jews in North Africa predates the Common Era, with communities established during the time of the Phoenicians and the Roman Empire. The ancient synagogues discovered in places like Carthage (in modern-day Tunisia) bear testament to a thriving Jewish life during antiquity. These communities, for the most part, would have used Hebrew primarily for liturgical purposes, as was common among diasporic Jewish communities. However, the first significant influx of Jews, and by extension the Hebrew language, into North Africa occurred after the fall of the Second Temple in Jerusalem in 70 CE. A second would follow, centuries later, with the expulsion of Jews from Spain.

In places like Fez in Morocco and Tlemcen in Algeria, Jewish academies or 'yeshivot' were established, becoming centres of Talmudic and Kabbalistic studies. These institutions played a vital role in ensuring the continuity of the Hebrew language, as they emphasized both its liturgical and scholarly use. Hebrew, in these centres, was the language for intellectual discourse, as well as that of prayer.

The daily life of Jews in North Africa, however, was mostly conducted in the vernacular languages of the region. In the Maghreb, which includes countries like Morocco, Algeria, and Tunisia, Jews spoke varieties of Maghrebi Arabic and Berber, depending on their location. Yet even in these languages Hebrew made its mark. Hebrew loanwords, especially those connected to religious practices and life-cycle events, were incorporated into their daily speech. Thus, for example, Hebrew 'שוורša' (saxor), meaning 'black', still denotes a type of black bread among older Bedouin today.

While Hebrew maintained its primary role as a religious language, the region's broader sociopolitical developments influenced its status. The colonial era, especially the French occupation of much of North Africa, brought European languages to the forefront, often pushing indigenous languages, including Hebrew, to the periphery. However, post-independence movements and the subsequent formation of Israel in the mid-twentieth century led to renewed interest in Hebrew, both among Jews and, for geopolitical reasons, the broader North African populace.

The eventual emigration of the majority of North African Jews to Israel, France, and other parts of the world in the twentieth century marked a shift in the role of Hebrew in the region. In Israel, many North African Jews began to use Hebrew as their daily language, infusing it with the intonations and expressions of their native North African tongues.

The history of Hebrew is also enfolded in Europe, and the two divergent threads met most significantly in the late fifteenth century. In 1492, a major event changed the course of Jewish history: the Spanish expulsion of Jews. The Alhambra Decree, ruled by the Catholic monarchs Ferdinand and Isabella, forced countless Jews to embark on a journey that would take them to unfamiliar lands and challenge their resilience. The Spain from which the Jews were expelled was one they had called home for centuries. There, Jews, Christians, and Muslims had coexisted, often peacefully, contributing to what is fondly remembered as a 'golden age' of cultural and intellectual collaboration. Jewish poets, scholars, and physicians held esteemed positions, and their contributions enriched both Spanish and Jewish heritage. However, with the rise of the Catholic Reconquista, this convivial atmosphere began to deteriorate. The 1492 decree gave Spanish Jews a painful ultimatum: convert to Christianity or leave the kingdom. While many chose to convert, either genuinely or superficially (the latter group becoming 'Conversos' or 'Marranos'), a large number decided to retain their Jewish faith and identity, which meant uprooting their lives.

Setting foot outside Spain, the Sephardic Jews (named 'Sephardic' from 'Sefarad', the Hebrew name for Spain) spread in multiple directions. The Ottoman Empire with its vast territories, including present-day Turkey, Greece, and parts of the Balkans, welcomed these refugees. Sultan Bayezid II, viewing the Spanish decree as folly, saw an opportunity in attracting the skills and expertise of the expelled Jews to his domains, so that cities like Salonica, Istanbul, and Izmir soon became new centres of Sephardic life. North Africa, with regions like modern-day Morocco, Algeria, and Tunisia, also drew significant numbers of Sephardic Jews. Here, they often mingled with pre-existing Jewish communities, enriching the local traditions with their Andalusian practices, music, and flavours.

Further afield, Sephardic Jews ventured to places like the Netherlands, particularly Amsterdam, where they played a role in the city's burgeoning mercantile prowess. Some even ventured across the Atlantic to the New World, finding their way to regions of the Caribbean and, later, the nascent colonies of North America. The Sephardic diaspora was a journey of not just miles but also of cultural displacement and dispersal. They took with them their Ladino language, a fusion of medieval Spanish with Hebrew, and their culinary traditions, merging Spanish tastes with those of their adopted lands and leaving us a legacy of food from the almond pastries of Morocco to the aubergine dishes of Turkey.

In Venice, the first complete Hebrew Bible was published in 1517. Venice's strategic position as a trade hub meant that it quickly became a centre for Hebrew printing. This wasn't limited to religious texts: works spanning various disciplines, including science and philosophy, were also printed in the language.

However, this growing interest in Hebrew wasn't just within Jewish communities. As scholars turned to original Greek and Latin sources, there was a similar movement towards studying the Hebrew Bible in its original language. Recognizing the importance of Hebrew for biblical studies, institutions like the University of Bologna even introduced formal courses in the language.

The Vatican in Rome, despite being the centre of Catholicism, also took a significant role in the language's revitalization; it accumulated a considerable collection of Hebrew manuscripts. These texts were often studied, and in some cases even directly commissioned, by the Church. They include numerous texts of Halakhah, Kabbalah, and Talmudic commentaries.[1] This enhanced focus on Hebrew among Christian scholars led to increased interactions between them and Jewish rabbis and scholars, who were sought for their expertise in the language. The printing press further amplified the spread and standardization of Hebrew. By the sixteenth century, Jewish texts, including the Talmud, were widely printed and disseminated.

In the new settled Jewish communities across Europe, the daily usage of Hebrew was overshadowed by vernacular languages, such as Yiddish in Eastern Europe and Ladino among Sephardic communities. But Hebrew retained a sacrosanct place in religious studies, and the yeshiva (religious academy) system ensured its continuity as the medium for Talmudic and biblical studies.

By the eighteenth and nineteenth centuries, the rise of the Haskalah, or Jewish Enlightenment, brought about a new paradigm in the use of the language. Maskilim (proponents of the Haskalah) viewed Hebrew as a tool to modernize Jewish culture. Poets and authors such as Moses Mendelssohn, Naphtali Herz Wessely, and, later, Hayim Nahman Bialik began using Hebrew to address contemporary issues, penning essays, poems, and stories that grappled with the challenges and aspirations of modern Jewish life. This literary movement set the stage for Hebrew's transition from a classical language to a potential vernacular for modern Jewish living.

In parallel, Eastern European Jewry, particularly in Russia, faced intense sociopolitical pressures that culminated in the pogroms of the late nineteenth century. As Zionist ideologies began to crystallize in response to these challenges, the vision of a national homeland for Jews became intertwined with the idea of a linguistic revival. The language of God, modernized for contemporary needs, was seen as an instrument for uniting a dispersed people.

Eliezer Ben-Yehuda, or Eliezer Yitzhak Perlman, (1858–1922) played a pivotal role in the modern revival of Hebrew as a spoken language. His work was rooted in the broader context of nineteenth-century European nationalism. Advocating the principle that language is central to national identity, as espoused by eighteenth-century philosopher Johann Gottfried Herder, Ben-Yehuda saw the restoration of Hebrew as essential to the Jewish national identity.

One main challenge in this restoration was the need to expand the lexicon of Hebrew to address modern concepts and technologies not present in biblical times. For example, the term 'bicycle' was developed as 'מיינפוא' (ofanayim) by adapting the root word for 'wheel'. Moreover, Ben-Yehuda borrowed and adapted words from other languages, as seen in the adaptation of 'telephone' to 'זופלט' (telephone). Existing Hebrew words were also given updated meanings: 'בכר' (rechev), for instance, shifted from 'chariot' in biblical contexts to 'vehicle' in modern usage.

In his personal life, Ben-Yehuda practised Hebrew as the sole language of communication in his household. His son, Itamar Ben-Avi, is cited as the first native speaker of Modern Hebrew. Publicly, Ben-Yehuda utilized media to promote Hebrew. He founded the *HaZvi* newspaper in 1884, which introduced and standardized new linguistic forms for the Yishuv, the Jewish community in Palestine.[2]

Recognizing the need for a central linguistic reference, Ben-Yehuda began compiling a Hebrew dictionary. Completed posthumously by his family, it documents the evolution of Hebrew across different periods. Ben-Yehuda also emphasized the role of education in the preservation and growth of Hebrew. He was instrumental in the establishment of Hebrew-based educational institutions. To maintain linguistic standards, he founded the Va'ad HaLashon in 1890, a precursor to the Hebrew Language Academy, which was responsible for the ongoing development of Modern Hebrew.

The language of the Māori people of New Zealand

Other languages, despite centuries of being victimized by colonization, are starting to reclaim their rightful position in the world. Te reo Māori is the indigenous language of the Māori people of New Zealand; its resurgence is a testament to the resilience of indigenous cultures worldwide. Beyond its history, te reo Māori also offers a plethora of unique linguistic features that set it apart from many of the world's languages, as well as a glimpse of how a successful language recovery can begin.

Te reo Māori's origins can be traced back to the Eastern Polynesian languages. Māori ancestors, often referred to as the great voyagers, arrived in Aotearoa (New Zealand) around the thirteenth century. These settlers brought with them a proto-Polynesian language that, over several generations, adapted to the new environment, eventually evolving into te reo Māori.

But the late eighteenth and early nineteenth centuries saw the arrival of European missionaries and settlers. Initially, there was some eagerness to learn each other's languages, and te reo Māori was an integral part of a developing multilingual society. The Māori, realizing the advantages of written communication, quickly adopted the Latin script, so that by the mid-nineteenth century a significant portion of the Māori population was literate in their own language, and numerous texts, including the Bible, were translated into te reo Māori. However, with the Treaty of Waitangi in 1840 and subsequent colonization, English became dominant, especially in administrative and legal domains. English-centric policies in schools actively discouraged Māori children from speaking their native tongue. Punishments, of the kind already discussed for many of the languages in other chapters, for using te reo were commonplace. The decline of the language was swift and continued long into the twentieth century. Young people believed that to do well they needed to focus on the English language and reject their own tongue. Only a few young people were able to succeed and gain influence, but they did not forget where they had come from. The Nga Tama Toa was a university-based Māori political movement that began to publicly question government language policy and the rights of its people. In conjunction with other grassroots movements, driven by Māori leaders and activists, the first kōhanga reo (language nests) and kura kaupapa (Māori immersion schools) were established.[3]

The kōhanga reo were not schools where only te reo Māori was spoken, but rather classrooms involving the whole family, with elders educating the youngest of extended family groups, not only in the language but also in cultural tradition and belief. In 1987, the Māori Language Act finally provided the much-needed legislative support, recognizing te reo Māori as an official language of New Zealand.

In 1987, after hundreds of years of discrimination, the Māori people in New Zealand finally had their language designated an official one. The commission established because of the Māori Language Act stated one of its core aims was to

'Promote the Māori language, and in particular its use as a living language and as an ordinary means of communication'.[4]

At the time, it might have seemed like a wish rather than an aim, but, against the odds, Māori has triumphed to become one of the great language success stories of our times. Māori bands singing in their language routinely get to the number-one position in the charts. The song 'Wairua' by the Māori group Maimoa Music is the most watched YouTube video of 2018 in the whole of New Zealand, with more than 5.5 million hits. Language classes in Auckland and Wellington have long waiting lists. Mainstream broadcasting includes Māori presenters, and the few words that were scattered into the New Zealand English-speaking vocabulary, like 'kia ora' (hello), Aotearoa (New Zealand), and 'aroha' (love), have expanded to include 'mahi' (work), 'puku' (belly), and 'kai' (food), as well as many others.

Linguistically, te reo Māori has many original and distinctive features. It is well-known in linguistic circles for its consistent phonemic inventory. With just ten consonants and five vowels (which can be short or long), the language's phonetic simplicity stands out. Long vowels, essential in differentiating word meanings, are represented by a macron (tohutō) above the vowel. For instance, 'keke' means 'cake', whereas 'kēkē' refers to 'armpit'.

It is primarily agglutinative, meaning it often uses prefixes and suffixes to change word meanings. For example, the word for 'child' is 'tamaiti', but for 'children' you'd say 'tamariki'. The morpheme '-riki' here acts as a pluralizer.

Particles play an interesting and pivotal role in te reo Māori. These are short words that can indicate tense, mood, or negation. For instance, the particle 'ka' is often used to denote the future tense or a change of state. In Māori, pronouns and possessive structures differ based on inclusivity and exclusivity. For example, 'tātou' means 'we' including the listener, while 'mātou' means 'we' excluding the listener.

Many Māori words encapsulate meanings often not directly translatable into English. Let's consider the term 'whakapapa'. At a superficial level, it might be translated as 'genealogy', but the concept it embodies is something far more complex. Whakapapa is the interwoven lineage of mountains and rivers, humans and gods, past and present. It is the narrative that binds the Māori to their ancestors, their environment, and each other.

Other lexical items illustrate the complex interconnectedness of their belief system: 'mana' refers to a combination of authority, power, and spiritual strength, while 'tapu' can mean sacred, but also encompasses notions of restriction and prohibition.

The digital age, marked predominantly by the rise of the internet, has offered an unparalleled platform for decolonization, for the revitalization and enhanced understanding of te reo Māori. With the advent of online learning platforms, tutorials, and mobile applications, acquiring foundational knowledge of the language has become more accessible than ever. Websites offer interactive courses, while apps facilitate daily practice, pronunciation guides, and vocabulary building.

Platforms like Duolingo have integrated te reo Māori into their offerings, making it feasible for anyone worldwide to engage with the language. Social media platforms, discussion forums, and dedicated websites provide spaces for Māori speakers, learners, and enthusiasts to connect. These digital communities foster discussions, offer clarifications, and share resources. The likes of Facebook and X, formerly Twitter, witness periodic challenges like 'Māori Language Week', encouraging users to post exclusively in te reo.

The internet has also democratized content creation. Today, there are numerous Māori podcasts, YouTube channels, music playlists, and online radio stations. Many classic Māori texts, stories, and educational materials, which were previously hard to access, have been digitized and are now freely available online. The integration of te reo Māori into software has further promoted its usage. Web browsers offer Māori as a language option, and there are Māori keyboards and predictive-text tools, making it simpler for users to communicate in the language digitally. The Te Whanake website, created by New Zealand academic Professor John Moorfield, offers a huge array of free resources for learning the language, and there's even a television language-learning show, *Tōku Reo*, based on the site.

The number of New Zealanders who are bilingual is steadily growing too, although not as quickly as some of the language's supporters might wish. At the time of writing, more than thirty per cent of the country described themselves as having a fair knowledge of the language, where that was defined as having more than a handful of words and phrases. In an article for the *Guardian* newspaper in 2022, Debbie Ngarewa-Packer, the co-leader of Te Pāti Māori (the Māori party), described the country's journey to reclaiming te reo Māori: 'It's like trying to spin a big-arse truck into a tiny little one-lane corner. It's a clumsy transformation, but the first steps to walking always are.'

10

---<o>---

Dare to Speak Your Language: Guarani and Gaelic

Ko tetã omoneĩva mokõimi umi ñe'ẽ	This country that claims those two languages
Hetave umíva ári ñe'ẽnguéra oĩva	among the many other languages that exist
Maymavénte ijuky, iporã joaite	all tasty, all beautiful
katu umíva pa'ũgui pe Castilla ñe'ẽ	perhaps among those, the language of Castile
Ojehe'a Guaraníre Ojeavýrõ Jepe	mixes with Guaraní even though they are contrary
ku omendáva oikoháicha ojospýri oikove	like the couple that walks together
há kiñénto ro'ýma ojospy gotyo oke.	and after five hundred years he does not sleep
	embraced/in the same sense.

— Gregorio Gómez Centurión Apysa (Ear),
Tetãygua Pyambu (2017)

Guarani

Paraguay has two official languages, Guarani and Spanish. Surprisingly, and in contradiction to many other cases encountered in this book, the language that is foremost is not the one with the majority of speakers. More Paraguayans speak Guarani than Spanish, yet the latter is regarded as the dominant language of the country. Even today, Guarani speakers, just like the Tamil in Sri Lanka or the Khoikhoi in South Africa, may be regarded as less intelligent and assumed to be of a low economic class. Respect for their culture has been eroded with their language, and, in recent history, the consequences for speaking Guarani have been even worse.

The military dictatorship of Alfredo Stroessner Matiauda is still recalled by Paraguayans as a period of torture and abuse. Matiauda was a Paraguayan military officer who ruled the country with an iron fist for nearly four decades. His dictatorship, which lasted from 1954 to 1989, is known for its authoritarianism, human-rights abuses, and economic mismanagement. This period in Paraguay's history had a profound impact on the nation and its people.

Alfredo Stroessner was born on 3 November 1912 in Encarnación, Paraguay. He joined the Paraguayan army and quickly rose through the ranks, displaying exceptional military skills. Stroessner's opportunity to seize power came on 4 May 1954, when he orchestrated a military coup that ousted the popular President Federico Chaves, who had been in office since 1949. Stroessner assumed the presidency and began his long reign as the country's leader. His right-wing regime was marked by a strong authoritarian rule and the suppression of political opposition. He established the Colorado Party as the sole legal political party in Paraguay, effectively eliminating any viable alternatives. Political opponents were systematically repressed, arrested, or exiled, and censorship was enforced to control the flow of information.

As with most dictators, one of the key aspects of Stroessner's rule was his promotion of nationalism and the cultivation of a cult of personality. He portrayed himself as a guardian of Paraguayan values and traditions, projecting an image of strength and stability. His vision of the past was heroic, harking back to an idyllically depicted heyday.[1] Only national history could be promoted, and protection of this nationalism legitimized the torture and human rights abuses that ensued. The Stroessner regime's economic policies were characterized by a combination of protectionism and crony capitalism. The government implemented protectionist measures to shield domestic industries from foreign competition, but this resulted in a lack of economic diversification and stagnation. Corruption was rampant, with Stroessner and his inner circle enriching themselves through embezzlement and bribery. Meanwhile, most of the population struggled with poverty and limited access to basic services.

Human rights abuses were pervasive during the dictatorship. The government employed a network of secret police and intelligence agencies to monitor and suppress dissent. Torture, extrajudicial killings, and forced disappearances were common tactics used against political opponents. Many individuals and families were forcibly displaced or exiled, leaving behind a legacy of fear and trauma. All these actions were promoted as being necessary to defend the nationalist ideals, the continuation of a nationalist historical narrative. The country's numerous indigenous languages faced severe restrictions and prohibitions. Stroessner's regime sought to promote cultural homogeneity, which led to the suppression of Paraguay's indigenous languages, including that spoken by the majority of the country's people, Guarani.

Stroessner's government implemented policies that favoured the Spanish language over Guarani, aiming to establish Spanish as the dominant language of education, government, and public life. This approach reflected a broader historical trend in Paraguay, where Guarani had long been marginalized in favour of Spanish due to the influence of colonialism and assimilation efforts. Under Stroessner's rule, the use of Guarani in schools was actively discouraged, and students were prohibited from speaking it in classrooms. Spanish became the sole language of instruction, which marginalized Guarani-speaking students and hindered their access to education. The regime saw the promotion of Spanish as a way to modernize the country and integrate Paraguay into the broader Latin American cultural and economic framework. In addition to education, the Stroessner regime also restricted the use of Guarani in official government pro-ceedings and public institutions. Spanish became the exclusive language of bureaucracy, law, and politics. This policy not only undermined the rights of Guarani-speaking Paraguayans but also perpetuated a social divide between those who spoke Spanish and those who primarily spoke Guarani.

The prohibitions on the Guarani language during Stroessner's dictatorship were part of a broader campaign to suppress indigenous cultures and promote a homogenized national identity. The regime's nationalist agenda sought to create a unified Paraguayan identity that aligned with European and Spanish-speaking traditions, while diminishing the importance of indigenous languages and cultures.

Throughout his tenure, Stroessner maintained a tight grip on power through a combination of repression, co-optation, and patronage. He skilfully managed divisions within the military and rewarded loyalty, ensuring his regime's survival for nearly four decades. However, as the 1980s progressed, international pressure and internal opposition began to mount against Stroessner's rule. Paraguayan literature began to develop in such a way that it offered alternatives to the official stories of a glorious past. The suppression of indigenous culture, the constructed narrative of historic heroism and success, were challenged by well-known Paraguayan writers such as Miguel Chase Sardi, Branislava Sušnik, and Helene Castres, while Helio Vera tackled the breakdown of the official stories of identity and race using humour.[2]

Stroessner's regime finally came to an end in 1989 when a military coup led by General Andrés Rodríguez successfully overthrew him. But Guarani remained a marginalized language, regarded as low status and unable to shake the devastating effects of the long dictatorship in its immediate aftermath, even as it continued to be spoken by a significant portion of the Paraguayan population. Guarani was still an integral part of everyday life, particularly in rural areas and among indigenous communities. Gradually, following the end of Stroessner's rule, a growing recognition of the importance of cultural difference and the rights of indigenous communities in the country's post-dictatorship era began to develop.

In 1992, Stroessner's successors enacted a national constitution. This granted indigenous peoples full citizenship, acknowledged them as distinct ethnic groups, and guaranteed their education as well as protection of their culture. Paraguayan Guarani was made the country's official second language and the right to education in Guarani stated in law. With this legislation, Guarani became the first non-European language to achieve official status in the whole of South America.[3]

Finally, in 2010, the Ley No. 4251 de lenguas (Law number 4.251 of Languages) was established to enhance, protect, and promote the use of indigenous languages. It highlighted the prominence and importance of Guarani and depicted the country as bilingual, with a further call for 'respect' of all indigenous languages.[4] It also established a government department that was tasked with liaising with schools to directly ensure indigenous language education. The use of Spanish and Guarani is guaranteed 'in court, in the national government's official communication, for the registration of public documents, for personal identification, for communication in public transit, in academic titles, in the naming of public institutions, and in toponyms'.[5]

Guarani has finally regained recognition as an official language alongside Spanish, and it is increasingly used in education, media, and public discourse. There has been a growing recognition of the importance of cultural autonomy and improved rights for indigenous communities in the country's post-dictatorship era, although the effects of Stroessner's authoritarian rule still linger in the memories of its victims.[6]

Carmen Barrios, now in her seventies, is small and white-haired. She lives in North London, in an apartment with views over heathland, so that on a midsummer afternoon we feel displaced, as if we are in another country, and her first remark to me is a comment on this. She asks that I don't record her so, unusually, I take notes on a pad while we chat, and occasionally ask her to repeat things when she goes too quickly for me to keep up with her. I can understand a little Spanish but not enough for this conversation, so she offers to speak in English, and I thank her, apologizing that I don't know Spanish well or Guarani at all. She tells me she hasn't spoken Guarani in decades and adds that moving to London did what 'that bastard Stroessner' never managed and stopped her using her own language for day-to-day life (she stresses that she loves watching things in Guarani online).

Her gracefulness is apparent as she curls her legs under herself and sits on the sofa opposite me, or perhaps I notice it more because of the image one of her first recollections leaves me with. She remembers being made to cross a classroom on her knees over scattered maize and salt because a teacher heard her speak with a girl sitting next to her in the language she used at home. Like PST, Guarani was a secret language of school classrooms, but whispered, not signed.

'It was the humiliation of it as much as the pain. Silent Guarani girls like me, and the others who just smirked. It made my friend and I more careful but we didn't stop. She was Carmen too,' she tells me. 'She's dead now.' I say I'm sorry and she shrugs, adds, 'It comes to all of us sooner or later. She was seventy when she passed, it's not a bad age for us.

'She was caught speaking Guarani a second time and they didn't give her any food for two days. I smuggled some in for her. It was fear on their part, I think, and also a kind of disgust.

'We disgusted them. Skinny, dark children, speaking nonsense. They said we smelled. Grown-ups disgusted by little innocent girls. Angaité che retã.'

I look lost.

'It means something like "the devil take them".' She smiles and offers me another cup of tea.

Scottish Gaelic

The memories of Carmen Barrios are mirrored by those of people far closer to my home. The persecution of Scottish Gaelic speakers throughout history has been a significant factor in the decline of the language and its struggle for survival. As early as the medieval period, Scottish Gaelic faced numerous threats that contributed to its marginalization as a language. These threats were driven by political, social, and cultural factors, as well as the influence of the English-speaking nobility and the centralization of power.

The Norman conquest of England in 1066 had brought the Norman French aristocracy to power, and this influence extended to Scotland during the reign of David I (1124–1153), who ascended to the throne during a period of political instability and Norse invasions in Scotland. His mother, Queen Margaret, was an Anglo-Saxon princess with ties to the English nobility, including Edward the Confessor and Edgar the Ætheling, and these familial connections helped to create a bridge between the Scottish and English noble families, with implications for the political dynamics of the time. It meant that Scottish nobles often had personal loyalties to and alliances with the English monarch, which influenced their interactions with the Scottish monarchy. But the Scottish nobility's connections to the English crown also created tensions and conflicts within Scotland, as they were torn between their loyalty to the Scottish monarch and their ties to the English crown. David I himself had spent much of his youth at court in England, a refugee from the political turmoil in Scotland, and, inspired by Norman and English practices, began to implement administrative reforms as king. He introduced a feudal system of land ownership, granting land to nobles in exchange for military service and other obligations. This brought him loyalty and established a large, developed hierarchy with the monarchy at its head.

But as land ownership became concentrated in the hands of the nobility, the influence and power of Gaelic-speaking chieftains declined. The feudal system's structure placed predominantly English- and Norman-speaking nobles and landowners at the top, while the Gaelic-speaking clans and their leaders were pushed to the periphery. The nobility's centralized power enabled them to exert control over land and resources so that Gaelic-speaking communities were often displaced or absorbed into the feudal structure, leading to the breakdown of traditional Gaelic-speaking networks and the inevitable loss of ancestral lands.

English was adopted as the official language of the Scottish court, thus excluding Gaelic speakers from positions of power and influence. As with so many other dominant languages, from Spanish to Singhalese, English-speaking officials were appointed to key administrative positions, and Gaelic was gradually replaced by English in legal proceedings, official documents, and diplomatic exchanges.

The king actively encouraged the establishment of towns and the growth of trade and commerce, granting charters to various towns, including Berwick-upon-Tweed, Roxburgh, and Stirling, which allowed them to govern themselves and engage in economic activities. Charters included provision for market rights, allowing towns to control trade within their boundaries according to rules established by the monarchy, as well as the right to collect taxes from these activities, thus

generating income for the court. But these economic trans-
formations also hastened the decline of Scottish Gaelic. The
shift from subsistence agriculture to a more commercialized
economy led to increased interactions with English-speaking
Lowland merchants and a greater reliance on trade with
England. English became not only the language of court and
the nobility, but also acted as a lingua franca for business and
trade, undermining the use of Gaelic.

David I had a close relationship with the Roman Catholic
Church. He founded numerous monastic institutions and
brought in religious orders from continental Europe such as
the Augustinians and Cistercians. The Church became an
important ally of the monarchy, further strengthening its
authority and legitimizing royal power internationally. But,
yet again, the rise of Christianity in Scotland brought further
marginalization to Gaelic. Latin became the language of the
Church and the educated clergy, the language of the Bible,
religious texts, and liturgical practices. The spread of Latin
as the language of the Church contributed to the erosion of
Gaelic's religious and cultural significance. Monastic institutions that provided education conducted lessons in Latin or
French, as did Scottish schools.

The erosion of Gaelic's status and significance was briefly
alleviated during the reign of Robert the Bruce, from 1306
to 1329. He was of Norman French and Anglo-Norman
descent but recognized the importance of Gaelic culture
and sought to navigate the linguistic and cultural diversity
within his kingdom while gaining loyalty from the chiefs in

the Highlands and islands, who still predominantly spoke Gaelic and were hugely influential in the north of the country. The Wars of Scottish Independence benefited hugely from the support of Gaelic chieftains and lords, and the fighting prowess of Highland clans like the MacDonalds, Frasers, and Campbells was crucial to their success. This was acknowledged just six years after the resounding Scottish victory for Robert the Bruce at the Battle of Bannockburn when, in 1320, the Declaration of Arbroath, the Scottish declaration of independence, was drafted.

Addressed to Pope John XXII and written in Latin, it was intended to confirm Scotland's status as an independent nation and assert its right to self-governance. It expressed the Scottish nobility's unwavering support for Robert the Bruce as their rightful king and outlined the legal and historical justifications for Scotland's independence, emphasizing its long-standing autonomy, the importance of popular consent in the choice of a monarch, and the duty to defend the nation's freedom. The signatories were both Gaelic and English speakers – the unity of the nation was represented by its distinctiveness.

But Scotland was multilingual, not bilingual. And by the fifteenth century, the English of Scotland, always written as 'Inglis', was being referred to as Scottis or Scots. Scots was the language of commerce and correspondence and, during the Reformation, would gradually become the language of the Church too. Initially still perceived as a dialect of English, Scots had significant linguistic differences to Southern

English and was widely spoken. But the Reformation would bring further change.

Southern English printed tracts had been circulated as widely as Scots ones and were comprehensible to Scots speakers; the languages were equally in use. But the similarity of the two forms also eroded the distinctiveness of Scots, a process that would have long-reaching consequences. When the Scottish court moved to England in 1603 and James VI brought the Union of the Crowns, the markers of Scots distinctiveness and any prestige that the language had carried dissolved.[7] This change is nowhere more apparent than in the *Basilicon Doron* (The King's Gift) of James VI, a book that was intended as a guide for his son on how to govern. The first edition, from 1599, is indisputably in the Scots language, while the second, from 1603, carries many features of what would come to be known as Standard English.[8]

The court and its creeping Anglicization did not openly target the Scots tongue, but instead used its power to openly target the Gaelic-speaking communities. The clans especially were deemed to be resistant to the new union, stubbornly clinging to their traditional customs and culture, and in many cases to the Roman Catholic religion. The Band and Statutes of Iona of 1609 decreed:

Every gentleman or yeoman in the Islands possessing 'thriescore kye' [60 cattle] and having children, to send at least his eldest son, or, failing sons, his eldest daughter, to some school in the Lowlands, there to be kept and brought up 'until they may be found sufficiently able to speak, read and write English'.[9]

Religion was to be standardized with Highlanders forced to follow the same observance of the Sabbath and of other moralities and the suppression of the inveterate Celtic practice of marriages for a term of years.[10] The statutes were further cemented by a 1616 act that states:

Forasmuch as the King's Majesty, having a special care and regard that the true religion be advanced and established in all the parts of this Kingdom, and that all his Majesty's subjects, especially the youth, be exercised and trained up in civility, godliness, knowledge, and learning, that the vernacular English tongue be universally planted, and the Irish language [i.e., Gaelic], which is one of the chief and principal causes of the continuance of the barbarity and incivility amongst the inhabitants of the Isles and Highlands, may be abolished and removed; and whereas there is no measure more powerful to further his Majesty's principal regard and purpose than the establishing of schools in the particular parishes of this kingdom where the youth may be taught at least to write and read, and be catechised and instructed in the grounds of religion.[11]

These various political decrees had a devastating effect, with Sir Thomas Craig noting: 'I myself remember a time when the inhabitants of the shires of Stirling & Dumbarton spoke pure Gaelic. But nowadays that tongue is relegated ... so that one rarely comes upon any who speak it.'[12]

But it was the eighteenth and nineteenth centuries that would sound the death knell for the vibrant Gaelic communities that still doggedly remained in the Highlands and Islands. The Clearances, ostensibly ordered to find more profitable use for land, were also meant to civilize what were seen as the recalcitrant and unassimilated Gaelic populations of the north. People who had been living in a subsistence farming system based on communal land tenure found themselves evicted from their plots. Homes were burned to the ground, communities devastated, land given over to sheep grazing. Forced emigrations saw Gaelic communities sent to Australia, Canada, and the United States, as well as other parts of the United Kingdom. Those who remained often became labourers on the land that had once been their home. The Highland population declined, rural communities were lost, and Gaelic became a scattered language – although many of the resettled diaspora communities took their language and culture with them, forming New World Gaelic-speaking communities that thrive today, such as that in Nova Scotia.

But, sadly, the Gaelic speakers who remained in Scotland had not seen the last of the discrimination against their language. The later years of the nineteenth century saw the establishment of a centralized education system whose primary aim was to assimilate Gaelic-speaking children into what was being regarded as an English-speaking country.

Children were punished for speaking Gaelic in school, and speakers were openly discriminated against. One unusual and cruel punishment involved the 'maide crochaidh', the punishment stick. Any child caught speaking Scottish Gaelic had to wear it around his or her neck; if they heard another child speaking Gaelic, they passed the stick on. When school was over, the teacher used the stick to beat every child who had carried it earlier in the day.[13]

Finally, in the closing years of the twentieth century and with the dawning of the twenty-first, Scottish Gaelic began to regain recognition and political support. Just as with Māori, bilingual Gaelic–English education is now widespread, and television programmes and films showcase the language. The European Charter for Regional or Minority Languages, signed by the UK government, means that funds must be available for its support, not in education alone, but also for media channels, for public information signs, and for speakers to be able to handle bureaucracy in the Scots Gaelic language.

The Gaelic Language (Scotland) Act of 2005 further ensured Gaelic's status as an official language. Passed by the Scottish parliament, however, it applies only to devolved powers and procedures and not to UK-wide agencies. The creation of the Gaelic Language Board (Bòrd na Gàidhlig) gave direct responsibility to a government body for the protection and promotion of the tongue. In terms of popularity, Gaelic has recently been enjoying a boom. In the past there was a marked reluctance to learn the language, which was often marked as being 'less useful' than a language that was more widely spoken, but in just over ten years there has been an increase of 90 per cent in the number of students in Gaelic-medium primary education, with fierce competition for places in some cities that previously had very little Gaelic presence at all.

The Book Nook coffee shop in Stirling is one of those rare places where you feel relaxed enough to just sit and browse books, or catch up with friends, or, indeed, conduct an informal interview. I meet the writer Kevin MacNeil, who is originally from Stornoway and a Gaelic speaker, there to listen to him speak about what he feels the position of the language is today. It's freezing outside, and we chat for a while before turning to the question of Gaelic. I think I'm expecting something positive from Kevin about the future of Gaelic in our country. There's quite a lot of government spin on how much Gaelic is being lifted from the doldrums of the past, and the only negative things I ever really see are ridiculous comments on social media from people complaining about bilingual road signs and saying the Gaelic ones are not only pointless but could cause an accident. I have always dismissed these as being representative of a tiny minority, minuscule, and picture them living odd lives, draped in Union Jacks and never, ever leaving the UK in case they encounter another language.

But Kevin doesn't paint the picture of a beckoning better future that I expect.

Even the most optimistic people wouldn't think of Gaelic as being in a healthy state now. It's in a perilous state. It's kind of on a life support machine. What's being done now may be too little too late. Education and the media could and should have been supportive but were not. I think of my father who went to school aged five as a monoglot Gaelic speaker and was taught from his first day at school through a foreign language, through English. And then was punished for speaking Gaelic. It's a very insidious form of colonialism, that kind of colonialism engenders an internalised form that is especially difficult to combat. Indigenous Gaelic speakers might say something like 'What's the point in speaking Gaelic?' You go to the mainland and Gaelic won't even get you a pint of milk.

We wander off topic briefly because Kevin's sweet-natured rescue greyhound, Molly, comes to my side of the table and puts her head on my knee.

A language isn't just a means of communication, it's a means of understanding life, and it influences the way you experience life, so it's precious beyond any dictionary definition. For that to be obliterated as people tried to do is really shameful. Even to this day when Gaelic arises, about road signs or whatever, these inane comments arise. I encounter antipathy towards Gaelic often in Scotland. And I'd say I encounter it more in Scotland than anywhere. We don't value it in Scotland the way that we should. Especially given that it was once spoken in most parts.

I ask Kevin what should happen to change the situation, and he focuses on education.

The education system didn't and doesn't teach people their own languages, their own indigenous languages, and it's a real failing. Some people think the miracle is that Gaelic still exists, but I think it exists only in a weak and sorry state. To survive at all in a real way it will take much more of a concerted cultural effort.

Kevin mentions, in a story already familiar from the accounts of Carmen and Singing Bird, that his dad remembers when they were punished for speaking Gaelic in the classroom but still spoke it in the playground. Now, he notes, there's a strange reversal with many Gaelic-medium schools, where kids use the language in the classroom but immediately revert to English outside of it. 'There are also lots of people who say, "I'm like the dog", meaning they can understand the language, referring to working dogs, like collies, but not speak it, and many who are not literate in it because of their education.'

We speak for a while about our attempts to learn languages. I talk about Finnish and how difficult it was to learn, and Kevin points out that even with a language like that, completely distinct from English, it's still possible to immerse yourself in it while you are learning. In Scotland you can't do that with Gaelic any more. He adds:

Even the name of the language, the way it's pronounced 'Gahlik' not 'Geilik', which is the Irish language, is often said wrongly in Scotland. I would say the level of wilfully instilled ignorance in Scotland is appalling. There are just small pockets of optimism. It's easier to learn. People look at Gaelic and think it's impossible to spell, but actually it's far more consistent than English orthography. There are eighteen letters in the alphabet; each one is associated with a different tree. Many place names are Gaelic, but they've been degraded and diminished.

I mention Khoikhoi and my discussion with Denver Toroxa Breda about the South African place names in a language that isn't acknowledged officially. I say how sad it is to think of place names in my own country losing their link to what they used to be called.

The way it was treated was despicable and shameful. Our future needs to include all of our indigenous languages. It's a kind of cultural colonialism. The treatment of the languages arises directly from the need to subdue a peoples.

It seems I have come full circle. Having chased languages around the world, I find that I'm living through a slow decline of one much closer to home. This diminishing, too, will carry away ecological knowledge and the stories of its speakers. I only know half a dozen phrases of Gaelic. I picked them up in my teens when I spent time on boats between Mull and the islands. I did try to learn it for a year or so after, at a hall in Glasgow, in a weekly class given for free by a woman from Tiree. But outside of that hour I never heard it spoken, and in those days even Gaelic broadcasting, which is more established now, was extremely limited. I abandoned my attempts, moved to London, and focused on other languages. I too was guilty of once forgetting, if I even knew at the time, that a language is valuable for its own sake and not only for what it can offer you in your life.

Yet I did know another language, although, while acknowledging its literary and historical importance, I had always thought of it as a modern-day dialect. My mother tongue. In 2015, Scots was officially recognized as one of the indigenous languages of Scotland by the Scottish government in the Scottish Language Act. I had grown up reciting Robert Burns because my dad was an enthusiast. What I referred to as my mum's dialect was broad, picked up in miners' row houses and in fields picking rhubarb and potatoes. Even the words I associated with that part of her early life – rhubarb is 'howked' not picked, literally dug deep out of the ground – were words that other parts of the country regarded as foreign. My parents were of the generation where Stanley Baxter's *Parliamo Glasgow* comedy show was a hit. For the first time the language that we heard when we were in Glasgow on a Saturday, not really that dissimilar to that of Lanarkshire, was on the telly. It was funny too. I saw reruns when I was old enough to appreciate them and smiled with friends at what seemed like an insider joke. The programme consisted of the comedian, Baxter, introducing a series of words (that we thought of as slang/dialect) in a Southern English accent with their meaning, then showing the phonetic spelling on the screen while his co-star provided some context. 'Izziahhiz', for example (is he off is), as in 'izziaffiz booz?' (is he relatively sober?) or 'zatnoa' (is that not a) as in 'zatnoa nabsaloot scunner?' (is that not disconcerting?). The meanings too were funny because they weren't quite right. 'A scunner' is a lot stronger than 'slightly disconcerting'! At school there was a probably apocryphal story that did the rounds of a French language assistant who asked a teacher, 'What does 'gizaleeny' mean?' (literally, give us a loan of something). The teacher's reply was 'Please may I borrow, but don't ever use it.'

As a working-class girl, I was encouraged to speak well, not to mimic my parents but to pronounce words 'properly', as my mum would say. In school I was often asked to give presentations and recite poetry because I was a 'good speaker'. The girls of my age I met in dance class were better off, had softer accents, did not use what we referred to as 'slang' words at home. They were privately educated or went to good comprehensive schools in the West End of Glasgow, in areas like Hyndland. To succeed, I would have to 'fit in' with them. To do that, it was better to sound like them. But it was a careful tightrope because sounding English, and therefore not native to the country, was to be avoided at all costs.

My dialect and my accent were markers of my education and my class, things that would only hold me back. I understand absolutely why my parents thought like this. For the most part, it was true. And even my softened regional accent would be mocked by some upper-class students when I moved to London. Had I sounded like my mum, many people would have struggled to understand me at all. Even when I came back to Scotland briefly after university, I found the accent and the Scots of my childhood returned, and I'd be the lucky recipient of remarks such as 'You've done well for a girl from Lanarkshire'. In an odd turnabout, I ended up craving the anonymity of London. I sounded Scottish, yes, but in a generic way that did not lead to patronizing preconceptions. Years later, I found there was another anomaly developing, both in the inclusion of a language question in the census and in the number of people who identified as knowing the language. Two years before the 2011 census, a survey by the Scottish government showed that my own feeling that the way I spoke at home was a dialect, rather than a language, was shared with 64 per cent of the population. One council in the predominantly working-class area of Lanarkshire where I grew up formally stated that it had 'serious reservations about the validity of Scots as a language' as well as questions as to how consistent the public understanding of 'Scots' as a language actually was. Should it even be in the census at all?

Interestingly, in an odd echoing of the issues around literacy rates in India, studies showed that the working-class Scots who spoke the language, like my mum, were the least

likely to know how to write it. Well-educated middle classes
had appropriated the language, could write it, and frequently
chose to use a little sprinkling of Scots words as an identity
marker. One noted linguist even commented that using
some Scots grammar and vocabulary in speech that was per-
formatively middle class and educated was, in 2009, a 'safety
net' that speakers used to differentiate themselves from the
working class while retaining their national identity.[14]

But the Scots of the fifteenth century was about to find its
place again. Political recognition came about largely because
in the Scottish census of 2011 a staggering one and a half
million people identified themselves as Scots speakers. In a
country of 5.28 million (in 2011) more than a fifth of those
regarded themselves as speakers of a language I had never
really considered to be a contemporary living one, even
though I spoke and understood it.

And impressions changed too. Education about the
language and its history is growing beyond the traditions
of Burns Night or comedy shows, in no small part due to
younger Scottish language activists who write popular poetry
and songs, set up websites, and have high-profile social media
accounts. It's no longer a language for academics or the middle
classes; instead, there's more recognition that it's always been
here, an essential part of our culture, our third language – it
was just that we didn't really know it as such. Most of the
people I know now, both on the estate where I grew up
and at university, broadly accept that Scots is a language and
that it's made up of several dialects, including Glaswegian,

Aberdonian, Shetland, and so on. Linguistically speaking, these dialects fit into four groups or dialect regions, which were first mapped in the 1870s, namely Insular, Northern, Central, and Southern.

Within these are sub-dialects, so-called because people within a primary dialect area have unique speech patterns, including specific words, phrases, or pronunciations, that are unique to smaller regions. Within these sub-dialects, there are even more localized variations, such as those found in individual cities. For instance, Central Scots is a primary dialect that includes a sub-dialect known as West Central Scots. Within this sub-dialect, the city of Glasgow has its own distinct dialect. Therefore, speakers of the Glasgow city dialect are actually using a form of West Central Scots and are part of the larger Central Scots region, sharing many linguistic features with others in this broader area. On a larger scale, those who speak the Glasgow city dialect are considered Scots speakers because Central Scots is one of the main dialects of the Scots language.[15]

The most recent census, in 2022, indicated that 1.76 million people can read, write, speak, or understand Scots, while the percentage of people aged three and over with some skills in Scots also increased to 46.2 per cent in 2022 from 37.7 per cent in 2011. The young singer Iona Fyfe sings in Doric, spoken in the north-east. However, she describes her personal dialect as being 'Glescadjacent' because she's lived in the city of Glasgow most of her life. The poet Len Pennie frequently appears on television and radio and does a 'Scots

Word of the Day' on her popular podcast. And the innovative and brilliant Scots Opera Project gives well-known works like Mozart's *The Magic Flute* a whole new dimension with performances sung in Scots. The overall impression is of a language not just being acknowledged but being nationally celebrated.

Conclusion

———◁◦▷———

The day and ever.
I am homesick, free, in love
with the way my mother speaks.

– Carol Ann Duffy, 'The Way My Mother Speaks',
The Other Country (Picador, 1990)

THIS BOOK IS a very personal journey. The languages included are here because they have resonated with me or meant something particular to me in the course of my life or studies. They are no more or less valuable and interesting than the thousands of other languages I do not even name. The connections I've drawn, such as that between the whistled mountainous calls on Gomera and the pre-mobile whistling and yodelling between council flats in Scotland, are only my own perceptions. The stories I've listened to and shared with you here, such as those of Carmen and Denver, have changed my understanding of the world. The knowledge of another language can do that too. Even if you have neither the wish nor the time to start learning, for example, Zulu or Hawaiian on Duolingo, just a glimpse of how their languages described their environments can show why it's important that they're not lost.

Halfway through researching this book, I moved back to Scotland. Following the death of my dad, my elderly mum was alone, and, like many others, my husband and I decided that moving to live closer to family was one of the most important changes to make after the pandemic. It was, as I said at the very beginning of this book, a kind of linguistic homecoming too. I found myself buoyed up and engaged in the many, many activities designed to promote the Scots language and curious about the position of Gaelic, which didn't seem to have enjoyed quite the resurgence that I'd thought it had and which I wish I had learned more diligently. There is other linguistic longing in my family too. My husband understands the dialect words I use with my mum, yet does not speak his father's language, Dutch. He carries a Dutch passport and continually laments that, growing up in New Zealand, the use of anything but English was actively discouraged. Dutch settlers in the post-war period were often separated, settled in towns far apart, so that the dominant language would be English for generations to come.

My husband apologizes for this constantly at passport control when we are entering the Netherlands. If we are visiting dear friends in Rotterdam and someone speaks to him in Dutch, he always begins, 'I'm sorry, I'm so sorry, I can't speak Dutch.' Although he tries to learn from time to time, he's not really a languages person – he finds numbers easier than words and says the words don't stick, no matter how hard he tries. Not usually given to poetic descriptions, he nevertheless explains to me one evening that new words for him are like smoke, floating into the atmosphere, impossible to keep. At the end of each attempt to learn, he feels slightly further from his antecedents, from the place he is descended from and to where he feels he belongs. And Dutch is still an Indo-European language, like English in a multitude of ways. How much more difficult, then, would it feel to have an unrelated language from a completely different culture and geography replace the one that described your home? And there are odd parts of his experience of the language too. His dad spoke nothing but Dutch till he was in his teens, yet now barely speaks it at all and regards English as his only language.

For me and my own efforts to learn over the years, the metaphor is different. It is that of water, the way it slips through your fingers and you can never hold it, no matter how you wish to or try to. The older I become, the more learning a language becomes like this. The words run over my fingers, I sense them, I touch their meaning, but then too soon they are lost to me. Regrets linger that when I was younger I didn't take the time. One consequence of the urbanization of society is that many words relating to human interaction with the elements are being lost, made redundant. Sometimes the power of these words is simply in the emotion they can invoke. I cannot even write the words 'coorie in thegither' (snuggle in together from cold or wet weather) without think-ing of the love I have for my parents. How we communicate with those closest to us is intrinsic to our sense of self. Other similarly semantic words that define situations we can all relate to, such as the Danish and Norwegian term 'hygge', meaning cosy together time, have entered English usage now, in lieu of a native term that encapsulates this experience.

But there's reluctance to multilingualism too, as with those in Scotland who are angered by Gaelic on road signs. 'Why should the majority have to put up with it? It's a tiny group of speakers who all know English anyway' is a common lament. 'Why are we paying for this extra signage?' I've heard from New Zealanders annoyed that their children now learn compulsory Māori in school because they think they would be better off knowing what they think of as a 'useful' language, like Spanish or German. Yet, if you ask them for a definition of 'useful' they cannot find one. Does having more speakers make a language better to learn, or is it about the information, the wisdom it carries, or is it just about community and kinship, rather than anything more easily quantifiable?

As we come to the end of this tour of unusual tongues, I hope that the value of investigating, studying, and revitalizing the intricacies of all languages is all too apparent. I like to think of this book as a kind of linguistic odyssey, moving from languages such as Māori, Hawaiian, Guarani, Ainu, Catalan, and Scottish Gaelic to Khoikhoi and Kunjen, each of these languages painting a distinct portrait of its speakers' experiences and surroundings while their narratives illuminate the connections between language, identity, and cultural survival.

There is every reason to hope that things are improving. Awareness of the relationship between ecology and language is now spreading across different faith groups. Both an encyclical issued by Pope Francis I and the Islamic Declaration on Global Climate Change explicitly refer to the link between climate change and the erosion of human cultural diversity. In 2019, the United Nations held their first International Year of Indigenous Languages, leading to the establishment of the International Decade of Indigenous Languages, which runs until 2032. In villages and communities around the world, small groups of speakers are learning about the support that global involvement and concern can offer them. They fight for acknowledgement that their home languages are an intrinsic part of their identity and history, while demonstrating they can be a valuable tool in the quest to protect the natural environment

New worldwide initiatives go far beyond linguistic classification. These include the National Geographic's Enduring Voices project and the Wikitongues collection, which aims not only to capture languages that are threatened but also to provide ways of learning them.

The languages we've looked at here offer a slightly different perspective on the value of linguistic variety in preserving threatened languages, but also what we can gain from listening to and learning about those that are not. The stories of Hawaiian and Nuxálk are examples of the resurgence of indigenous languages in post-colonial contexts. Their revitalization is more than linguistic: it's also a cultural reawakening, affirming the values, traditions, and knowledge of their speakers. By studying these languages, we may uncover the centrality of ecological stewardship and communal kinship, themes that also resonate across a hemisphere with Mongolian and Sámi, whose lexical richness in environmental knowledge reveals a similar respect for, and understanding of, the natural world as well as a defined appreciation of sustainable living.

In contrast, the accounts of Catalan, Khoikhoi, Guarani, and Scottish Gaelic bring to the fore the intersection of language and politics. Their narratives are steeped in struggles for cultural recognition and autonomy, mirroring broader sociopolitical movements. Here, language is a symbol of identity and resistance, and its preservation is inextricably caught up with the assertion of regional distinctiveness against homogenizing forces.

For some of the languages discussed here, such as Dyirbal or Kunjen, the growing contemporary interest in and awareness of the importance of native knowledge has come too late. But there are several others that can serve as a powerful testament to indigenous resilience. Languages such as Ainu and Machaj Juyai in the Andes embody a heritage that has withstood the pressures of assimilation and marginalization. The recent revitalization of these and of others included here are initiatives that highlight a global awakening to the rights of indigenous peoples, acknowledging the intrinsic value of linguistic diversity as a cornerstone of cultural richness and human heritage. Even beyond that, the very words we use to describe the loss of a language are now interrogated and challenged as an attempt to reclaim words, syntax, and meaning and to fight against a colonial legacy.

El Silbo, with its unique adaptation of Spanish into a whistled form, the bird language of Turkey, and the lullabies whistled in the Himalayas demonstrate the ingenuity inherent in human communication. They are a reminder of the capacity of languages to evolve and adapt to the specific needs of their speakers and to the landscapes they inhabit, a phenomenon observed across different contexts and cultures. In examining these diverse languages, I've looked at the many, many roles languages play in shaping human societies. They are not only tools for communication but keepers of collective memory, ecological wisdom, and artistic expression. They provide frameworks through which communities interpret their worlds, construct their identities, and connect with their pasts. The study of these languages serves a larger purpose. It's an act of recognizing and valuing the richness of human experiences. It challenges the notion of a monolithic human narrative and opens new spaces for multiple voices and accounts. It may make us listen more, ask more, care more, and perhaps even be the beginning of a moral imperative encouraging all of us to foster respect and understanding in an increasingly interconnected world. The preservation of linguistic variety is intrinsically linked to the continued existence of human diversity, but it requires effort and awareness. The character of Tancredi in the novel *Il Gattopardo* by Giuseppe Tomasi di Lampedusa famously declares, 'Se vogliamo che tutto rimanga come è, bisogna che tutto cambi' (If we want everything to stay the same, then everything needs to change). Likewise, just to maintain the historically diminished but nevertheless still gloriously pluralistic world of voices we live in now, so many things must change.

APPENDIX

―◦―

A Note on Some Linguistic Terms and the Idea of Linguistic Universality

Languages do have *life, purpose and form,* each of which can be studied and analyzed as soon as we strip them of their metaphorical or mystical content and look upon them as aspects of human behaviour.

—Einar Haugen, 'The Ecology of Language' (2001)

THROUGHOUT THIS JOURNEY of world languages, we used some linguistic terms to describe how a language works or to compare it to other languages. This brief appendix will serve as a general guide to those terms for those of you who aren't familiar with them. I'll use mostly English examples here, to make the explanation clear, but add in a few other words and phrases from very different languages so you can start to see the commonality and contrast that exists.

Phonetics

Phonetics is the study of the physical properties of speech sounds, including their production, transmission, and perception. It looks at how sounds are articulated by the human vocal tract (articulatory phonetics) but also considers acoustic properties of different sounds (acoustic phonetics).

British English has a diverse range of consonant and vowel sounds, each with its own unique characteristics. Consonants can be voiced or unvoiced. In other words, during the production of some consonantal sounds the air coming up from the lungs makes the vocal folds vibrate. This happens in sounds like /b/ or /d/ or /l/ or /g/ or /v/, for example, but not in /p/, /t/, /k/ or /f/, which we therefore label as being unvoiced, or voiceless.

The distinctive sound of a particular consonant is also produced by restricting or obstructing the airflow through various parts of the vocal tract, such as the lips, teeth, tongue, and hard and soft palate of the mouth. This feature is known as their place of articulation. Labial sounds are those made with the lips ('labial' is Latin for lips) and so /p/ or /b/ would be classed in this way, as would a sound like /m/. The 'th' sound in 'thin', which is written in phonetic script as /θ/, involves placing the tongue between the teeth, so it is called a lingua (Latin for tongue) dental consonant, while the 'r' sound in most Scottish accents, or in an Italian word like 'caro' (dear), is produced by vibrating the back of the tongue against the soft palate.

The third feature that distinguishes different consonantal sounds is known as the manner of articulation. The sound /t/, for example, is made with the tongue briefly touching the alveolar ridge, the hard bone just behind your front teeth, and then releasing it, and is accordingly known as an alveolar stop (because the air is momentarily stopped and then released). However, /s/ is also an alveolar sound because it too is formed as a result of the positioning of the tongue and the alveolar ridge. But in this case a small gap exists between them, and air is pushed through it, resulting in friction; thus /s/ is labelled as an alveolar fricative.

Vowels, on the other hand, are produced with an open vocal tract, allowing the air to flow freely without obstruction. The shape of the vocal tract, and in some cases the lips, is what gives us different vowel sounds.

British English has a system of short and long vowels, as well as diphthongs (a combination of two vowel sounds in one syllable). For instance, the short vowel sound in 'cat' is different from the long vowel sound that a speaker with a Southern English accent has in 'cart', while the diphthong in 'boy' contains two different vowels and involves a glide from one to the other.

The shape of the inside of the mouth is varied by raising different sections of the tongue, so a high front vowel, the sound in the English word 'sea' or in the Māori word 'pī' (to ignore, take no notice of), is the result of the front of the tongue being slightly raised (but not enough to make contact with the roof of the mouth or teeth because that would then give us a consonant sound). The vowel sound in 'bed' or in French 'mer' (sea) is labelled a mid-front vowel because the tongue is lifted halfway between an open and a closed vowel and is positioned forward in the mouth.

These various articulatory properties can result in acoustic cues, patterns that we can observe when we record the sound and break down its wave forms. These can be crucial in understanding how humans perceive the difference between sounds and what properties of the sound are crucial for this purpose. When we speak on a phone, the signal is distorted, compared to speaking to someone face to face, and yet comprehension, assuming we have good reception, is not an issue. It therefore follows that this loss or change of information in the production of the sounds cannot be one that is essential for us to communicate with each other.

Acoustic phonetics focuses on the physical aspects of speech sounds, looking at how sounds are produced, transmitted, and perceived as waves of sound in the air. The characteristics of sound waves, such as frequency, amplitude, and duration, are important in understanding speech sounds and how humans perceive them. Frequency refers to the number of cycles or vibrations per second and is measured in Hertz (Hz). In speech, it determines the pitch of a sound. Higher-frequency waves correspond to higher-pitched sounds, while lower-frequency waves correspond to lower-pitched sounds.

Amplitude refers to the intensity or strength of a sound wave. It is measured in decibels (dB). In speech, it determines the perceived loudness of a sound. Larger-amplitude waves correspond to louder sounds, while smaller-amplitude waves correspond to softer sounds. In the chapter about whistling languages, we saw how this property in particular gives an advantage to such languages over certain kinds of terrain.

We can view these properties of sound on a spectrogram, a visual representation of the acoustic properties of speech sounds. It displays the frequency, amplitude, and duration of different sounds over time. Spectrograms are often used to analyse speech and identify specific phonetic features. Formants are resonant frequencies that occur in the vocal tract during speech production. They are displayed as dark bands or regions in a spectrogram. Formants play a crucial role in distinguishing different vowel sounds and contribute to the unique quality of each vowel.

British English also has distinctive features in its intonation and stress patterns. Intonation refers to the rise and fall of pitch during speech, which can convey nuances such as emphasis, emotion, and sentence structure. Stress refers to the prominence or emphasis given to certain syllables within a word or in a sentence. These stress patterns differentiate words like 'present' (noun) and 'present' (verb).

Like Russian, Italian, Swahili, and many others, English is a non-tonal language, one in which the pitch or tone does not play a significant role in distinguishing word meanings. In non-tonal languages, the pitch is typically used for intonation patterns or to convey emotions rather than conveying lexical or grammatical distinctions.

In tone languages, such as Yoruba or Mandarin, the actual meaning of words or phrases is determined by the pitch or tone at which they are spoken. The pitch or tone carries linguistic distinctions that differentiate words or convey additional grammatical or semantic information. For example, Mandarin Chinese has four main tones and a neutral tone. Each tone is associated with a specific pitch contour, which can change the meaning of a word. For instance:

'*mā*' (妈) with a high-level tone means 'mother'
'*má*' (麻) with a rising tone means 'hemp'
'*mǎ*' (马) with a falling-rising tone means 'horse'
'*mà*' (骂) with a falling tone means 'scold'[1]

Yoruba, a language spoken in Nigeria and Benin, is another example. It has three basic tones: high, mid, and low. Tonal distinctions in Yoruba can differentiate words. For example:

'*ọkọ*' with a high tone means 'husband'
'*ọkò*' with a low tone means 'farm'
'*okò*' with a mid-tone means 'stomach'

Phonology

Phonology is a linguistic study field closely related to phonetics; it is concerned with examining the patterns and organization of sounds within a particular language or dialect, including their distribution, their variation, and the different rules that restrict possible combinations.

There are different theoretical approaches to phonology, a variety of ways of representing these structures, some of which are concerned with looking for universals, of finding an abstract way of representing commonalities that exist between all languages. This is the area of phonology that most interests me because one of its aims is to look at how language is represented in the human brain and what common factors we can use to describe and represent this.

Other phonological approaches are concerned with describing what is and isn't allowed within any given language. For the purposes of this book, we will mainly be concerned with the latter, although I may from time to time make some mention of a particular phonological framework and what it suggests about a language we're speaking about.

Phonemes are the smallest units of sound that can differentiate word meanings in a language. They are abstract representations of sounds, and each language has a specific set of phonemes.

For example, in English the phonemes /p/ and /b/ differentiate words like 'pat' and 'bat', and in Spanish the phonemes /k/ and /g/ differentiate words like 'casa' (house) and 'gasa' (gauze).

Allophones are variant pronunciations of a phoneme that do not change word meanings. They occur due to phonetic variations influenced by specific phonetic contexts. So we can find that the aspirated /pʰ/ sound in 'pat' and the unaspirated /p/ sound in 'spot' are allophones of the phoneme /p/ in English. While in French the nasalized /ã/ sound in 'vent' (wind) and the oral /a/ sound in 'vanne' (valve) are allophones of the phoneme /a/.

Phonological rules describe the patterns and regularities in the pronunciation of sounds within a language. They explain how phonemes and allophones interact and change in specific phonetic contexts. Thus, in US English final /t/ becomes voiceless [t] in words like 'cat' but is pronounced as a flap [ɾ] in words like 'better'. A flap is a version of /r/ where the tongue briefly touches the alveolar ridge and then moves immediately away. And similarly, in Japanese the /r/ sound is pronounced as a flap [ɾ] between vowels, as in 'kirei' (beautiful).

Phonotactics refers to the permissible sound combinations and patterns within a language. It specifies which sounds can occur in specific positions within a word. For example, in Hawaiian words cannot start with two consonants or end with a consonant cluster, as in 'aloha' (hello) and 'mauna' (mountain), and in Swahili consonant clusters are strictly limited to specific patterns, such as those in 'kamba' (rope) and 'pembe' (horn).

Syntax

As well as the sounds of words, it's important to know some terms for different grammatical features. Grammar encompasses the rules and structures that govern how words are organized and combined to create meaningful sentences. Again, we will focus on familiar English examples here, with a scattering of others, just to give an idea of the variation and distinction demonstrated right across the languages of the world.

Unlike some other languages, British English does not have a complex case system. Nouns have generally lost the endings that would denote case. However, by looking at pronouns we can see the three cases of English. They (subject case), them (object case), and their (possessive case). In contrast, a language like Finnish has fifteen different noun cases, which express different functions. For example, 'Hän on talossa' (He/She is in the house) shows the inessive case, marked by the ending 'ssa'; and 'Hän tuli talosta' (He/She came from the house), with the 'sta' at the end of the word for house, shows the elative case, which means to move away from something. Most of these functions would be performed using prepositions in English. Prepositions are words that establish relationships between nouns, pronouns, and other words in a sentence and indicate location, direction, time, or relationships between different elements (e.g., 'in', 'on', 'at', 'from', 'with').

In English we find possessive prepositions like 'my', 'your', and so on, whereas in Quechua, an indigenous language spoken in the Andean region of South America, these are all marked by suffixes – so we find 'Wasiyki' (your house) and 'Wasiy' (my house).

Languages can have both regular and non-regular plural forms. In English, we find plurals made by adding '-s' or

'-es' to the end of a noun (e.g., 'cat' becomes 'cats' and 'box' becomes 'boxes') as well as irregular plural forms that do not follow this pattern (e.g., 'child' becomes 'children' and 'mouse' becomes 'mice').

British English uses definite and indefinite articles ('a', 'an', 'the') to indicate the specificity of a noun. 'A' and 'an' are used for nonspecific or general cases (e.g., 'a book', 'an apple'), while 'the' is used for specific or previously mentioned nouns (e.g., 'the book', 'the apple'). A language like Japanese, in contrast, has no word at all for the definite or indefinite article, so we find '猫が来た' (Neko ga kita), 'A cat came', which breaks down into 'neko' (cat), 'ga' subject marker to show the case (note in Japanese the subject marker isn't attached to the noun it refers to!), and 'kita' (came).

Syntax refers to the arrangement of words and phrases to form grammatically correct sentences. British English follows a subject-verb-object (SVO) word order in most sentences. For example, 'She (subject) eats (verb) an apple (object)'. However, questions and some other sentence types may have a different word order, such as 'Are you (verb) coming (object)?'

Basque is of interest here because, unlike neighbouring languages like French or Spanish, which are SVO, it is SOV. So we find:

'*Ni liburua irakurri dut*' (I have read the book)
'*Ni*' (I) – subject
'*liburua*' (book) – object
'*irakurri*' (read) – verb

English uses a variety of tenses to express different time frames. So, for example, we have the past simple, used to express completed actions in the past, 'He fed the cat', and the present continuous, used to describe ongoing actions in the present, giving us 'It is always sunny in Glasgow'. Verbs can undergo inflection to indicate tense, person, and number. For example, 'sing' becomes 'sang' in the past tense and 'singing' in the present participle. Verbs can also be modified to form the continuous aspect (e.g., 'is walking') or the perfect aspect (e.g., 'has walked').

Semantics and pragmatics

Semantics is the study of meaning in language. It examines the meaning of individual words, including their definitions, lexical categories, and relationships with other words, and focuses on how words, phrases, and sentences convey meaning and how meaning is structured in a language. Semantics examines the relationships between words, their definitions, and, importantly, their interpretations (by the person who perceives them). Simply put, in English the word 'dog' refers to a domesticated mammal of the Canidae family. It is associated with characteristics such as loyalty, companionship, and barking. Semantics analyses how these meanings are encoded and understood by speakers.

Many Aboriginal languages in Australia have a complex system of semantic categories related to Dreamtime concepts.

Dreamtime refers to the Aboriginal spiritual and cultural belief system that encompasses creation stories, ancestral beings, and the relationship between people and the land. These languages often have specific vocabulary and semantic distinctions to describe different Dreamtime-related phenomena, such as songlines, ancestral spirits, and sacred sites. The semantic richness in these languages reflects the cultural and spiritual significance of Dreamtime concepts.[2]

Semantics also focuses on the meaning of sentences and how the combination of words within a sentence conveys a particular message or proposition. It explores how sentence structure, word order, and grammatical relationships contribute to meaning. The sentence 'The cat is on the mat' conveys a proposition about the location of a cat. Semantics investigates the meanings of 'cat', 'mat', and their relationship through grammatical and syntactic analysis.

It also explores the relationships between words and how they contribute to meaning. These relationships include synonyms (words with similar meanings), antonyms (words with opposite meanings), hyponyms (words that are more specific or less general), and homonyms (words with the same sound but different meanings). Thus 'big' and 'large' are synonyms that both convey the idea of size, while 'hot' and 'cold' are antonyms representing opposite temperature extremes. Semantics studies these relationships and their impact on meaning.

Different words within a sentence are examined to ascertain how they contribute to the overall meaning by assigning them semantic roles or functions. These roles include agent, patient, theme, and experiencer, and indicate the participants and their relationships in an event or situation. In 'Alan gave Lorna roses', 'Alan' is the agent performing the action, 'Lorna' is the recipient or goal, and 'roses' is the theme or object being transferred. Semantics allows us to analyse how these roles affect the interpretation of the sentence.

Semantics intersects with pragmatics, the study of meaning in context. Roger Bacon was a maverick Franciscan friar of the thirteenth century, a kind of British Leonardo da Vinci, with interests in mathematics, optics, and alchemy as well as linguistics. He designed a flying machine with flapping wings, predicted motorized vehicles, and was the first European to give exact instructions on how to make gunpowder, also realizing its importance as an instrument of war. Bacon postulated that it was not only the symbol or content that mattered in an exchange but the intention of the speaker/writer and interpretation of the listener/reader.[3] This was the beginning of the study of pragmatics.

Pragmatic meaning goes beyond the literal definitions of words and involves speaker intentions, presuppositions, implicatures, and cultural factors that influence interpretation. Pragmatics explores how speakers use language to convey meaning beyond the literal definitions of words.

For example, in Chinese culture two concepts of 'face' – 'mianzi' and 'lian' – play a significant role in pragmatics. 'Mianzi' tends to be more the positively evaluated aspects of face, while 'lian' tends to be more negative. Face refers to social reputation, dignity, and maintaining harmony in inter-actions.[4] Speakers often use indirect language, euphemisms, or silence to save face or avoid causing embarrassment or discomfort to themselves or others.

Historical linguistics

Historical linguistics is the study of language change over time. It involves the reconstruction of extinct languages, the tracing of language families, and the examination of language evolution. Historical linguists investigate sound changes, grammatical changes, and lexical changes, and they seek to understand the factors that drive language change.

The cornerstone of historical linguistics is the comparative method, which was formalized in the nineteenth century by scholars such as August Schleicher and Franz Bopp. This method involves comparing phonological, morphological, syntactic, and lexical elements across related languages to reconstruct their ancestral forms, known as protolanguages. The principle of regularity in sound change, which posits that phonological changes occur systematically rather than sporadically, underpins this methodology.

Historical linguistics also draws on the theory of linguistic relatedness, which groups languages into families based on shared ancestry. The Indo-European language family is a quintessential example, encompassing a wide array of languages from Sanskrit to English, all tracing back to a common protolanguage. Indo-European languages are believed to have originated from a common ancestral language known as Proto-Indo-European (PIE). PIE is reconstructed by linguists based on comparative linguistic analysis of its descendant languages. It is estimated to have been spoken around 4500–2500 BCE, although the exact time and place of its origin are still debated. Around 4000–3000 BCE, speakers of PIE began to migrate from their homeland, dispersing into different regions. These migrations led to the divergence of the Indo-European languages into various branches. Nine such divisions are now recognized, including two, Celtic and Germanic, which include languages native to the British Isles and others as diverse as Indo-Iranian (encompassing tongues such as Pashto, Hindi, and Kurdish) and Hellenic (Greek).

The primary methodological approach in historical linguistics is the comparative method, which entails systematic comparison of cognates, or words with a common etymological origin, across different languages. By identifying regular correspondences in sound and meaning, historical linguists reconstruct protolanguages and postulate about their phonological and grammatical features. Historical linguists also employ methods from other disciplines, such as archaeology, genetics, and palaeography, to corroborate linguistic hypotheses with external evidence. This interdisciplinary approach enriches the understanding of language evolution in its broader historical and cultural contexts.

Historical linguistics has far-reaching implications across various fields. In linguistics, it provides a framework for understanding language change and diversity. In anthropology and history, it offers insights into human migrations, cultural contacts, and the development of civilizations. Historical linguistics also contributes to the study of literature by elucidating the linguistic backgrounds of ancient texts. And it can play a crucial role in language preservation and revitalization: by reconstructing extinct or endangered languages, historical linguists provide invaluable resources for linguistic and cultural revitalization efforts.

Ecolinguistics

Ecolinguistics is an emergent and interdisciplinary field that explores the intricate relationship between language and the ecological environment. It investigates and analyses the ways in which linguistic practices reflect, shape, and are influenced by ecological realities. This nascent discipline traverses the boundaries of linguistics, ecology, anthropology, and environmental studies, aiming to elucidate the interconnections between language and the lived environment.

It resides at the confluence of linguistic inquiry and ecological awareness and is predicated on the understanding that language is not merely a tool for communication, but also a medium that reflects and influences human interactions with the natural world. Ecolinguistics interrogates the role of language in shaping environmental perception and action, recognizing that linguistic patterns can both reflect and perpetuate ecological ideologies. It is sometimes couched within the theory of linguistic relativity, which posits that the structure of a language affects its speakers' perception and categorization of the world.

This theory, often associated with the work of Edward Sapir and Benjamin Lee Whorf, suggests that language not only mirrors reality but also shapes it. In the context of ecolinguistics, this implies that linguistic structures and vocabularies can influence individuals' environmental perceptions and behaviours. However, languages are constantly evolving, and individuals within a linguistic community may vary in their usage and proficiency. The Sapir–Whorf hypothesis often treats languages as monolithic entities with fixed structures, failing to account for language change and variation within communities over time. Many researchers advocate for an interactionist perspective, which acknowledges the dynamic interplay between language, cognition, and culture. According to this view, language influences thought, but thought also shapes language. Additionally, both language and thought are influenced by cultural and environmental factors, leading to complex and bidirectional relationships. Ecolinguistic analysis employs a variety of methodological approaches to investigate this intricate interplay between language and ecology. Discourse analysis is a primary tool, enabling scholars to examine how environmental issues are framed and discussed in various communicative contexts. This involves analysing texts, conversations, and media representations to discern underlying ecological ideologies and values.

Another approach is ethnolinguistics, which explores the ecological knowledge embedded in the languages and practices of indigenous and local communities. This involves documenting and analysing linguistic expressions related to flora, fauna, and environmental phenomena, recognizing that language can encapsulate traditional ecological knowledge. Additionally, ecolinguistics employs cognitive linguistic methods to investigate how metaphor and other figurative language influence ecological thought. By examining the conceptual metaphors underlying environmental discourse, ecolinguists aim to understand how abstract ecological concepts are grounded in human experience.

Ecolinguistics has profound practical implications, especially in the realms of environmental education, policymaking, and activism. By elucidating the linguistic underpinnings of ecological thought, it can inform more effective communication strategies for environmental advocacy and education and can also contribute to the development of policies that recognize and respect the linguistic multiplicity and ecological knowledge of local communities.

Moreover, ecolinguistics has a role in language preservation, because the loss of linguistic diversity usually entails the loss of unique ecological knowledge. By documenting and revitalizing endangered languages, ecolinguists can help preserve the rich ecological wisdom they embody.

Sociolinguistics

Sociolinguistics explores the relationship between language and society. It investigates how language varies across different social groups and contexts and how social factors such as class, gender, ethnicity, and age influence language use. Sociolinguistics also examines language attitudes, language policy, and language change in social contexts. It decodes information about how we may also use specific functions of language to convey social meaning or aspects of our identity. In this regard, it often focuses on dialect, register, and style as the three key areas of variation.

This is a very brief introduction to a group of linguistic sciences that have each individually filled many books, far bigger than this one. Some of these are listed in the bibliography for anyone keen to explore further some of the exciting discoveries and debates they open. The different branches offer a multifaceted view of language, each providing unique insights into its structure, function, and role in human life. From the minute analysis of speech sounds to the exploration of language's social implications, linguistics is a rich and diverse field that intersects with numerous other disciplines. Understanding the various branches of linguistics not only deepens our appreciation of language's complexity but also highlights its central place in human culture and cognition.

Language universals

As early as four hundred thousand years ago, a man found a sturdy stone with a particular shape and heft and, in a sheltered area of a quartzite cave in Bhimbetka, Central India, used it to carefully hammer cup-shaped hollows into the rock. It was not an easy endeavour. The shape he created was almost perfectly circular as well as symmetrical. A twenty-first-century attempt to recreate its production indicated that it took one person six hours to make a single indentation and that most modern humans are incapable of matching the combination of precision and strength needed.[5] Yet today there are well over five hundred cupules still to be seen just in this one particular site.

We do not know what those shapes meant, nor can we tell what message or meaning they gave to the people who saw them, but we do know that they were left there deliberately, with great effort, using time that was precious for hunting and collecting food, in a space that had communal use. Even more intriguingly, identical shapes are found in other ancient sites in different continents around the world, from Europe to Australia. One possibility, some scientists would even call it a probability, is that these non-utilitarian cupules are an example of a very early symbol.[6] Moreover, these petroglyphs are culturally uniform, an ancient precursor of what modern linguists might call language universals. The man and his arduous rock-pounding was communicating to the people around him, the people who could see his cupules, and in India, France, Panama, and the Northern Territory of Australia, other groups were communicating using these very same shapes, produced in an identical way.

Something similar can be seen in the development of writing, with systems emerging independently, during the Bronze Age, in Egypt, China, and Pakistan as well as Peru and Mexico.[7]

These examples of evolutionary synchronicity are mirrored by another idea, that language itself developed from a common, innate basis and that these structures are consistent across all the languages of the world.

The suggestion that our different languages might have a common core again dates back to the thirteenth century and our unconventional monk, Roger Bacon. In his *Grammatica Graeca*, Bacon posited that 'Grammar is substantially the same in all languages, even though it may undergo in them accidental variations'.[8]

Bacon was writing in Latin, and in that language the term 'grammatica' is ambiguous and does not necessarily refer to what we might think of as grammar in plain language, but rather to the underlying structure of language, a use of the word 'grammar' that would seem more familiar to a contemporary linguist.

The existence of language universals, underlying properties that are common to all human languages, is still a debated topic amongst modern linguists. Theories from Chomsky and Montague in the latter half of the twentieth century even resulted in what became known as 'linguistic wars'. But while opinions over the past fifty years or so have moved to definitely favour the existence of a universal grammar, a few contemporary linguists are beginning to question this hypothesis.[9] And even among those who defend language universality, conflicting theories that attempt to analyse the languages we use, the way we speak and understand them, vie for popularity and support. Yet to many, these strictly defended academic positions seem obscure and unhelpful; the problems of identifying, then describing, these fundamental similarities persist. The theoretical underpinnings of the units we choose to encapsulate our predominant means of interacting with each other only detract from the observation of seven centuries past.

Linguistic universals demonstrate our common humanity, our shared biology, the need to interact that links all of our kind. The varied realizations of those common properties bind us to social groups and communities and are thus both a tool for harmony and relationship and a means of creating division.

But, like the cupules, language does not always involve words, either spoken or written. Often these different means have developed to unite communities, facilitate exchange in particular circumstances, or share secret information in a public space. There is a myriad of historical examples, including a language of flowers, the smoke signalling of North American indigenous peoples, the whistling languages, and the 127 intricate signs of silent monks preserved in the eleventh century *Monasteriales Indicia* manuscript in the

British Library. Each of these also has a private or public function inherent within it. Some of the whistling natives use whistled messages to announce public events, such weddings, religious celebrations, and births, that they want to share with everyone. In this case, there is no intimacy of exchange: it is a means of announcing and declaring, one that overcomes the difficulties of the mountainous, jagged terrain. The gestures of the monks to communicate with each other in monasteries where silence was observed were first codified in the seventh and eighth centuries. This type of sign language, used by hearing, speaking individuals in special contexts as a supplementary form of communication, is distinct from that used by people who use it instead of auditory/oral language because they are Deaf or want to communicate with those who use it as their first or only language.

But once again in support of Bacon's hypothesis, and just as with spoken languages, there are striking similarities between sign languages that have developed independently in internationally disparate and culturally diverse communities.

Select Bibliography

Armstrong, David, *A Show of Hands, A Natural History of Sign Language* (Washington, DC: Gallaudet University Press, 2011).

Bearden, E., 'Before Normal, There Was Natural: John Bulwer, Disability, and Natural Signing in Early Modern England', *PMLA*, 132.1 (2017).

Bednarik, R. G. et al., 'Preliminary Results of the EIUP Project', *Rock Art Research*, 22.2 (2005), pp.147–97.

Ben-yehuda, E., *A Dream Come True.* (London: Taylor and Francis Group, 2019).

Blacker, J., *The Faces of Time: Portrayal of the Past in Old French and Latin Historical Narrative of the Anglo-Norman Regnum* (Austin: University of Texas Press, 1994).

Bradley, David, 'Ancient Connections of Sinitic', *Languages*, 8.3 (2023), p.176. https://doi.org/10.3390/languages8030176

Bromham, L., X. Hua, C. Algy, F. Meakins. 'Language Endangerment: A Multidimensional Analysis of Risk Factors', *Journal of Language Evolution*, 5.1 (January 2020), pp.75–91. https://doi.org/10.1093/jole/lzaa002

Bromham, L., R. Dinnage, H. Skirgård et al., 'Global Predictors of Language Endangerment and the Future of Linguistic

Diversity', *Nature Ecology and Evolution*, 6 (2022), pp.163–73. https://doi.org/10.1038/s41559–021–01604-y

Chatwin, Bruce, *Songlines*, (Harmondsworth: Penguin, 1988).

Chatwin, Bruce, *In Patagonia* (Harmondsworth: Penguin Classics, 2003).

Clark, Billy, 'Pragmatics and Inference', in *Cambridge Handbook of Stylistics*, eds Peter Stockwell and Sara Whiteley (Cambridge: Cambridge University Press, 2014), pp.300–314.

Coulmas, Florian, *The Blackwell Encyclopedia of Writing Systems* (Oxford UK & Cambridge MA: Blackwell, 1996).

Crystal, D., *Language Death* (Cambridge: Cambridge University Press, 2002).

Cummins, Jim, 'Cultural and Linguistic Diversity in Education: A Mainstream Issue?', *Educational Review*, 49.2 (1997), pp.105–114. https://doi.org/10.1080/0013191970490202

Cunliffe, Daniel and Susan C. Herring, 'Introduction to Minority Languages, Multimedia and the Web', *New Review of Hypermedia and Multimedia*, 11.2 (2005), pp.131–7. https://doi.org/10.1080/13614560512331392186

Davis, J. E., *Hand Talk: Sign Language among American Indian Nations* (Cambridge: Cambridge University Press, 2014).

De Witte, Bruno, *The Protection of Linguistic Diversity through Fundamental Rights*, PhD thesis (Florence: European University Institute, EUI, LAW, 1985). https://hdl.handle.net/1814/4825

Dorian, N., *Language Death: The Life Cycle of a Scottish Gaelic Dialect* (Philadelphia: University of Pennsylvania Press, 1981).

——, 'Western Language Ideologies and Small-Language Prospects' in *Endangered Languages: Current Issues and Future Prospects*, eds Lenore A. Grenoble and Lindsay J.

Whaley (Cambridge: Cambridge University Press, 1998), pp.3–21.

Duggirala, V., 'Metaphoric Expressions and Temporality in Telugu', *Journal of South Asian Languages and Linguistics*, 10.1 (2023), pp.19–40. https://doi.org/10.1515/jsall-2023–1008

Dutta, Piyashi and Kedilezo Kikhi, 'Folk Practices of the Khasi Tribe: A Description of Jingrwai Iawbei in Kongthong Village', *Indian Sociological Bulletin*, 65 (2016), pp.237–52. https://doi.org/10.1177/0038022920160205

Evans, Nicholas, *Dying Words: Endangered Languages and What They Have to Tell Us*, Oxford and New York: Wiley-Blackwell, 2009).

Evans, N. and S. Levinson, 'The Myth of Language Universals: Language Diversity and Its Importance for Cognitive Science', *Behavioral and Brain Sciences*, 32.5 (2009) pp.429–48.

Flottum, K., *The Role of Language in the Climate Change Debate* (New York and Abingdon: Routledge, 2019).

Ghatage, A. M. 'Indian Linguistics', *Bulletin of the Deccan College Research Institute*, 21 (1963), pp.28–37. http://www.jstor.org/stable/42929878

Grenoble, Lenore A. and Lindsay J. Whaley, eds, *Endangered Languages: Current Issues and Future Prospects* (Cambridge: Cambridge University Press, 1988).

Groff, C. and Wendy Zwaanswijk, Ann Wilson and Nadira Saab, 'Language Diversity as Resource or as Problem? Educator Discourses and Language Policy at High Schools in the Netherlands', *International Multilingual Research Journal*, 17.2 (2023), pp.157–75. https://doi.org/10.1080/19313152.2022.2162761

Gynan, Shaw N. 'Attitudinal Dimensions of Guaraní-Spanish

Bilingualism in Paraguay', *Modern & Classical Languages*, 61 (1998), pp.35–59. https://cedar.wwu.edu/mcl_facpubs/61

Gynan, Shaw N., 'Linguistic Demography and Attitudinal Dimensions of Intergenerational Transmission of Guaraní and Spanish in Paraguay', *Modern & Classical Languages*, 62 (2011), pp.57–94. https://cedar.wwu.edu/mcl_facpubs/62

Hale, K., 'Endangered Languages: On Endangered Languages and the Safeguarding of Diversity', *Language*, 68.1 (1992), pp.1–42. https://doi.org/10.1353/lan.1992.0052

Hammarström, H., Linguistic Diversity and Language Evolution, *Journal of Language Evolution*, 1.1 (2016), pp.19–29. https://doi.org/10.1093/jole/lzw002

Hancock, Dawson R., 'The Effects of Native Language Books on the Pre-Literacy Skill Development of Language Minority Kindergartners', *Journal of Research in Childhood Education*, 17.1 (2002), pp.62–8.

Harmon, David, *In Light of Our Differences: How Diversity in Nature and Culture Makes Us Human* (Washington, DC: The Smithsonian Institute Press, 2002).

Harmon, David and Jonathan Loh, 'The Index of Linguistic Diversity: A New Quantitative Measure of Trends in the Status of the World's Languages', *Language Documentation & Conservation* 4 (2010), pp.97–151.

Harrison, K. David, *When Languages Die: The Extinction of the World's Languages and the Erosion of Human Knowledge* (Oxford: Oxford University Press, 2007).

Harshav, B., *Language in Time of Revolution.* (Berkeley: University of California Press, 1993).

Haugen, Einar, 'The Ecology of Language', in *The Ecolinguistics*

Reader: Language, Ecology, and Environment (London: Continuum, 2001 [1972]), pp.57–66.

Hill, J. H., '"Expert Rhetorics" in Advocacy for Endangered Languages: Who Is Listening, and What Do They Hear?', *Journal of Linguistic Anthropology*, 12.2 (2002), pp.119–33. http://www.jstor.org/stable/43104007

Ishtiaq, M., 'Determinants and Correlates of Language Shift among the Tribals of Central India', *GeoJournal* 45 (1998), pp.189–200. https://doiorg/10.1023/A:1006910132008

Ito, H., 'With Spanish, Guaraní Lives: A Sociolinguistic Analysis of Bilingual Education in Paraguay', *Multilingual Education*, 2.6 (2012). https://doi.org/10.1186/2191–5059-2-6

James, Carl E. and Sandra R. Schecter, 'Mainstreaming and Marginalization: Two National Strategies in the Circumscription of Difference', *Pedagogy, Culture & Society*, 8.1 (2000), pp.23–41.

Janni, Kevin D. and J. W. Bastien, 'Exotic Botanicals in the Kallawaya Pharmacopoeia', *Economic Botany*, 58 (2004), pp.S274–S9. http://www.jstor.org/stable/4256924

Janson, T., *A Natural History of Latin* (Oxford: Oxford University Press, 2006).

Joos, M., *Readings in Linguistics* (New York: American Council of Learned Societies, 1958).

Kaye, J. D. et al, 'The Internal Structure of Phonological Elements: A Theory of Charm and Government', *Phonology Yearbook*, 2 (1985), pp.305–28.

Kaye, J., *Phonology, A Cognitive View* (New Jersey: Lawrence Erlbaum Associates, 1989).

Kenstowicz, M., *Phonology in Generative Grammar* (Cambridge, MA: Blackwell, 1994).

Kisch, S., 'Deaf Discourse', *Medical Anthropology*, 27.3 (2008), pp.283–313.

Koch, Harold and L. Hercus, *Aboriginal Place Names: Naming and Re-naming the Australian Landscape* (Canberra: ANU Press, 2011).

Krauss, Michael, 'The World's Languages in Crisis', *Language*, 68.1 (1992), pp.4–10.

Kukulska-Hulme, Agnes and Mark Pegrum, 'Linguistic Diversity in Online and Mobile Learning', in *The Routledge Handbook of Language and Superdiversity*, eds Angela Creese and Adrian Blackledge (Abingdon: Routledge, 2018), pp.518–32.

Ladd, Paddy, *Understanding Deaf Culture: In Search of Deafhood* (Clevedon: Multilingual Matters, 2003).

——, 'Colonialism and Resistance: A Brief History of Deafhood', in *Open Your Eyes: Deaf Studies Talking*, ed. H-Dirksen L. Bauman (Minneapolis: University of Minnesota Press, 2008), pp.42–59.

Ladefoged, P., *A Course in Phonetics* (New York: Harcourt Brace Jovanovitch, 1982).

Leonard, W. 'Challenging "Extinction" through Modern Miami Language Practices', in *Global Language* Justice, eds L. Liu and A. Rao (New York and Chichester: Columbia University Press, 2023), pp.126–65. https://doi.org/10.7312/liu-21038–007

——, 'Refusing "Endangered Languages" Narratives', *Daedalus* 152.3 (2023), pp.69–83. https://doi.org/10.1162/daed_a_02018

Linkov, V., K. O'Doherty, E. Choi and G. Han, 'Linguistic Diversity Index: A Scientometric Measure to Enhance the Relevance of Small and Minority Group Languages', *SAGE Open*, 11.2 (2021). https://doi.org/10.1177/21582440211009191

Macfarlane, R. *Landmarks* (London: Penguin, 2016).

Majumdar, Sarmistha R. and Michael O. Adams, 'Diversity in Master of Public Administration Programs at Minority-Serving Institutions', *Journal of Public Affairs Education*, 21.2 (2015), pp.215–28.

Mar-Molinero, C., *The Politics of Language in the Spanish-Speaking World: From Colonisation to Globalisation* (London and New York: Routledge, 2000).

Marks, S., 'Khoisan Resistance to the Dutch in the Seventeenth and Eighteenth Centuries', *The Journal of African History*, 13.1 (1972), pp.55–80. doi:10.1017/S0021853700000268

Matos, S., 'Can Languages Be Saved? Linguistic Heritage and the Moving Archive', in *Memory in Motion*, eds Ina Blom, Trond Lundemo and Eivind Røssaak (Amsterdam: Amsterdam University Press, 2016), pp.61–84. https://library.oapen.org/bitstream/handle/20.500.12657/32015/1/619950.pdf#page=62

Mayer, J., *Whistled Languages: A Worldwide Inquiry on Human Whistled Speech* (Berlin: Springer-Verlag, 2015).

Mehta, S., 'Localization, Diversification and Heterogeneity: Understanding the Linguistic and Cultural Logics of Indian New Media', *International Journal of Cultural Studies*, 23.1 (2020), pp.102–20. https://doi.org/10.1177/1367877919880304

Mostowlansky, Till, 'Dying Dreams in Tajikistan's Global Borderland', *Current History*, 121.837 (2022), pp.277–82. https://doi.org/10.1525/curh.2022.121.837.277

Mühlhäusler, Peter, *Linguistic Ecology: Language Change and Linguistic Imperialism in the Pacific Region* (London: Routledge, 1996).

——, *Language of Environment – Environment of Language: A Course in Ecolinguistics* (London: Battlebridge, 2003).

Nathan, D. and M. Fang, 'Language Documentation and Pedagogy for Endangered Languages: A Mutual Revitalisation', *Language Documentation and Description*, 6 (2009), pp.132–60.

Nelson, Diane, Nhenety Kariri-Xocó, Idiane Kariri-Xocó and Thea Pitman, '"We Most Certainly Do Have a Language": Decolonizing Discourses of Language Extinction', *Environmental Humanities*, 15.1 (2023), pp.187–207. https://doi.org/10.1215/22011919–10216239.

Nettle, Daniel, *Linguistic Diversity* (Oxford: Oxford University Press, 1999).

Nevins, M. E., 'Learning to Listen: Confronting Two Meanings of Language Loss in the Contemporary White Mountain Apache Speech Community', *Journal of Linguistic Anthropology*, 14 (2004), pp.269–88. https://doi.org/10.1525/jlin.2004.14.2.269

Olko, J. and J. Sallabank, eds, *Revitalizing Endangered Languages: A Practical Guide* (Cambridge: Cambridge University Press Open Access, 2018).

Ostler, Nicholas, *Empires of the Word: A Language History of the World* (London: Harper Perennial, 2006).

Pakendorf, B. and M. Stoneking, 'The Genomic Prehistory of Peoples Speaking Khoisan Languages', *Human Molecular Genetics*, 30.R1 (2021), pp.R49–R55. https://doi.org/10.1093/hmg/ddaa221

Payne, D. L. 'Review of *Endangered Languages: Current Issues and Future Prospects*, by L. A. Grenoble & L. J. Whaley', *Journal of Linguistics*, 35.3 (1999), pp.618–24. http://www.jstor.org/stable/4176554

Pedley, Malika and Alain Viaut, 'What Do Minority Languages

Mean? European Perspectives', *Multilingua*, 38.2 (2019) pp.133–39. https://doi.org/10.1515/multi-2018–0025

Pinker, Stephen, *The Language Instinct* (London: Penguin, 2015).

Rialland, A., 'Phonological and Phonetic Aspects of Whistled Languages', *Phonology*, 22.2 (2005), pp.237–71.

Rosiak, Karolina, 'The Role of Language Attitudes and Ideologies in Minority Language Learning Motivation: A Case Study of Polish Migrants' (De)motivation to Learn Welsh', *European Journal of Applied Linguistics*, 11.1 (2023), pp.26–52. https://doi.org/10.1515/eujal-2021–0018

Ruffin, F. A., L. J. Teffo and H. O. Kaya, 'African Indigenous Languages and Environmental Communication', BBC. com, 24 October 2017. https://www.bbc.com/future/article/20190320-the-man-bringing-dead-languages-back-to-life

Sáenz-Badillos, Á., *A History of the Hebrew Language* (Cambridge: Cambridge University Press, 1996).

Sallabank, J., 'Diversity and Language Policy for Endangered Languages', in *The Cambridge Handbook of Language Policy*, ed. B. Spolsky (Cambridge: Cambridge University Press, 2012), pp.100–23. doi:10.1017/CBO9780511979026.008

Sasse, Hans-Jürgen, 'Theory of Language Death', in *Language death: factual and theoretical explorations with special reference to East Africa*, ed. Matthias Brenzinger (Berlin: Mouton de Gruyter, 1992), pp.7–30.

Schutz, A. J., *The Voices of Eden: A History of Hawaiian Language Studies* (Honolulu: University of Hawaii Press, 1994).

Shatil, N., 'Noun Patterns and Their Vitality in Modern Hebrew', *Hebrew Studies*, 55 (2014), pp.171–203. http://www.jstor.org/stable/43151471

Shimizutani, Satoshi and Eiji Yamada, 'Long-Term Consequences of Civil War in Tajikistan: The Gendered Impact on Education and Labor Market Outcomes', *Defence and Peace Economics*, 35.1 (2022), pp.72–85. https://doi.org/10.108 0/10242694.2022.2141946

Simons, Gary F. and M. Paul Lewis, 'The World's Languages in Crisis: A 20-Year Update', in *Responses to Language Endangerment: In Honor of Mickey Noonan—New Directions in Language Documentation and Language Revitalization*, eds Elena Mihas, Bernard Perley, Gabriel Rei-Doval and Kathleen Wheatley (Amsterdam and Philadelphia: John Benjamins, 2013), pp.3–20.

Skirgård, Hedwig et al., 'Grambank Reveals the Importance of Genealogical Constraints on Linguistic Diversity and Highlights the Impact of Language Loss', *Science Advances*, 9.16 (2023), eadg6175. https://doi.org/10.1126/sciadv. adg6175

Skutnabb-Kangas, Tove and David Harmon, 'Biological Diversity and Language Diversity: Parallels and Differences', in *The Routledge Handbook of Ecolinguistics*, eds Alwin F. Fill and Hermine Penz (New York: Routledge, 2015).

Smith, Andrew, 'The Origins and Demise of the Khoikhoi: The Debate', *South African Historical Journal*, 23.1 (1990), pp.3–14. https://doi.org/10.1080/02582479008671668

Soyolt, G., Y. Wunenbayar and L. G. Khasbagan, 'Wild Plant Folk Nomenclature of the Mongol Herdsmen in the Arhorchin National Nature Reserve, Inner Mongolia, PR China', *Journal of Ethnobiology and Ethnomedicine*, 9.30 (2013).

Sridhar, K., 'Bilingualism in South Asia (India): National/ Regional Profiles and Verbal Repertoires', *Annual Review of Applied Linguistics* 6 (1985), pp.169–86. https://doi. org/10.1017/S0267190500003123

Stibbe, A., *Ecolinguistics: Language, Ecology and the Stories We Live* (London and New York: Routledge, 2020).

Tapp, N., 'The Impact of Missionary Christianity Upon Marginalized Ethnic Minorities: The Case of the Hmong', *Journal of Southeast Asian Studies*, 20.1 (1989), pp.70–95. https://doi.org/10.1017/S0022463400019858

Tomkins, W., *Indian Sign Language* (New York: Dover Publications, 1989).

Tsimpli, Ianthi Maria, Margreet Vogelzang, Anusha Balasubramanian, Theodoros Marinis, Suvarna Alladi, Abhigna Reddy and Minati Panda, 'Linguistic Diversity, Multilingualism, and Cognitive Skills: A Study of Disadvantaged Children in India', *Languages*, 5.1 (2020), p.10. https://doi.org/10.3390/languages5010010

Tsitsipis, L. D., 'Language Shift and Narrative Performance: On the Structure and Function of Arvanítika Narratives', *Language in Society*, 17.1 (1988), pp.61–86. https://doi.org/10.1017/S0047404500012598

Turin, Mark, 'Language Endangerment and Linguistic Rights in the Himalayas: A Case Study from Nepal', *Mountain Research and Development*, 25.1 (2005), pp.4–9.

UNESCO, 'Indigenous Languages Decade (2022–2032)' [accessed 3 May 2022]. https://www.unesco.org/en/decades/indigenous-languages.

United Nations Department of Economic and Social Affairs, 'International Decade of Indigenous Languages

2022–2032'. https://www.un.org/development/desa/indigenouspeoples/indigenous-languages

Uriarte, J. R. and S. Sperlich, 'A Behavioural Model of Minority Language Shift: Theory and Empirical Evidence', *PLoS One*, 16.6 (4 June 2021), e0252453. https://doi.org/10.1371/journal.pone.0252453. Erratum in: *PLoS One* 16.7 (9 July 2021), e0254625.

Van Mensel, L., H. F. Marten and D. Gorter, 'Minority Languages through the Lens of the Linguistic Landscape', in *Minority Languages in the Linguistic Landscape*, eds D. Gorter, H. F. Marten and L. Van Mensel (London: Palgrave Macmillan, 2012). https://doi.org/10.1057/9780230360235_18.html

Weatherwax, M. *Indian Sign Language*, VHS (Browning: Department of Blackfeet Studies, Blackfeet Community College, 2002).

Wendel, J. N., 'Notes on the Ecology of Language', *Bunkyo Gakuin University Academic Journal*, 5 (2005), pp.51–76.

West, L. *The Sign Language: An Analysis, 2 Vols*, PhD dissertation (Bloomington: Department of Anthropology, Indiana University, 1960).

Whorf, B. *Language, Thought and Reality* (Cambridge: MIT Press, 1956).

Wiltshire, B. S. Bird and R. Hardwick, 'Understanding How Language Revitalisation Works: A Realist Synthesis', *Journal of Multilingual and Multicultural Development* (2022), pp.1–17. https://doi.org/10.1080/01434632.2022.2134877

Woodward, J., 'Implications for Sociolinguistic Research among the Deaf', *Sign Language Studies*, 1 (1972), pp.1–7.

Woolard, K., *Double Talk: Bilingualism and the Politics of Ethnicity in Catalonia* (Stanford: Stanford University Press, 1989).

Zaugg, I., 'Language Justice in the Digital Sphere', in *Global Language Justice*, eds L. Liu and A. Rao (New York and Chichester: Columbia University Press, 2023), pp.244–74. https://doi.org/10.7312/liu-21038–011

Acknowledgements

Many, many people have shared their languages and experiences with me while I was writing this book. Some of them are named in the text, others asked not to be. But every single one of them helped me understand just a little more about our shared chaotic Tower of Babel. The book would not exist without their help.

Erika Koljonen at Atlantic Books has been an incredibly hard-working and insightful editor. The book wouldn't be what it is without her careful and informed reading and comments and the support of all the fabulous team at Atlantic. Peter Straus at RCW has been my agent for almost two decades now, and none of this would have been possible without him, not to mention the fact that the book might not have a name! I appreciate his honesty, his wit, and above all his support. Emma Dunne has been a tireless and precise copy-editor and I am immensely grateful for her care.

The Society of Authors generously gave me a grant to support some travel for this book and did not withdraw the funding when the journeys were delayed by the pandemic. Like many authors, I am indebted to them. They are a truly fantastic organization, and I am honoured to have been one of their many recipients. The University of Stirling paid for me to visit Wilamowice and spend time with the fascinating and knowledgeable Tymoteusz Król. I am very grateful to them for making both my visit to the village and this wonderful encounter possible. Colleagues at Stirling University, in particular Dr Liam Bell and Professor Katie Halsey, have been supportive. Dr Kevin MacNeil was generous with his time and gave invaluable suggestions to help me understand the Gaelic situation today. Dr Bethan Benwell and Dr Cristina Johnson both kindly gave detailed answers to queries I put to them, and Dr Andrew Smith took the time to explain the Chinese characters for the tone examples used. I'm indebted to him for his careful exposition. Any errors in the retelling are, of course, mine. Former colleagues, many still friends, at the University of Hertfordshire were encouraging, both with some small research funding and with a huge amount of moral support, even when I wasn't working with them any more. Thanks especially to Dr Saskia Kersten (now at the University of Munich), Dr Sharon Maxwell, Dr Penny Pritchard, Dr Rowland Hughes, and Dr Daniel Grey. Early conversations with Professor Paul Cobley at Middlesex University and Professor Billy Clark, now at Northumbria University, helped the book to grow when it was just an embryo.

There have been a huge number of informants for these different languages, as well as many generous hosts and a handful of linguists offering reading suggestions, tips, and corrections. Thanks to all of them for taking the time to share their knowledge and helping me to appreciate just a few of the secrets of their fascinating tongues. This book would not exist without them. Special gratitude to Claude Chasset, Kelly Liang, Denver Toroxa Breda, and my dear friend Alessia Biancardia, for hospitality as well as Japanese and Italian expertise. Maria Medrano invited my husband and me to her community's powwow in Laughlin so we could share an amazing experience that we will never forget.

Also great thanks to Dr Anna Zbierska-Sawala, Dr Sylvia Shaw, Carmen Barrio, the late and much missed Ylmas Vural, Melisande Bernant, Lotte Toivanin, Auntie Wakiwa, Little Bird, Professor Thanawat Sondirhatna, Maria Varga, Jose Fernandez, Gonul Cevik, Amalia Korkanitsu, Krist Kindt Sarojarvi, Timo Sarojarvi, Dr Valentina Bold, Arabella Lasciata, Dr Colin Reilly, Gary and Kelly Liang, Ching Mai, Professor Paul Komesaroff, Abdul Mohammed, Noor Mohammed, Aisha Althani, Francois Thierry, Guillaume Thierry, Gigliola Ruscelli, Marco Di Costa, Maya Chimbata, Abeba Luo, Otieno Achebe, Rebecca Jacobson, Zara Mehdi, Denver Toroxa Breda, Angela Micchetti, Nga Perodu, Elaine Patchett, Jennifer Muir, Catherine Mercat, Jean Dupont, Vita Rognasson, Carmela Battista, Ashati Da, Melissa Warner, the late Professor Felicia Campbell, and Liz Sommerville.

As always, friends have played their part. Zana Elisabeth Gul offered beautifully cooked lunches and horsey chat, as well as brisk walks in the woods when I was struggling to get through a chapter. Dr James Charlton, Andrew Roberts, Robin Fairfield, Diego Lourenco, Colvin Stewart, Jill Nicholls,

Gonul Cevik, and Chris Burkinshaw still share friendship with me, even after these many years, and have cajoled and distracted me. Thank you for dinners, galleries, walks, and theatre. Dr Michael Newton has cheered me with the moral support and kindness we've offered each other for several decades now. Hannah Wells is the best riding instructor I could ever hope for, and the most patient, and Yvonne Lyon, the best piano teacher.

My late dad instilled in me a love of Scots poetry and prose. My husband, Alan Wesselson, and my mum, Jessie, have, as always, steadfastly supported me while I was working on this book. They have done so with everything from surprise gifts of earrings to long walks by Scottish lochs when I couldn't face another minute of looking at a computer screen. The elderly cats who sat beside me when I began this book have gone now. But there are another four who now occupy the cushions beside my desk and nudge me for treats. They are an essential part of my writing process and my comfort on the days that words don't come easily or well.

Notes

1. Latin and How Languages Develop

1. Unlike England, in large parts of Scotland 'chapel' usually indicates an RC place of worship, whereas 'church' means a place of worship for any of the Protestant religions, but I've kept it 'church' here for general understanding.
2. M. Kleijwegt, 'Creating New Citizens: Freed Slaves, the State and Citizenship in Early Rome and under Augustus', *European Review of History: Revue européenne d'histoire*, 16.3 (2009), pp.319–30.
3. For a full and amusing guide to the graffiti of both Herculaneum and Pompei, see http://ancientgraffiti.org/Graffiti
4. Ashley Marie Maxwell, 'Digging for Truth: How Chaucer, Boccaccio, and Ovid Gave Life to Ancient Tales', conference paper, *Excavations* at McGill University, February 2020.
5. Estimated numbers taken from the Google Endangered Languages Project.
6. Yin Pumin, 'Preserving Ethnic Identity', *Beijing Review*, 3 July 2017 [accessed 6 November 2023]. https://www.bjreview.com/Lifestyle/201707/t20170703_800099496.html

2. Khoisan – The Languages with Many Sounds

1. Huge thanks to Dr Niklaas Fredericks, who kindly sent me these.
2. See, for example, A. Traill, 'Do the Khoi Have a Place in the San? New Data on Khoisan Linguistic Relationship', *Sprache and Geschichte im Afrika*, 7 (1986), pp.407–30.
3. See https://www.scientificamerican.com/article/why-click-speech-is-rare/ [accessed 3 January 2023]
4. For a much fuller account of Herero, see Wilhelm J.G. Möhlig and Jekura U. Kavari, *Reference Grammar of Herero (Otjiherero): Bantu Languages of Namibia; With a Glossary Otjiherero–English–Otjiherero*. Southern African Languages and Cultures, vol. 3. (Köln: Rüdiger Köppe Verlag, 2008).
5. *The Namibian*, 1 June 1990, translated in Martin Pütz (ed.), *Discrimination through Language in Africa? Perspectives on the Namibian Experience* (Berlin: Mouton de Gruyter, 1995), p.19.
6. B. Brock-Utne and G. Garbo, *Language and Power: The Implications of Language for Peace Development* (Dar-es-Salaam: Mkupi na Nyota, 2010), p.144.
7. Pütz (ed.), p.2.
8. K. Iipinge, *English Lingua Franca as Language of Learning and Teaching in Northern Namibia: A Report on Oshiwambo Teachers' Experiences* (Stellenbosch: Stellenbosch University, 2013), pp.21–3.
9. https://rising.globalvoices.org/blog/2020/05/20/language-revolt-this-activist-tweets-against-erasure-of-first-languages-in-south-africa/ [accessed 13 June 2023].
10. Ibid.

3. Lost and Reclaimed

1. Christine is a pseudonym. I met her when researching *Childless Voices*. This quote is an amalgamation of two emails from January 2017 and February 2019. Christine was reluctant to speak about her own experience of her native language and asked that I didn't mention her name or any identifying features so that she remained anonymous within her own and the wider community.

2. Many, but not all – we will see later in this chapter that these terminologies are now often recognized as problematic.

3. See D. Nettle and S. Romaine, *The Extinction of the World's Languages* (New York: Oxford University Press, 2000) for a detailed and full account. The discussion of types of extinction is on pp.51–2.

4. https://archive.org/details/dyirballanguageo00dixo/page/n5/mode/2up?view=theatre [accessed 1 May 2023].

5. Nettle and Romaine, p.67.

6. Ibid., p.54.

7. See P. Segupta, 'Endangered Languages: Some Concerns', *Economic and Political Weekly*, 45.32 (2009), p.18.

8. M. N. Alexiades, *Mobility and Migration in Indigenous Amazonia: Contemporary Ethnoecological Perspectives* (New York and Oxford: Berghahn Books, 2009).

9. Simon Van de Kerke, 'El Leko', in *Ambito Andino*, eds Mily Crevels and Pieter Muysken (La Paz: Plural Editores, 2009), p.288.

10. J. Wong, *Selected Poems* (London: Excalibur Press of London, 1995), pp.34.

11. Mashiho Chiri, *Bunrui Ainugo Jiten: Sokubutsu Hen* [Classified dictionary of the Ainu: plants] (Tokyo: Jomin Bunka Kenkyujo, 1953), preface.

12. These examples come from Takako Yamada, *The World View of the Ainu* (London: Kegan Paul, 2001). https://www.academia.edu/1478933/The_World_View_of_the_Ainu [accessed 21/6/2023]. I recommend this book for many more fascinating and intriguing examples.

13. The inhabitants of the town generally consider themselves to be of Flemish origin.

14. Sarah G. Thomason, *Language Contact: An Introduction* (Edinburgh: Edinburgh University Press, 2001), pp.58–9.

15. https://www.cambridge.org/core/services/aop-cambridge-core/content/view/344D725FB56D4E46 AF76E2A7DB66CAD9/S1062798717000424a.pdf/ awakening-the-language-and-speakers-community-of-wymysioerys.pdf

16. It translates as 'You cocky guy, who lives in a big house, you are a piece of garbage'.

17. For a fuller introduction to this, see the various articles in Geoffrey Khan and Paul Noorlander (eds), *Studies in the Grammar and Lexicon of Neo-Aramaic* (Cambridge: Open Book Publishers, 2021).

18. The remarkable story of this language being brought back into the world can be read in its entirety in Diane Nelson, Nhenety Kariri-Xocó, Idiane Kariri-Xocó, and Thea Pitman, '"We Most Certainly Do Have a Language": Decolonizing Discourses of Extinction', *Environmental Humanities*, 15.1 (2023), pp.187–207. https://doi.org/10.1215/22011919-10216239

19. Cited and translated to English in ibid., p.200.
20. Ibid. p.196.

4. Languages and Ecosystems: An Environmentalist Vocabulary

1. https://www.seagardens.net/lokoia [accessed 11 September 2023].
2. V. Walsey and J. Brewer, 'Managed out of Existence: Over-Regulation of Indigenous Subsistence Fishing of the Yukon River', *GeoJournal*, 83.5 (2018), p.174.
3. https://doi.org/10.1016/j.marpol.2020.103971 [accessed 11 September 2023].
4. S. Klain et al., 'Ecologically Sustainable but Unjust? Negotiating Equity and Authority in Common-Pool Marine Resource Management', *Ecology and Society*, 19.4 (2014); A. Frid et al, 'Rapid Recovery of Dungeness Crab within Spatial Fishery Closures Declared under Indigenous Law in British Columbia', *Global Ecology and Conservation*, 6 (2016), p. 54.
5. R. Macfarlane, *Landmarks* (London: Penguin Random House, 2016), pp.1–2.
6. Ibid., p.53 and p.88.
7. R. Cámara-Leret and J. Bascompte, 'Language Extinction Triggers the Loss of Unique Medicinal Knowledge', *Proceedings of the National Academy of Sciences of the USA*, 118.24 (2021), e2103683118. https://doi.org/10.1073/pnas.2103683118
8. See the Kallawaya Language Project at https://livingtongues.org/kallawaya/ [accessed 12 September 2023]

and Kevin D. Janni and J. W. Bastien, 'Exotic Botanicals in the Kallawaya Pharmacopoeia', *Economic Botany*, 58 (2004), pp.S274–S9. http://www.jstor.org/stable/4256924

9. F. A. Ruffin, L. J. Teffo, and H. O. Kaya, 'African Indigenous Languages and Environmental Communication', *Journal of Human Ecology*, 53.2 (2016), p.185.

10. Ibid., p.186.

11. Ibid.

12. Ibid., p.187.

5. Plains Sign Talk – The Sound of Silence

1. The term 'Indian' is regarded as pejorative by some, although not all, Native American and First Nations people.

2. *The Journey of Alvar Nuñez Cabeza de Vaca and His Companions from Florida to the Pacific*, 1528–1536, pp.180–1, https://archive.org/details/journeyofalvarnu00nune_1/page/n9/mode/2up [accessed 01/01/2023].

3. L. Allan (ed.), *North American Exploration* (Lincoln: University of Nebraska Press, 1997), p.95.

4. Jefferson's instructions for Lewis [ante 20 June 1803], 'Thomas Jefferson and Early Western Explorers', transcr. and ed. Gerard W. Gawalt, Manuscript Division, Library of Congress. https://www.loc.gov/exhibits/lewisandclark/transcript57.html

5. All quotations from the Lewis and Clark journals come from https://lewisandclarkjournals.unl.edu/journals.

6. W. P. Clark, *The Indian Sign Language* (Philadelphia: L. R. Hamersly & Co., 1885), p.5.

7. Ibid., p.17.

8. Ibid., p.315.

9. A topic–comment structure has two parts, a topic and a comment. If we take the sentence 'He loved his cat', 'He' is the topic and 'loved his cat' is the comment. If we said 'The cat is loved by him', the cat would be the topic, and 'loved by him' would be the comment.

10. See L. West, *The Sign Language: An Analysis, 2 vols.*, PhD dissertation (Bloomington: Department of Anthropology, Indiana University, 1960).

11. Maria Medrano, Mohave Nation, personal communication.

12. James P. Ronda, *Lewis & Clark among the Indians* (Lincoln: University of Nebraska Press, 1984). https://lewisand-clarkjournals.unl.edu/item/lc.sup.ronda.01.06

13. A. Chapman, *European Encounters with the Yámana People of Cape Horn, Before and After Darwin* (New York: Cambridge University Press, 2010).

14. Ibid., p.56.

6. Whistled Languages

1. Julien Meyer, 'Environmental and Linguistic Typology of Whistled Languages', *Annual Review of Linguistics*, 7.1 (2021), pp.493–510.

2. Ibid.

3. Ibid., p.497.

4. A. Classe, 'Phonetics of the Silbo Gomero', *Archivum Linguisticum*, 9 (1957), pp.44–61.

5. Example from Julien Meyer, *Whistled Languages: A Worldwide Inquiry on Human Whistled Speech* (Heidelberg: Springer, 2015), p.113.

6. R. G. Busnel and A. Classe, *Whistled Languages* (Berlin: Springer, 1976).

7. Meyer, *Whistled Languages*, p.162.

8. Annie Rialland, 'Phonological and Phonetic Aspects of Whistled Languages', *Phonology*, 22.2 (2005), p.14.

9. See ibid., p.261.

10. https://www.bbc.com/future/article/20170525-the-people-who-speak-in-whistles

11. Meyer, 'Environmental and Linguistic Typology', p.498.

12. https://ich.unesco.org/en/USL/whistled-language-00658

13. Ibid.

14. C. Leroy, 'Étude de phonétique comparative de la langue turque sifflée et parlée', *Revue de Phonétique Appliquée*, 14/15 (1970), pp.119–61. Cited in Rialland, p.255. http://www.jstor.org/stable/4615531

15. https://www.newyorker.com/tech/annals-of-technology/the-whistled-language-of-northern-turkey [accessed 12 June 2023].

16. See http://themileage.org/2018/03/kongthong-whistling-village-india.html and https://www.mlcuniv.in/kongthong-whistling-and-song-village/ and https://indianexpress.com/article/lifestyle/destination-of-the-week/bjp-mla-seeks-unesco-heritage-tag-for-meghalayas-whistling-village-7221060/ [accessed 1 May 2022].

17. Meyer, *Whistled Languages*, p.47.

18. An incredible collection of material, including recordings, translations, and analysis of the Gaviao and Surui languages, can be found here: Julien Meyer, *Documentation of Gavião and Suruí Languages in Whistled and Instrumental*

Speech, Endangered Languages Archive (2010). http://hdl.
handle.net/2196/00-0000-0000-000D-851F-4 [accessed
13 May 2023].

19. J. Meyer. M. O. Magnasco, and D. Reiss, 'The Relevance of
Human Whistled Languages for the Analysis and Decoding
of Dolphin Communication', *Frontiers in Psychology*, 12
(2021). https://doi.org/10.3389/fpsyg.2021.689501

7. Rare Tongues in Europe: Sicilian, Corsican, Catalan, and Monégasque

1. O. Tribulato, 'Non-Classical Languages', in *Language
and Linguistic Contact in Ancient Sicily*, ed. O. Tribulato
(Cambridge: Cambridge University Press, 2012), p.10.

2. Salvatore Giarrizzo, *Dizionario etimologico siciliano* (Palermo:
Herbita, 1989).

3. Thanks to Gianni Certo, native Sicilian speaker, for these
examples (personal communication).

4. Laura Lanzafame, 'Relevant Influences of Siculo-Arabic
Dialect on the Sicilian Language and Culture', *Review of
Historical Geography and Toponomastics*, 6.11–12 (2011),
pp.69–79.

5. Dionisius A. Agius, *Siculo Arabic* (London and New York:
Routledge, 2012), pp.392–6.

6. For a full account of this see A. Jaffe, 'Poeticizing the
Economy: The Corsican Language in a Nexus of Pride and
Profit', *Multilingua*, 38.1 (2019), pp.9–27. https://doi.
org/10.1515/multi-2018-0005

7. https://en.wal.unesco.org/languages/monegasque
[accessed 18 April 2024]

8. I am grateful to M. Claude Passet for giving up so much of a sunny afternoon to meet with me. He was a real treasure trove of information about Monégasque and other languages in the area, almost another book in themselves.

8. Language in Conflict

1. Joxerra Garzia, 'History of Improvised Bertsolaritza: A Proposal', *Oral Tradition Journal*, 22.2 (2007), pp.77–115.
2. Ibid. See also https://www.bertsozale.eus/en/bertsolaritza/history-of-bertsolaritza [accessed 7 July 2023].
3. Peter Trudgill, 'Time to Make Four into One', *The New European* (30 November 2017), p.46.
4. Text of the declaration, https://jezicinacionalizmi.com [accessed 21 July 2023].
5. See https://www.lawnet.gov.lk/tamil-language-special-provisions-2 [accessed 17 August 2023].
6. Minority Rights Group, 'Pamiris in Tajikistan', March 2023. https://minorityrights.org/communities/pamiris/#:~:text=Profile,branch%20of%20Shi'a%20Islam
7. https://www.languageconflict.org/conflict/pamiris-in-tajikistan/?wpv_view_count=694-TCPID2086&wpv_paged=2 [Accessed 1 February 2024].
8. Leila R. Dodykhudoeva and B. Ivanov Vladimir, 'Data Elicitation in Endangered Pamiri Communities: Interdependence of Language and History', Institute of Linguistics, Russian Academy of Sciences, Bolshoy Kislovskiy pereulok 1/12, 125009 Moscow, Russia (2022).

9. Language Revival

1. The Vatican Hebrew texts, as well as those at the Bodleian in Oxford, can be viewed online here: http://bav.bodleian.ox.ac.uk/digitized-items-hebrew-manuscripts [accessed 27 October 2023].
2. Itamar Even-Zohar, 'The Emergence of a Native Hebrew Culture in Palestine 1882–1948', in *Essential Papers on Zionism*, eds Jehuda Reinharz and Anita Shapira (New York & London: New York University Press, 1996), pp.727–44.
3. For a full account of kōhanga reo see A. R. Tangaere, 'Te kohanga reo: More Than a Language Nest', *Early Childhood Folio*, 3 (1997), pp.41–7. https://doi.org/10.18296/ecf.0268
4. Maori Language Act 1987, http://www.legislation.govt.nz/act/public/1987/0176/latest/whole.html#DLM124142

10. Dare to Speak Your Language: Guarani and Gaelic

1. For a detailed and readable account of the Paraguayan background to suppression, see P. Lambert, 'Paraguayan National Identity', in *Oxford Research Encyclopedia of Latin American History* (2016). https://doi.org/10.1093/acrefore/9780199366439.013.88
2. Ibid. p.8.
3. J. Elliott and R. Heaton, 'Languages and Language Politics in the Paraguayan Chaco', in *Handbook of the Changing World Language Map*, eds S. D. Brunn and R. Kehrein (Cham: Springer, 2020), pp.1–27. https://doi.org/10.1007/978-3-319-73400-2_226-1

4. Ibid.

5. Ibid.

6. The championing of Guarani is not without controversy, as some researchers claim that it is now done so at the expense of other, smaller indigenous languages. For a full account of this, please see Elliott and Heaton.

7. S. Pons-Sanz and A. MacCoinnich, 'The Languages of Scotland', in *The International Companion to Scottish Literature, 1400–1650*, ed. N. Royan (Glasgow: Scottish Literature International, 2018), pp.19–37 (see version at https://orca.cardiff.ac.uk/id/eprint/125635/2/AA_Draft_Sara__Aonghas_6_Sep_2012.pdf, p.3).

8. Ibid., p.17.

9. https://exploringcelticciv.web.unc.edu/statutes-of-iona [accessed 1 June 2023].

10. Ibid. Celtic marriages were contracts of agreement that did not involve the church or religious ceremony.

11. https://exploringcelticciv.web.unc.edu/1616-education-act-scottish-privy-council [accessed 2 June 2023].

12. C. S. Terry (ed.), *De Unione Regnorum Brittaniae Tratatum by Sir Thomas Craig*. Edited from a manuscript in the Advocates' Library (Edinburgh: Scottish History Society, 1909), pp.288–89.

13. https://bellacaledonia.org.uk/2019/12/04/education-and-the-colonisation-of-the-gaidhlig-mind-2/ [accessed 1 March 2023].

14. F. Douglas, *Scottish Newspapers, Language and Identity* (Edinburgh: Edinburgh University Press, 2009).

15. Scots Language Centre, 'The Main Dialects of Scots', https://www.scotslanguage.com/articles/node/id/69.

Appendix: A Note on Some Linguistic Terms and the Idea of Linguistic Universality

1. Ninety per cent of Chinese characters are semantic-phonetic compounds, with one part denoting the meaning and the other part denoting the sound, but others (often words for natural objects) are pictographic, ideographic, and rebuses (see Coulmas). If you look at the characters for each of these words closely, you'll notice that the sign for horse is included in two of the examples, thus both 'mother' and 'scold' include the sign for horse, indicating 'sounds like the word horse', while the word for 'hemp' is an ideographic compound representing hemp leaves.

2. For a full and detailed account of this see Cliff Goddard and Anna Wierzbicka, 'What Does Jukurrpa ("Dream-time", "Dreaming") Mean? A Semantic and Conceptual Journey of Discovery', *Australian Aboriginal Studies* (2015), pp.43–65.

3. MS. Digby 67, No. 1, Part 8, *Summa de sophismatibus et distinctionibus*, Bodleian Library.

4. Ling Zhou and Shao-jie Zhang, 'How Face as a System of Value-Constructs Operates through the Interplay of Mianzi and Lian in Chinese: A Corpus-Based Study', *Language Sciences* 64 (2017), pp.152–66.

5. See R. G. Bednarik et al., 'Preliminary Results of the EIUP Project', *Rock Art Research*, 22.2 (2005), pp.147–97.

6. See, for example, R. G. Bednarik, 'The Oldest Rock Art in the World', *Anthropologie* 39.2–3 (2001), p.96.

7. See M. T. Poe, *A History of Communications* (Cambridge: Cambridge University Press, 2011), pp.69–71.

8. E. Gilson, *A History of Christian Philosophy* (London: Sheed and Ward, 1955), p.19 n.1.

9. On arguments against universality see, for example, N. Evans and S. Levinson, 'The Myth of Language Universals: Language Diversity and Its Importance for Cognitive Science', *Behavioral and Brain Sciences* 32.5 (2009), pp.429–48.

Index